W9-ALW-643

ACADEMIC CONNECTIONS 3

ACADEMIC CONNECTIONS 3

JULIA WILLIAMS

Renison University College
University of Waterloo

DAVID HILL

ELT Support Services

PEARSON
Longman

Academic Connections 3

Copyright © 2010 by Pearson Education, Inc.
All rights reserved.

No part of this publication may be reproduced, stored in a retrieval system, or transmitted in any form, or by any means, electronic, mechanical, photocopying, recording, or otherwise, without the prior permission of the publisher.

Pearson Education, 10 Bank Street, White Plains, NY 10606

Staff credits: The people who made up the *Academic Connections 3* team, representing editorial, production, design, and manufacturing, are Pietro Alongi, Andrew Blasky, Aerin Csigay, Christine Edmonds, Ann France, Gosia Jaros-White, Caroline Kasterine, Sherry Preiss, Karen Quinn, Robert Ruvo, Debbie Sistino, Paula Van Ells, and Adina Zoltan.

ETS staff credits: The ETS people who made up the *Academic Connections* team, representing research, test design and scoring, item development, statistical analysis, and literature reviews, are Matthew Chametzky, Terry Cryan, Phil Everson, Elizabeth Jenner, Kate Kazin, Dawn Leusner, Brad Moulder, Jan Plante, Jonathon Schmidt, and Jody Stern.

Project editors: John Beaumont, Nan Clarke
Cover art: Art on File/Corbis
Text composition: Kirchoff/Wohlberg, Inc.
Text font: 10.5/12.5 Times Roman
Reviewers: See page 190

Library of Congress Cataloging-in-Publication Data

Academic connections. -- 1st ed.
    p. cm.
  ISBN 0-13-233843-2 (Level 1) -- ISBN 0-13-233844-0 (Level 2) -- ISBN 0-13-233845-9
(Level 3) -- ISBN 0-13-233841-6 (Level 4) 1. English language--Rhetoric--Problems, exercises, etc. 2. Report writing--Problems, exercises, etc. 3. Listening--Problems, exercises, etc. 4. Reading comprehension--Problems, exercises, etc. 5. College readers. I. Cassriel, Betsy. II. Martisen, Marit ter Mate III. Hill, David. IV. Williams, Julia
  PE1408.A223 2010
  428.0071'1--dc22

                                                    2009017781

ISBN-10: 0-13-233845-9
ISBN-13: 978-0-13-233845-5

Printed in the United States of America
3 4 5 6 7 8 9 10—V011—14 13 12 11 10

CONTENTS

WELCOME TO **ACADEMIC CONNECTIONS**

Academic Connections is a four-level, integrated skills course designed for students **preparing for academic study** as well as for **standardized tests**. A systematic, building-block approach helps students develop and sharpen their language skills as well as their academic and test-taking abilities.

The ACADEMIC CONNECTIONS Series Is

INTEGRATED

- *Academic Connections* **integrates** all four language skills—reading, listening, writing, and speaking.
- *Academic Connections* teaches students **how to integrate skills** and **content** in real-world academic contexts.
- **Integration of various media** empowers students and instills confidence.

ACADEMIC

- Academic skills and content prepare students for **success in the classroom** and on **standardized tests**.
- Explicit, **step-by-step skill development** leads to student mastery. With careful instruction and engaging practice tasks, students learn how to **organize information**, **make connections**, and **think critically**.
- Key **academic skills** are introduced, reinforced, and expanded in all four levels to facilitate acquisition.

AUTHENTIC

- **High-interest** and **intellectually stimulating authentic material** familiarizes students with content they will encounter in academic classes. Readings and lectures are excerpted or adapted from textbooks, academic journals, and other academic sources.

- Course content covers five **academic content areas**: Social Science, Life Science, Physical Science, Business and Marketing, and Arts and Literature.

- **Authentic tasks**, including listening to lectures, note-taking, participating in debates, preparing oral and written reports, and writing essays, prepare students for the demands of the content class.

ASSESSMENT-BASED

Academic Connections provides a **variety of assessments** that result in more effective student practice opportunities based upon individual needs:

- A *placement* test situates students in the appropriate level.
- *Pre-course* and *post-course* tests allow teachers to target instruction and measure achievement.
- *Multi-unit* tests track individual and class progress.
- *Formative assessments* monitor student skill mastery, allowing teachers to assign individualized exercises focused on the specific learning needs of the class.

RESEARCH-BASED

- *Academic Connections* was developed in cooperation with the **Educational Testing Service (ETS)**, creators of the TOEFL® test. The blend of curriculum and assessment is based on research that shows when English language learners are provided with authentic tasks, individualized and target practice opportunities, and timely feedback, they are better able to develop and integrate their reading, writing, speaking, and listening skills.

PERSONALIZED

MyAcademicConnectionsLab, an easy-to-use **online** learning and assessment program, is an integral part of the *Academic Connections* series.

MyAcademicConnectionsLab offers:

- **Unlimited access** to reading and listening selections with online glossary support.
- **Original activities** that support the *Academic Connections* program. These include activities that build academic skills and vocabulary.
- **Focused test preparation** to help students succeed academically and on international exams. Regular **formative** and **summative assessments**, developed by ETS experts, provide evidence of student learning and progress.
- **Individualized instruction**, **instant feedback**, and **personalized study** plans help students improve results.
- **Time-saving tools** include a **flexible gradebook** and **authoring features** that give teachers **control of content** and help them **track student progress**.

THE **ACADEMIC CONNECTIONS** UNIT

UNIT OPENER

Each unit in the *Academic Connections* series begins with a captivating opener that outlines the unit's content, academic skills, and requirements. The outline mirrors an authentic academic syllabus and conveys the unit's academic purpose.

The content in *Academic Connections* is organized around five academic disciplines: Social Sciences, Life Sciences, Physical Sciences, Business and Marketing, and Arts and Literature.

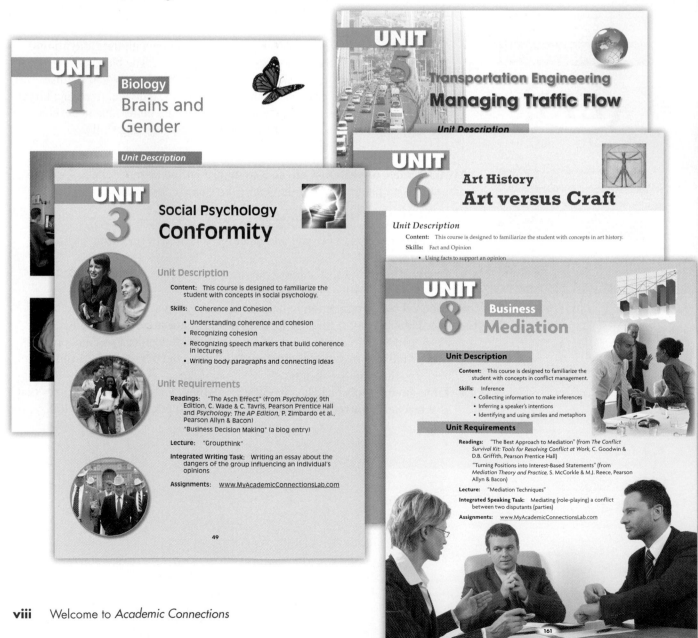

UNIT 1

Biology
Brains and Gender

Unit Description

UNIT 5

Transportation Engineering
Managing Traffic Flow

Unit Description

UNIT 6

Art History
Art versus Craft

Unit Description

Content: This course is designed to familiarize the student with concepts in art history.

Skills: Fact and Opinion

- Using facts to support an opinion

UNIT 3

Social Psychology
Conformity

Unit Description

Content: This course is designed to familiarize the student with concepts in social psychology.

Skills: Coherence and Cohesion

- Understanding coherence and cohesion
- Recognizing cohesion
- Recognizing speech markers that build coherence in lectures
- Writing body paragraphs and connecting ideas

Unit Requirements

Readings: "The Asch Effect" (from *Psychology*, 9th Edition, C. Wade & C. Tavris, Pearson Prentice Hall and *Psychology: The AP Edition*, P. Zimbardo et al., Pearson Allyn & Bacon)

"Business Decision Making" (a blog entry)

Lecture: "Groupthink"

Integrated Writing Task: Writing an essay about the dangers of the group influencing an individual's opinions

Assignments: www.MyAcademicConnectionsLab.com

49

UNIT 8

Business
Mediation

Unit Description

Content: This course is designed to familiarize the student with concepts in conflict management.

Skills: Inference

- Collecting information to make inferences
- Inferring a speaker's intentions
- Identifying and using similes and metaphors

Unit Requirements

Readings: "The Best Approach to Mediation" (from *The Conflict Survival Kit: Tools for Resolving Conflict at Work*, C. Goodwin & D.B. Griffith, Pearson Prentice Hall)

"Turning Positions into Interest-Based Statements" (from *Mediation Theory and Practice*, S. McCorkle & M.J. Reece, Pearson Allyn & Bacon)

Lecture: "Mediation Techniques"

Integrated Speaking Task: Mediating (role-playing) a conflict between two disputants (parties)

Assignments: www.MyAcademicConnectionsLab.com

161

1

Preview

This section introduces students to the theme of the unit.

Previewing the Academic Content gives an overview of the topic, engages students in it, and exposes them to key words they will need in order to proceed.

In this unit, you will practice using strategies for identifying main ideas and supporting details in readings and lectures. You will also look at how the introduction of an essay has one main idea, which is supported in the rest of the essay. Finally, you will practice writing essays.

Neurons are the smallest structures of the brain.

Previewing the Academic Skills Focus

1. *Read the paragraph. Underline the sentence that you think is the author's most important idea or point.*

There are some things we know about the brain, and there are other things that are still a big mystery. For one thing, the physical structures within the brain are quite well known. We also know that each structure has at least one function, sometimes more. For example, the front part of the brain, the frontal lobe, deals with decision making and problem solving. We also know something about the important kind of brain cells, the neurons. These are very small but sometimes very long, up to a meter (around 3 feet). Incredibly, there are 100 billion of them in a human brain, and each connects to others: One neuron can connect to up to 10,000 other neurons. As a consequence of this complexity, we are only at the very early stages of finding out in detail how the brain works. One reason for this is that we have only recently developed technology that can see deep inside a living brain. New discoveries are being made each day. Who knows what we'll find out next week or next year?

2. *Compare the sentence you have underlined with a partner's. Answer the questions.*
- Did you both underline the same sentence?
- What is the most important idea of this paragraph?

Main Ideas and Supporting Details

The **main idea** is the most important idea or point in a text, part of a text, lecture, or part of a lecture. A **supporting detail** is a piece of information that tells us more about the main idea. Sometimes you will need all the details, so you will have to read everything. Other times, you will only need the main ideas of a text or lecture. Reading or listening for main ideas only is reading or listening for the gist.

When you read a text or listen to a lecture, it is important to notice which points are main ideas and which are supporting details. Fortunately, a common pattern in English can help you do this. In this pattern, the main idea usually comes first. Later ideas provide support for this main idea.

So, a good strategy to find the main idea is to look for this pattern:
- The main idea of a lecture or essay is usually in the introduction. The supporting details follow, in the body paragraphs.
- The main idea of a paragraph is usually at or near the beginning of the paragraph. The supporting ideas come later in the paragraph.

There are many types of supporting ideas. The most common ones are:
- examples
- reasons
- consequences
- solutions to problems

Unit 1 ■ Brains and Gender **3**

1

Preview

For online assignments, go to

`myacademicconnectionslab`

Previewing the Academic Content

Buildings surround us and are an important part of our lives. People have strong opinions about them. For example, many say that modern architecture is boring and ugly and that the buildings of the past were far more attractive. Others claim that modern buildings are far more varied and interesting than what was previously possible.

In this unit, we will explore, from an architectural viewpoint, some ideas about what makes a building a good building, with an emphasis on aesthetics.

Pompidou Center,
Paris, France

Taj Mahal, India

Hundertwasser Apartments,
Vienna, Austria

Key Words

aesthetics *n* the study of beauty, especially beauty in art; **aesthetic** *adj;* **aesthetically pleasing** *exp*

form *n* the shape of something

ornamentation *n* decoration on an object; **ornamental** *adj*

scale *n* the size or level of something, when compared to the things around it

Look at the pictures of the three buildings. Then discuss the questions in small groups.

1. Which of these buildings have you seen pictures of or heard about?
2. What do you know about these buildings?
3. What do you like about each of the buildings? What do you dislike?
4. Overall, do you think these buildings are attractive? For each, circle a number on the scale from one to six to express your opinion. Explain your opinion.

	Very aesthetically pleasing					Not at all attractive
Pompidou Center	1	2	3	4	5	6
Taj Mahal	1	2	3	4	5	6
Hundertwasser Apartments	1	2	3	4	5	6

5. Choose at least one other building that you like. Tell your partner about it. You can draw a rough sketch if you think it will help with your description. Use a dictionary for any vocabulary you need.

74 Unit 4 ■ Architecture

Previewing the Academic Skills Focus gives an overview of the academic skill for the unit. The material activates students' awareness of the skill and then prompts them to use it on a global level.

2 and 3
Building Academic Reading and Listening Skills

Sections 2 and 3 focus on academic reading and listening skills. First, students read a text or listen to a lecture on a topic related to the unit's academic discipline. They acquire reading and listening skills through careful instruction and engaging practice tasks.

Every unit includes both reading and listening.

Before You Read/Listen introduces students to the topic of the selection with pre-reading or pre-listening activities. The activities may include discussions that activate students' prior knowledge of the topic; they may also include vocabulary or brief academic skill practice.

2
Building Academic Reading Skills

In this section, you will learn some common vocabulary related to genetics and how dominant and recessive genes create physical characteristics in individuals. You will also consider the primary and secondary purposes of a textbook excerpt. For online assignments, go to

`myacademicconnectionslab`

Key Words

allele *n /ə'liːəl/* one of several possible forms of gene

chromosome *n /'krəʊməsəʊm/* a thread-shaped part of every living cell that contains the genes controlling size, shape, and other physical characteristics

gene *n /dʒiːn/* a part of a chromosome that controls what an organism looks like, how it grows, and how it develops

Before You Read

1. Read the key words and their definitions, and look at the illustration. Then read the statements. Decide if they are true or false. Write T (true) or F (false). Correct the one false statement.

A pair of chromosomes

A **homologous pair** of chromosomes carries genes for the same traits. One member of each pair was inherited from the mother and the other from the father.

A **gene** is a segment of DNA located in a specific site on a specific chromosome that contains information for producing a particular protein (polypeptide).

A pair of **alleles**. An allele is an alternative form of a gene located on a specific site of a specific chromosome. One allele is inherited from the mother, and the other from the father.

_____ 1. Chromosomes come in pairs and contain paired genes. One gene is inherited from the mother, and one comes from the father.

_____ 2. A homologous pair of chromosomes carries genes for the same physical trait.

_____ 3. An allele is a kind of chromosome.

2. Look at the photographs. Then complete the tasks on the next page.

Freckles: *FF* or *Ff*   No freckles: *ff*   Widow's peak: *WW* or *Ww*   Straight hairline: *ww*

Attached earlobes: *EE* or *Ee*   Unattached earlobes: *ee*   *tt   Tt   TT* Tongue rolling

Genotypes and phenotypes of selected inherited human traits

MyAcademicConnectionsLab icons remind students to complete their online assignments.

2
Building Academic Listening Skills

In this section, you will practice distinguishing between major and minor points and between essential and non-essential information in a lecture. For online assignments, go to

`myacademicconnectionslab`

Before You Listen

1. Work in small groups. Look at the photographs and information about the buildings that the professor will discuss in the lecture. Then read the Claim to Fame statements. These statements describe features of the buildings that made them famous. Decide which building each Claim to Fame statement describes. Write the statement in the correct places in the chart.

Claim to Fame

A. It is still the largest wooden building in the world.

B. The curved shape of the concrete roof is uniquely elegant.

C. It is said by UNESCO to be the largest and most perfect example of its style of architecture.

D. It was the world's tallest reinforced concrete office building when it was built.

E. It was the world's tallest building for just 11 months after construction; it is still the world's tallest brick building.

F. It was built in memory of an emperor's wife.

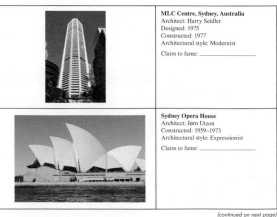

MLC Centre, Sydney, Australia
Architect: Harry Seidler
Designed: 1975
Constructed: 1977
Architectural style: Modernist

Claim to fame: _____

Sydney Opera House
Architect: Jørn Utzon
Constructed: 1959–1973
Architectural style: Expressionist

Claim to fame: _____

(continued on next page)

Global Reading/Listening presents a selection that is adapted or excerpted from higher education textbooks or other academic sources. Comprehension and critical thinking activities lead students to an understanding of the selection on a global level. Students are also introduced to an academic skill that they practice by completing engaging tasks.

Global Reading

Skimming: Finding the Main Ideas Quickly

Skimming is reading quickly to understand the general meaning of a whole text. One way to skim is to look only for the main ideas.

Here are some strategies to use when skimming:

Do:
- Read the first and last parts of each paragraph.
- Look at captions, diagrams, and illustrations.
- Read the title, headings, and subheadings.
- Look out for **bold**, *italicized*, or <u>underlined</u> words.
- Keep your eyes moving over the text.

Don't:
- Don't use a dictionary.
- Don't think about the meaning of difficult words (you can do that later).
- Don't read every word.

It is a good idea to skim every text before you read it in detail. This will help you determine what the text is about and where each main idea is.

Key Words

assumption *n* something that you think is true although you have no proof; **assume** *v*

hormone *n* a chemical produced by your body that influences how your body develops or works

infer *v* to form an opinion that something is probably true because of information that you have; if something is inferred, it is not explained directly

instinct *n* natural behavior; something you do without having to learn; **instinctive** *adj*

proportionately *adv* if something increases proportionately, it increases by the same percentage; **proportionate** *adj*

relative *adj* having a particular quality, such as size, compared with something else

signal *n* a simple message; **signal** *v*

transmit *v* to send a message

1. Skim the article for the main ideas. Use some of the skimming strategies from the box. Try to remember where the main ideas are—in the introduction, the middle (up to the diagram), or the end (after the diagram) of the passage. You have one minute.

ONE HUMAN BRAIN, OR TWO?
The human brain is complex enough. But what if there were not one, but two?

1   Anyone who knows the opposite sex well will tell you that, at times, men and women seem to be from different planets. The sexes often appear to think very differently from each other. However, until recently, researchers thought that these differences were caused by two things: social pressures, which have encouraged males and females to behave in a certain way, and secondly, hormones—chemical signals which tell different parts of the body, including the brain, what to do. Researchers didn't think the brain itself caused differences—on the contrary, they thought the brain's structure was mostly the same for both sexes. Interestingly, though, new research is casting doubt on these assumptions: There may be a third factor that had not previously been considered seriously. Research is now revealing that male and female brains have many differences in structure. There are also differences in how the various parts of the brain are linked and in the chemicals that transmit messages between neurons. All this suggests that there is not just one kind of human brain, but two.

Global Listening

Distinguishing Major from Minor Points and Essential from Non-essential Information

Major points are main ideas and supporting details that are necessary for understanding—the essential information. These include evidence and explanations. **Minor points** are additional details or information that add interest to the lecture but are not necessary for understanding—non-essential information. These often include examples.

Noticing the difference between major and minor points is important because it will make your note-taking and study more efficient—you only need to focus on the essential information. Also, in summarizing, only major points should be used.

You have already learned about some ways to identify main ideas:
- Think about the focus of the lecture beforehand. The major points will support the focus.
- Listen carefully to the introduction. The thesis will state the main point or opinion of the lecture, and the scope will give the main ideas to be covered.
- Listen for logical connectives and certain phrases that often introduce main ideas and supporting details, for example:
  Let's begin with . . .
  Most importantly, . . .
  One of the main reasons is . . .

Here are some other ways to identify main ideas:
- Sometimes a lecturer also gives emphasis to a point <u>after</u> saying it. Notice that in the following sentences, *this* and *that* refer to the previous idea.
  I believe this is a key point.
  I think that goes a long way to explaining why . . .
- Pay attention to <u>how</u> the lecturer is talking about major points. Ideas that the lecturer emphasizes—perhaps by speaking more slowly, more clearly, more loudly, or more quietly—and ideas that the lecturer repeats are most likely the major points.

As a check, ask yourself these questions:
- Is this information important for me to understand the purpose of the lecture?
- Is it an important detail that supports the main idea (such as an explanation or reason)?

Key Words

serene *adj* very calm and peaceful

surface *n* the outside or top layer of something

temple *n* a religious building in which people from several religions, including Buddhism and Hinduism, worship

texture *n* the way that a surface, material, etc. feels when you touch it, and how smooth or rough it looks

1. Professors often post course notes on their websites. Look at the overview of the lecture you will listen to. Work in pairs. Think of at least three questions that you think you may be answered in the lecture. Write them on the next page.

www.architecture101.com/spring

Lecture 4: In this lecture, we'll look at three techniques that architects use to inspire an emotional response to their buildings. We'll see that, perhaps, modern architects can learn at least one lesson from the architects of the past.

In **Focused Reading/Listening**, students begin to explore the complexities of the selection. Comprehension, critical thinking, and/or inference activities in this section test students' detailed understanding of the text and lecture. This section might introduce another academic skill related to reading/listening and offer practice of the skill.

At the end of Sections 2 and 3, students are prompted to take an online test on **MyAcademicConnectionsLab**. These section tests (Checkpoints) monitor student progress and allow the teacher to assign individualized exercises focused on students' specific needs.

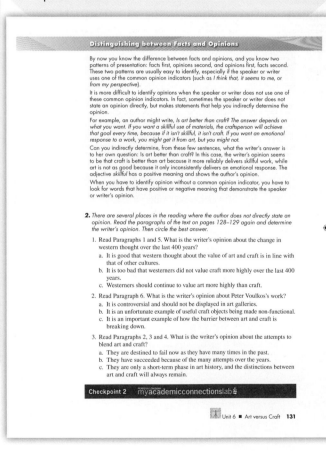

Focused Listening

Recognizing Relationships between Two Spoken Sources

As you learn about a topic, you will gather information from a variety of sources. You will certainly learn from textbooks and your own research; you will also learn from lectures and conversations with classmates. As you listen to your lectures and speak with your classmates about a topic, it is important to notice the relationships among the pieces of information that you hear. Recognizing the relationships among pieces of information will help you to understand the information more deeply and quickly.

Here are some common relationships that you might notice among pieces of information. The pieces of information might be:

- similar
- contrasting
- solutions to a problem
- reasons why something is true
- unrelated

In this activity, you will practice recognizing relationships between two spoken sources. Follow the instructions to complete the tasks.

1. Before you can recognize the relationship between two sources, you must clearly understand the first source. For this activity, the lecture will be your first source of information. In the first row of the chart, write the four main challenges for transportation engineers that you learned about in the lecture. You will complete the rest of the chart later. Listen to the lecture again if necessary.

Four Main Transportation Challenges:	
Student Opinions	**Relationship between Student Opinion and Main Lecture** (similar, contrasting, solutions to a problem, reasons why something is true, unrelated)
Student 1:	
Student 2:	

(continued on next page)

Unit 5 ■ Managing Traffic Flow **105**

Distinguishing between Facts and Opinions

By now you know the difference between facts and opinions, and you know two patterns of presentation: facts first, opinions second, and opinions first, facts second. These two patterns are usually easy to identify, especially if the speaker or writer uses one of the common opinion indicators (such as *I think that, it seems to me,* or *from my perspective*).

It is more difficult to identify opinions when the speaker or writer does not use one of these common opinion indicators. In fact, sometimes the speaker or writer does not state an opinion directly, but makes statements that help you indirectly determine the opinion.

For example, an author might write, *Is art better than craft? The answer depends on what you want. If you want a skillful use of materials, the craftsperson will achieve that goal every time, because if it isn't skillful, it isn't craft. If you want an emotional response to a work, you might get it from art, but you might not.*

Can you indirectly determine, from these few sentences, what the writer's answer is to her own question: Is art better than craft? In this case, the writer's opinion seems to be that craft is better than art because it more reliably delivers skillful work, while art is not as good because it only inconsistently delivers an emotional response. The adjective *skillful* has a positive meaning and shows the author's opinion.

When you have to identify opinion without a common opinion indicator, you have to look for words that have positive or negative meaning that demonstrate the speaker or writer's opinion.

2. *There are several places in the reading where the author does not directly state an opinion. Read the paragraphs of the text on pages 128–129 again and determine the writer's opinion. Then circle the best answer.*

1. Read Paragraphs 1 and 5. What is the writer's opinion about the change in western thought over the last 400 years?
   a. It is good that western thought about the value of art and craft is in line with that of other cultures.
   b. It is too bad that westerners did not value craft more highly over the last 400 years.
   c. Westerners should continue to value art more highly than craft.

2. Read Paragraph 6. What is the writer's opinion about Peter Voulkos's work?
   a. It is controversial and should not be displayed in art galleries.
   b. It is an unfortunate example of useful craft objects being made non-functional.
   c. It is an important example of how the barrier between art and craft is breaking down.

3. Read Paragraphs 2, 3 and 4. What is the writer's opinion about the attempts to blend art and craft?
   a. They are destined to fail now as they have many times in the past.
   b. They have succeeded because of the many attempts over the years.
   c. They are only a short-term phase in art history, and the distinctions between art and craft will always remain.

Checkpoint 2   myacademicconnectionslab

Unit 6 ■ Art versus Craft **131**

4
Building Academic Writing/ Speaking Skills

This section emphasizes development of productive skills for writing or speaking. It presents language and academic skills needed for the integrated task. Students also read or listen to another selection that expands on or otherwise complements the earlier selections.

Each unit concludes with an integrated writing or speaking task based on the authentic needs of the academic classroom. Units alternate between focusing on writing and speaking.

Before You Write/Speak introduces the language skill that students will need in the integrated task.

4
Building Academic Writing Skills

In this section, you will practice writing body paragraphs and connecting ideas. Then you will write an essay about the dangers of a group influencing an individual's opinions. For online assignments, go to
my.academicconnectionslab

Before You Write

1. Read the short student essay. In the introduction,
- underline the general statement once
- underline the thesis twice
- underline the scope with a squiggly line

Then compare your answers with a partner's.

In all walks of life—in companies, government, and even families—effective decision making is important. The right decision can lead to success, while the wrong one can cause disaster. Organizations must consider a range of ideas and choose the best from these. An excellent way to ensure that the widest possible range of ideas is considered is to consult with people outside the organization. This is because different people have different experiences, all of which may help in dealing with the issue. Also, consulting with external people helps to avoid groupthink.

A common expression in English is "two heads are better than one," meaning that two people's minds working together can think of better ideas than just one person. This is especially true when it comes to decision making. The more people who are consulted, the more experiences will be considered, and thus the more likely it is that the best idea will be found. Further, running the ideas by more people will mean that the ideas are examined more carefully. Thus, it is more likely that possible problems can be predicted in advance and solutions can be found. So, in short, the more heads, the better.

There is another reason to consult with others. That is to avoid the danger of groupthink. Groupthink occurs when people who get along well and know each other well reinforce each other's ideas rather than questioning them. This can reduce the level of critical thinking and lead to bad decisions. Someone from outside brings in new ideas, especially if that person is encouraged to freely express them. And that person will not allow old habits of the organization to prevent questioning of old ideas.

In conclusion, fresh ideas from outside an organization can greatly assist in decision making. Thus, it is important for organizations to consult with others whenever possible.

68   Unit 3 ■ Social Psychology

4
Building Academic Speaking Skills

In this section, you will practice emphasizing important information when speaking. Then you will orally express an opinion about an object and support your opinion with facts that you have learned from the unit. Your short presentation should explain whether you think the object is art, craft, or a blend of the two based on characteristics presented in the unit. For online assignments, go to
my.academicconnectionslab

Before You Speak

In the unit lecture you learned about the differences between art and craft, as defined by R. G. Collingwood. In the unit reading you learned about the blending of art and craft. In this reading you will learn another reason why craft and art are drawing together.

1. Read the text and answer the questions.

JAPANESE SWORDS

Today we are governed by rationalism and efficiency, and we live in the midst of mechanized and mass-produced objects. As a result, traditional crafts are becoming more valuable and important for modern people.

Craftspeople still make traditional craft items one by one with painstaking care. They use elaborate techniques dating back several hundreds or even thousands of years. These crafts are the exact opposite of rationalism and efficiency; they are full of unique beauty that can never be expected of mass production. When we see these traditional craft items, their beauty fascinates us.

In the past, crafts were a combination of function and ornament, while paintings and sculptures were made purely for the expression of beauty and existed only because of their beauty. This was the traditional view held by people who felt that works of craft should be clearly differentiated from the pure works of art like paintings and sculptures. Nevertheless, in modern society, traditional craft items have lost their function. For instance, Japanese swords were originally made to kill the enemy and were never intended to create beauty. Nowadays, however, they have completely lost their function as weapons. Yet because of their very beauty, they are now valued as one of the best of Japan's traditional arts. Excellent craft items with a long tradition necessarily possess superb artistry. We have only to appreciate their artistic value and beauty just as we do with paintings and sculptures.

Source: Japan Times, Ltd. (1972). *Japanese crafts.* Tokyo: The Japan Times.

1. Do you believe that modern people are governed by the principles of rationalism and efficiency? Support your opinion with some facts from your own experience. (State your opinion first, and provide facts second.)

2. Why are crafts the opposite of rationalism and efficiency?

3. Over time, what has happened to traditional crafts? Give an example.

132   Unit 6 ■ Art History

Focused Writing

Elaborating on Information from Sources

When you do not feel comfortable working in a language, you may try to write or say as little as possible in that language. While this may help you to avoid making mistakes, it is usually a clear sign that your language skills are weak.

To show that you are comfortable speaking or writing in your alternative language, there will be times when you will want to elaborate. Elaborating on ideas or information means giving more details or information about something. Look at the two responses to the question. Which answer demonstrates that the speaker is comfortable using his or her alternative language?

Question: *What are intelligent transportation systems (ITS)?*

Answer 1: *An ITS applies electronic and communications technology to solve transportation challenges.*

Answer 2: *An ITS uses technology, like road sensors and smart traffic signals, to sense the flow of traffic, and then it sends that information to a traffic operations center. Using this traffic flow information, dispatchers can control traffic signals to clear traffic jams and permit emergency vehicles to pass through a congested area.*

While Answer 1 is correct, it is abstract and not supported by concrete information. Also, it doesn't show the ability to work comfortably in an alternative language. Answer 2 is a more elaborate answer to the question and would demonstrate that you are a strong user of your alternative language.

1. *Work with a partner. Answer the questions either in writing or by speaking (or both), elaborating on your answers by adding concrete information. This will help your listener to understand the content, and you will demonstrate your comfort writing and speaking in English.*

1. Why is building extra highway capacity not always the best solution to rush-hour traffic?

_____

_____

_____

2. What are the three alternatives that must be considered when traffic congestion causes problems?

_____

_____

_____

3. What is a freeway management system?

_____

_____

_____

2. *Share your written and/or spoken answers with another pair or group. Share your best answers with the class.*

Focused Writing/Speaking
explains the skill that will be used in the integrated task. Students use the additional reading or listening selection in this section to practice the skill and prepare for the integrated task activity.

Focused Speaking

Preparing Spoken Summaries

You will often have to prepare spoken summaries in college. For example, you might be asked to give a summary of some articles you have read during a class. Or, you may have to include a summary at the end of an oral presentation.

A summary is a kind of paraphrase, in that it uses your own words and has the same meaning as the original.

Follow these steps to prepare a spoken summary:

1. Take notes while reading source texts or listening to lectures.
2. Close the source texts and cover your notes.
3. Make a list of main points.
4. Check the main points against your notes and, if necessary, the source texts. Adjust the list if necessary.
5. Cover your notes again.
6. Think about what you're going to say, and practice it in your mind.
7. Practice your summary with a partner.

Write a summary of the article on page 93. Follow the steps.

1. Follow steps 1–4 in the skills box.
2. Compare your notes with a partner's. Explain the reasons for your choices of main points, and discuss any differences.
3. Adjust your list of main points if necessary.
4. Follow steps 5–7 in the same skills box. At step 7, your partner will use the checklist.

Is/Does the summary. . .	Yes
short?	
include only important ideas?	
leave out detailed information such as numbers and dates, unless they are important?	
avoid including the personal opinions of the speaker?	
use the speaker's own words?	
have a conclusion that summarizes the main ideas?	

5. Listen to your partner's summary. Use the checklist to give feedback to your partner. Then discuss the results.

The **Integrated Writing/Speaking Task** challenges students to organize and synthesize information from the reading and listening selections in a meaningful way. Students follow clear steps that require them to use the vocabulary and academic skills they have learned in the unit. Completing the task is a productive achievement that gives students the tools and the confidence needed for academic success.

Integrated Writing Task

You have listened to and read information from various sources about some transportation challenges and solutions to those challenges. You will now use your knowledge of the content, key vocabulary, and report format to complete your writing assignment: **Write a conclusion to the report that recommends the best solution to traffic congestion in Markdale.**

Synthesizing Information

When you write in an academic context, you need to combine different pieces of information into whatever you are writing—an essay, a report, a response paper, or even a lab report. This is called synthesizing information. To synthesize well, you need to identify your pieces of information, determine the relationships among the pieces of information, and express these relationships clearly in writing.

To help you synthesize the information from this unit into a **Recommended Solution** section in the report, use the chart. Write your recommended solution in the first row of the chart.

Information from the readings and the lecture has been included in the first column of the chart. In the second column, indicate the relationship of this information to your recommended solution (*similar, contrasting, solutions to a problem, reasons why something is true, unrelated*). In the third column, place a check (✓) next to information you will include in your section.

Your Recommended Solution:		
Information Sources	**Relationship to Recommended Solution** *similar, contrasting, solutions to a problem, reasons why something is true, unrelated*	**Included in the Report? (✓ or X)**
Reading: Location, Time, and Cost Utility • Location utility • Time utility • Cost utility		
Lecture: Transportation Challenges Four transportation challenges: • Inconsistent demand (efficiency) • Lack of money • Environmental concerns • Safety		

(continued on next page)

🌐 Unit 5 ■ Managing Traffic Flow **115**

Integrated Speaking Task

You have listened to and read about ideas of what makes buildings examples of good architecture. You will now use your knowledge of the concepts, ideas, key vocabulary, and skills from this unit to choose a building and discuss this question: **Is the building you have chosen an example of good architecture?** Following your discussion, you will present a summary of the discussion to other students.

Follow the steps to prepare for the discussion.

Step 1: Work with a partner. Choose a building that you both know about and like. Together, come up with reasons why it is an example of good architecture. Use the chart to help you. Remember that you will need to justify your answer. You can use paraphrases of ideas from the texts.

Example

Let's think about Alberti's idea—you know, that a building's good looks come from its proportions and ornamentation.

	Idea about the Building
Proportions: subjective (your own impressions)	
Proportions appropriate? (for example, golden ratio)	
Durability	
Utility	
Beauty	
Ornamentation	
Does form follow function?	
Form	
Texture	
Scale	
Emotional response	
Profit?	
Spectacular and/or inspiring?	

🏛 Unit 4 ■ Aesthetics **97**

Welcome to *Academic Connections* **xv**

MyAcademicConnectionsLab

MyAcademicConnectionsLab, an integral part of the *Academic Connections* series, is an easy-to-use online program that delivers personalized instruction and practice to students and rich resources to teachers.

- Students can access reading and listening selections, do practice activities, and prepare for tests anytime they go online.
- Teachers can take advantage of many resources including online assessments, a flexible gradebook, and tools for monitoring student progress.

The **MyAcademicConnectionsLab** WELCOME page organizes assignments and grades, and facilitates communication between students and teachers. It also allows the teacher to monitor student progress.

For Sections 1–3, MyAcademicConnectionsLab provides Vocabulary Check activities. These activities assess students' knowledge of the vocabulary needed for comprehension of the content and follow up with individualized instruction.

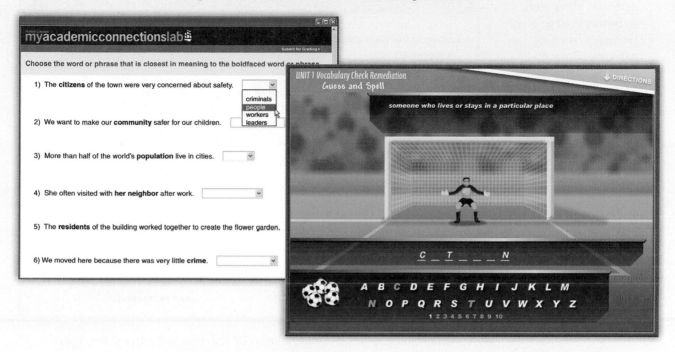

Reading and listening selections from the student book and additional practice activities are available to students online. Students benefit from virtually unlimited practice anywhere, anytime.

- Reading-based activities allow students to further engage with the unit's reading selection. Students practice comprehension, academic skills, grammar, and content vocabulary.

- Listening-based activities allow students to further engage with the unit's listening selection. Students practice comprehension, listening skills, and note-taking skills.

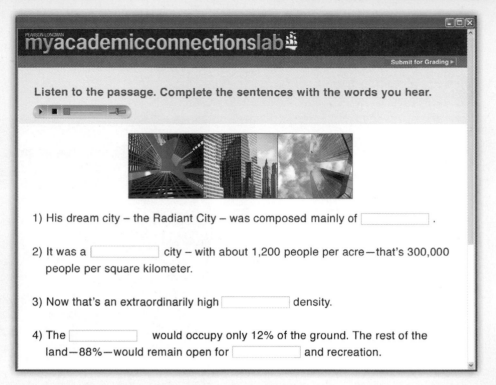

PEARSON LONGMAN
myacademicconnectionslab

Submit for Grading ▶

Listen to the passage. Complete the sentences with the words you hear.

1) His dream city – the Radiant City – was composed mainly of [   ] .

2) It was a [   ] city – with about 1,200 people per acre—that's 300,000 people per square kilometer.

3) Now that's an extraordinarily high [   ] density.

4) The [   ] would occupy only 12% of the ground. The rest of the land—88%—would remain open for [   ] and recreation.

MyAcademicConnectionsLab offers additional activities that support the *Academic Connections* program.

- Fun, interactive games reinforce academic vocabulary and skills.
- Internet-based and discussion-board activities expand students' knowledge of the topic and help them practice new vocabulary.

UNIT 1 Key Vocabulary
Jumble

Clues	Answers
1. a wide, main street **BVEROULAD**	b o u l u v _ _ _
2. a pattern of straight lines that cross, used to organize streets **IRDG**	_ _ _ _
3. business that provides goods or services **IRTSUDNY**	_ _ _ _ _ _ _ _
4. extreme, very different **RIAADCL**	_ _ _ _ _ _ _
5. very poor **IOPMSEEIHRVD**	_ _ _ _ _ _ _ _ _ _ _
6. someone whose job is to design buildings **AICTHCERT**	_ _ _ _ _ _ _ _ _
7. a building, statue, or other large	_ _ _ _ _ _

_ _ _ _ _ _ _ o _ _ _ _ _ _
_ _ _ _ _ _ n _ _ _ _ _ _ _ .

New message

PEARSON LONGMAN
myacademicconnectionslab

Submit for Grading ▶

RESEARCH TASK
ACTIVITY: Making a Better Market Street
WEBSITE: www.streetfilms.org/archives/making-a-better-market-street

Just about everyone who visits San Francisco's grand Market Street is awed by its hustle and bustle, the myriad modes of transportation, and some of the most beautiful architecture in the city. But just about everyone also agrees that Market Street has much bigger potential as a space that accommodates its users in more efficient and human terms.

- Go to the website.
- Watch the video.
- Use the box below to take notes.
  o What problems are mentioned?
  o What are people doing about these problems?
  o What can people do to make Market Street better in the future?

NOTES

The MyAcademicConnectionsLab ASSESSMENT tools allow instructors to customize and deliver tests online.

- A placement test situates students in the appropriate level (also available in the paper format).
- Pre-course and post-course tests allow teachers to target instruction.
- Section tests monitor student progress.

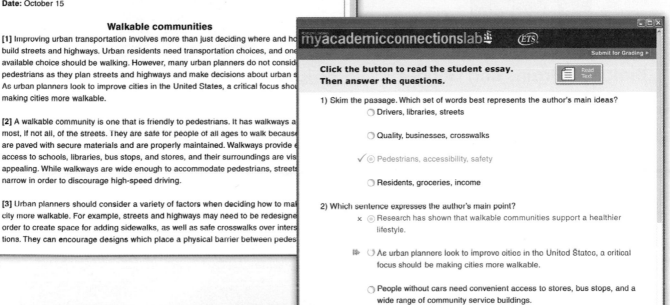

Student: Bob Travertine
Unit: City Planning 201
Date: October 15

Walkable communities

[1] Improving urban transportation involves more than just deciding where and ho build streets and highways. Urban residents need transportation choices, and one available choice should be walking. However, many urban planners do not consid pedestrians as they plan streets and highways and make decisions about urban s As urban planners look to improve cities in the United States, a critical focus shou making cities more walkable.

[2] A walkable community is one that is friendly to pedestrians. It has walkways a most, if not all, of the streets. They are safe for people of all ages to walk because are paved with secure materials and are properly maintained. Walkways provide e access to schools, libraries, bus stops, and stores, and their surroundings are vis appealing. While walkways are wide enough to accommodate pedestrians, streets narrow in order to discourage high-speed driving.

[3] Urban planners should consider a variety of factors when deciding how to mal city more walkable. For example, streets and highways may need to be redesigne order to create space for adding sidewalks, as well as safe crosswalks over inters tions. They can encourage designs which place a physical barrier between pedes

myacademicconnectionslab (ETS)

Submit for Grading ▶

Click the button to read the student essay. Then answer the questions.

📄 Read Text

1) Skim the passage. Which set of words best represents the author's main ideas?
   ○ Drivers, libraries, streets

   ○ Quality, businesses, crosswalks

   ✓ ◉ Pedestrians, accessibility, safety

   ○ Residents, groceries, income

2) Which sentence expresses the author's main point?
   x ◉ Research has shown that walkable communities support a healthier lifestyle.

   ➡ ○ As urban planners look to improve cities in the United States, a critical focus should be making cities more walkable.

   ○ People without cars need convenient access to stores, bus stops, and a wide range of community service buildings.

Teacher support materials in MyAcademic ConnectionsLab offer tips and suggestions for teaching the *Academic Connections* material and make lesson planning easier.

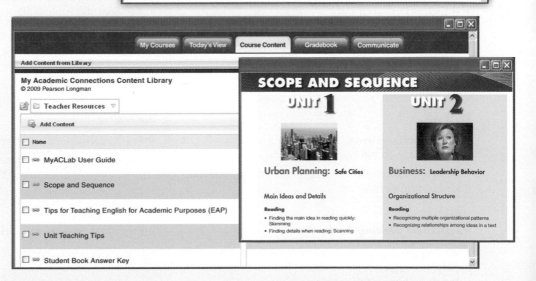

My Courses | Today's View | **Course Content** | Gradebook | Communicate

Add Content from Library

My Academic Connections Content Library
© 2009 Pearson Longman

📁 Teacher Resources ▽

➕ Add Content

☐ Name

☐ 📄 MyACLab User Guide

☐ 📄 Scope and Sequence

☐ 📄 Tips for Teaching English for Academic Purposes (EAP)

☐ 📄 Unit Teaching Tips

☐ 📄 Student Book Answer Key

SCOPE AND SEQUENCE

UNIT **1**

UNIT **2**

Urban Planning: Safe Cities

Business: Leadership Behavior

Main Ideas and Details

Organizational Structure

Reading
- Finding the main idea in reading quickly: Skimming
- Finding details when reading: Scanning

Reading
- Recognizing multiple organizational patterns
- Recognizing relationships among ideas in a text

SCOPE AND SEQUENCE

UNIT 1

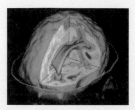

Biology: Brains and Gender

Main Ideas and Supporting Details

Reading

- Skimming: Finding the main ideas quickly
- Scanning: Finding specific information quickly
- Identifying supporting details

Listening

- Preparing to listen
- Getting the gist: Understanding a speaker's main ideas
- Listening for supporting details

Writing

- Understanding essay introductions and their relationship to the body of the essay
- Planning for writing: Thesis, major points, and supporting details

Integrated Writing Task

- Writing an essay about the implications of the differences between male and female brains for the development of medicine

UNIT 2

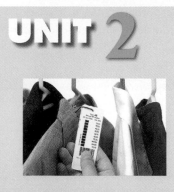

Business: Pricing

Organizational Structure

Listening

- Recognizing relationships between parts of a lecture
- Recognizing detailed relationships between ideas in lectures
- Note-taking

Reading

- Recognizing organization and purpose of written texts
- Recognizing relationships within a written text

Speaking

- Showing relationships between ideas
- Using notes to assist speaking

Integrated Speaking Task

- Choosing pricing strategies

UNIT 3

Social Psychology: Conformity

Coherence and Cohesion

Reading

- Understanding coherence and cohesion
- Recognizing cohesion

Listening

- Recognizing speech markers that build coherence in lectures

Writing

- Writing body paragraphs and connecting ideas

Integrated Writing Task

- Writing an essay about the dangers of the group influencing an individual's opinions

UNIT 4

Architecture: Aesthetics

Summarizing

Listening

- Distinguishing major from minor points and essential from non-essential information
- Identifying non-essential information, including digressions and asides

Reading

- Recognizing summary statements and conclusions
- Distinguishing essential from non-essential information in written texts

Speaking

- Paraphrasing
- Preparing spoken summaries

Integrated Speaking Task

- Discussing the aesthetics of buildings and summarizing the main points on the discussion

Transportation Engineering: Managing Traffic Flow

Synthesizing Information

Listening

- Recognizing the relationship between abstract concepts and concrete information
- Recognizing relationships between two spoken sources

Reading

- Recognizing the relationship between abstract concepts and concrete information in reading

Writing

- Elaborating on information from sources
- Synthesizing information

Integrated Writing Task

- Writing a conclusion to a report about a traffic challenge in the city of Markdale

Art History: Art versus Craft

Fact and Opinion

Listening

- Using facts to support an opinion
- Evaluating information used to support an opinion
- Recognizing degree of certainty when expressing opinions

Reading

- Distinguishing between facts and opinions

Speaking

- Emphasizing important information

Integrated Speaking Task

- Giving an oral presentation that expresses and supports an opinion about an object

UNIT 7

Biology: Genetic Testing

Purpose

Reading

- Recognizing a writer's or speaker's primary purpose
- Recognizing a writer's secondary purpose

Listening

- Recognizing a speaker's purpose
- Recognizing a speaker's secondary purpose
- Recognizing how thought groups, stress, and intonation express a speaker's attitude

Writing

- Understanding the intended audience

Integrated Writing Task

- Writing a pamphlet about genetic testing, keeping in mind the purpose and audience

UNIT 8

Business: Mediation

Inference

Reading

- Collecting information to make inferences

Listening

- Inferring a speaker's intentions

Speaking

- Identifying and using similes and metaphors

Integrated Speaking Task

- Mediating (role-playing) a conflict between two disputants (parties)

ACKNOWLEDGMENTS

Thank you to the following people, who have greatly influenced the direction of this book in these ways.

To Judi Jewinski who creates opportunities for those around her.

To Ron Williams whose interest in art defined the art versus craft topic.

To Dean and Janet Murray who provided a quiet room when my regular room was too noisy.

To Gosia Jaros-White who waited patiently and coordinated admirably.

To Wayne, Samuel, and Scott Parker who help me keep my balance.

To Carolyn and Ron Williams who cheer me on.

Julia Williams

While it is always the case that a book is a team effort, this was especially so with the *Academic Connections* series. I would like to thank all of those at Pearson involved from the initial concept through to editing, production and marketing. It's impossible to name everyone, but special thanks with level 3 go to Gosia Jaros-White, Development Editor, whose incredible efficiency and organisational ability played a powerful role in getting this book into its final form and into your hands.

Of course no author is without influence, and I would also like to acknowledge the numerous friends and colleagues as well as students I have worked with and learned so much from over the years. And on the home front, I extend my special thanks to Chie, whose encouragement, support and above all, patience, have been immensely valuable.

David Hill

The publisher would like to thank the following people.

Matthew Chametzky, R&D Capability Manager at ETS, who coordinated all assessment work for this project, bringing order when chaos seemed imminent.

Terry Cryan, Assessment Specialist at ETS who helped us all better understand (and appreciate) the many differences between testing and teaching.

Kate Kazin, Director of Client Management at ETS, whose clear vision kept the project true to its objective of evidence-based design.

For a complete list of reviewers and affiliations, see page 190.

UNIT 1

Biology
Brains and Gender

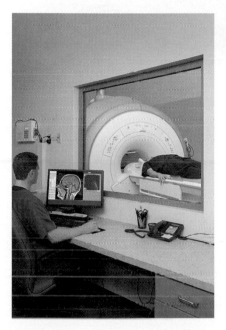

Unit Description

Content: This course is designed to familiarize the student with concepts in neuroscience.

Skills: Main Ideas and Supporting Details

- Skimming: Finding the main ideas quickly
- Scanning: Finding specific information quickly
- Identifying supporting details
- Preparing to listen
- Getting the gist: Understanding a speaker's main ideas
- Listening for supporting details
- Understanding essay introductions and their relationship to the body of the essay
- Planning for writing: Thesis, major points, and supporting details

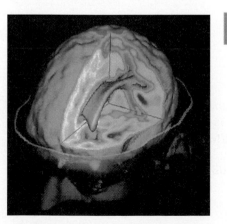

Unit Requirements

Readings: "One Human Brain, or Two?" (from *New Scientist, Australasian Edition,* H. Hoag, and from *Discover Magazine,* L. Marsa)

"Brain scan images" (captions)

Lecture: "Different Genders, Different Medicines?"

Integrated Writing Task: Writing an essay about the implications of the differences between male and female brains for the development of medicine

Assignments: www.MyAcademicConnectionsLab.com

1
Preview

For online assignments, go to

PEARSON LONGMAN
myacademicconnectionslab

Key Words

dimensional *adj* length, width, and height are dimensions, so a two-dimensional image (e.g., a television screen) has height and width, and a three-dimensional object (e.g., a book) has height, width, and length

finding *n* the information that someone has learned as a result of their studies, work, research, etc.

function *n* the purpose of something; what it is used for

imaging *n* producing pictures of something; **image** *n*

implication *n* a possible future effect or result of a plan, action, etc; **imply** *v*

neuron *n* a type of cell that is a part of the brain (neurons also send messages from the brain to other parts of the body)

neuroscientist *n* a scientist who studies the brain

Previewing the Academic Content

Studying the human brain in action was difficult in the past—we couldn't easily see inside a live brain! But new technology has changed that dramatically. *change a lot of* Using imaging techniques such as functional magnetic resonance imaging (fMRI) and positron emission tomography (PET), we can now produce detailed real-time movies and three-dimensional pictures of what is happening deep inside the brain. On a screen, scientists can watch different areas of the brain light up while a person performs actions, reacts to pictures, or holds conversations. In this way, secrets of how the brain works are quickly being discovered.

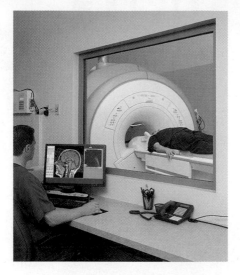

One very surprising finding is that there are much greater differences between male and female brains than neuroscientists expected. Some neuroscientists now say there are two human brains: one male, one female. This has great implications for many areas of medicine and biology, because in the past many drugs were tested only on males.

In this unit, we will look at some of the questions raised by this new understanding of the brain.

1. *Work in small groups. For each statement, predict and discuss what you think the most likely answer is and why. Circle the best answer. Which group gets the most correct answers?*

1. Scientists understand _____ about the human brain.
   a. nothing
   b. a little
   c. a lot

2. A typical human brain has around _____ neurons, each of which can be connected to up to _____ other neurons.
   a. 100 billion; 10,000
   b. 1,000; 100
   c. 100 billion; 10

3. The brain _____.
   a. has many different parts; all parts carry out the same functions
   b. is the same all over; different functions can be carried out anywhere
   c. has different parts; each part carries out a different function

2. *Work with a partner. Discuss what the brain does. List as many functions of the brain as you can. Then share your ideas with the class.*

In this unit, you will practice using strategies for identifying main ideas and supporting details in readings and lectures. You will also look at how the introduction of an essay has one main idea, which is supported in the rest *other part* of the essay. Finally, you will practice writing essays.

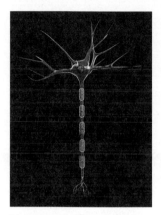

Neurons are the smallest structures of the brain.

Previewing the Academic Skills Focus

1. Read the paragraph. Underline the sentence that you think is the author's most important idea or point.

There are some things we know about the brain, and there are other things that are still a big mystery. *don't know* For one thing, the physical structures within the brain are quite well known. We also know that each structure has at least one function, sometimes more. For example, the front part of the brain, the frontal lobe, deals with decision making and problem solving. We also know something about the important kind of brain cells, the neurons. These are very small but sometimes very long, up to a meter (around 3 feet). *some can't believe* Incredibly, there are 100 billion of them in a human brain, and each connects to others: One neuron can connect to up to 10,000 other neurons. *result* As a consequence of this complexity, we are only at the very early stages of finding out in detail how the brain works. One reason for this is that we have only recently developed technology that can see deep inside a living brain. New discoveries are being made each day. Who knows what we'll find out next week or next year?

2. Compare the sentence you have underlined with a partner's. Answer the questions.
- Did you both underline the same sentence?
- What is the most important idea of this paragraph?

Main Ideas and Supporting Details

The **main idea** is the most important idea or point in a text, part of a text, lecture, or part of a lecture. A **supporting detail** is a piece of information that tells us more about the main idea. Sometimes you will need all the details, so you will have to read everything. Other times, you will only need the main ideas of a text or lecture. Reading or listening for main ideas only is reading or listening for the gist. *main idea*

When you read a text or listen to a lecture, it is important to notice which points are main ideas and which are supporting details. Fortunately, a common pattern in English can help you do this. In this pattern, the main idea usually comes first. Later ideas provide support for this main idea.

So, a good strategy to find the main idea is to look for this pattern:
- The main idea of a lecture or essay is usually in the introduction. The supporting details follow, in the body paragraphs.
- The main idea of a paragraph is usually at or near the beginning of the paragraph. The supporting ideas come later in the paragraph.

There are many types of supporting ideas. The most common ones are:
- examples
- reasons
- consequences *result*
- solutions to problems

3. Work with a partner to answer the questions.

1. Look again at the paragraph in Exercise 1 on page 3. After reading the information in the skill box on page 3, will you change the sentence you chose as the main idea? If so, what will you change it to?

2. Is the strategy you used to find the main idea the same as the strategy explained in the box? If not, what strategy did you use to find the main idea?

4. Read the paragraph in Exercise 1 on page 3 again. Underline the different types of supporting details. Then list the clues that helped you identify the different details.

1. **An example**

   Clue:_____

2. **A reason**

   Clue:_____

3. **A consequence**

   Clue:_____

2
Building Academic Reading Skills

In this section, you will practice reading for main ideas and supporting details.
For online assignments, go to

myacademicconnectionslab

Key Word

stereotype *n* a commonly held idea of what a particular group of people is like, especially one that is wrong or unfair. For example: *stereotype of girls being helpless and weak*

Before You Read

1. Which stereotype do these cartoons illustrate? Work with a partner. Complete the sentences. How true do you think these cartoons are?

Women always ___*talks*___,
and men never ___*listens*___.

"This meeting of The Male stereotype's Club is cancelled. Everyone is lost and won't ask for directions."

Men never ___*ask for directions*___

2. *Read the paragraph. Then work with a partner to answer the questions.*

In 1992, John Gray wrote a book called *Men Are from Mars, Women Are from Venus.*[1] His aim was to help people improve their relationships by showing how men and women think, communicate, and behave differently, almost as if they are from different planets. For example, he looked at how men and women try to solve problems. He said that men try to solve them quietly by themselves, whereas women discuss the problem with other people. However, many people criticized him because they thought the book encouraged stereotypes.

In 2007, Professor Deborah Cameron wrote a book called *The Myth of Mars and Venus: Do Men and Women Really Speak Different Languages*? In it, she examined many years of research and showed that there are far more similarities than differences in how men and women think and communicate. She also pointed out that the differences that do exist are very small. The differences between *individuals* are usually greater than the typical differences between males and females.

Cameron also reminded us that most people are not typical, and individual people's behavior may be different from the stereotypes. It is very dangerous to predict one person's behavior based on a stereotype.

_____

[1] Venus and Mars are two planets that go around the Sun. Venus is the second planet from the Sun. Earth, the planet on which we live, is the third. Mars is the fourth planet from the Sun.

1. Have you heard of either of these books? If so, what do you know about it/them?

2. Do you think that men and women communicate differently? If so, in what ways? Give some examples from your own experience.

3. Think about the example from Gray's book. In your experience, do you think men solve problems by themselves while women discuss the problems with other people? Do you think this is a stereotype?

4. Is your opinion closer to Gray's (that men and women are from different planets)? Or is it closer to Cameron's (that the differences between men and women are small)? What are the reasons for your opinion?

5. How would you qualify the differences between men and women that you discussed in questions 2–4? For example, would you say (you can use more than one):
   - . . . always . . .
   - Some people . . .
   - Generally, . . .
   - . . . never . . .
   - (other)

3. *Work with the same partner. What do you think causes the differences between males and females that you talked about in Exercise 2? Do you think the differences are caused by:*
   - biology ("nature")?
   - the way children are taught to behave when they are young ("nurture")?
   - a combination of nature and nurture?

Global Reading

Skimming is reading quickly to understand the general meaning of a whole text. One way to skim is to look only for the main ideas.

Here are some strategies to use when skimming:

Do:
- Read the first and last parts of each paragraph.
- Look at captions, diagrams, and illustrations.
- Read the title, headings, and subheadings.
- Look out for **bold**, *italicized*, or underlined words.
- Keep your eyes moving over the text.

Don't:
- Don't use a dictionary.
- Don't think about the meaning of difficult words (you can do that later).
- Don't read every word.

It is a good idea to skim every text before you read it in detail. This will help you determine what the text is about and where each main idea is.

1. *Skim the article for the main ideas. Use some of the skimming strategies from the box. Try to remember where the main ideas are—in the introduction, the middle (up to the diagram), or the end (after the diagram) of the passage. You have one minute.*

Key Words

assumption *n* something that you think is true although you have no proof; **assume** *v*

hormone *n* a chemical produced by your body that influences how your body develops or works

infer *v* to form an opinion that something is probably true because of information that you have; if something is inferred, it is not explained directly

instinct *n* natural behavior; something you do without having to learn; **instinctive** *adj*

proportionately *adv* if something increases proportionately, it increases by the same percentage; **proportionate** *adj*

relative *adj* having a particular quality, such as size, compared with something else

signal *n* a simple message; **signal** *v*

transmit *v* to send a message

ONE HUMAN BRAIN, OR TWO?

The human brain is complex enough. But what if there were not one, but two?

[*not simple*]

[*Introduction – 2 different kinds of brains*]

1   Anyone who knows the opposite sex well will tell you that, at times, men and women seem to be from different planets. The sexes often appear to think very differently from each other. However, until recently, researchers thought that these differences were caused by two things: social pressures, which have encouraged males and females to behave in a certain way, and secondly, hormones—chemical signals which tell different parts of the body, including the brain, what to do. Researchers didn't think the brain itself caused differences—on the contrary, [*opposite*] they thought the brain's structure was mostly the same for both sexes. Interestingly, though, new research is casting doubt on these [*showing question*] assumptions: There may be a third factor that had not previously [*something you guess*] been considered seriously. Research is now revealing that male and female brains have many differences in structure. There are also differences in how the various parts of the brain are linked and in the chemicals that transmit messages between neurons. [*brain cells*] All this suggests that there is not just one kind of human brain, but two.

Body =
-Researchers just looked at males before.

2   This is giving neuroscientists something of a headache, because most of what we know about the brain comes from studies of male animals and male humans. Generally, neuroscientists avoided using females in their research. This was because the monthly ups and downs of female hormones made it more complicated to interpret the results. If even a small proportion of what has been inferred from these studies does not apply to females, a huge body of research could be wrong.

-gender differences in brain structure are getting clear.

3   Male-female differences in brain structure are now becoming clear. In the past, the one structure that had long been known to differ slightly in males and females was the hypothalamus, which helps to control basic human instincts *behavior* such as regulating food intake. But new technology has helped scientists find other differences. For a start, the relative sizes of many of the structures inside female brains are different from those of males. In 2001, Jill Goldstein of Harvard Medical School and colleagues measured and compared 45 brain regions in healthy men and women. They found that parts of the frontal lobe, which houses decision-making and problem-solving functions, were proportionately larger in women, as was the limbic cortex, which controls emotions. Other studies have found that the hippocampus, involved in short-term memory and spatial navigation,[1] is proportionally larger in women—perhaps surprisingly, given women's reputation as poor map readers. In men, proportionately larger areas include the parietal cortex, which processes signals from the sensory organs and is involved in spatial perception, and the amygdala, which controls emotions and social behavior.

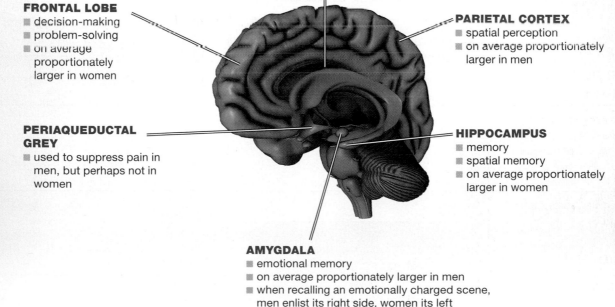

LIMBIC CORTEX
- regulates emotions
- on average proportionately larger in women

FRONTAL LOBE
- decision-making
- problem-solving
- on average proportionately larger in women

PERIAQUEDUCTAL GREY
- used to suppress pain in men, but perhaps not in women

PARIETAL CORTEX
- spatial perception
- on average proportionately larger in men

HIPPOCAMPUS
- memory
- spatial memory
- on average proportionately larger in women

AMYGDALA
- emotional memory
- on average proportionately larger in men
- when recalling an emotionally charged scene, men enlist its right side, women its left

---

[1]**spatial** *adj* relating to the position, size, and shape of things; **navigation** *n* planning which way to go when you are traveling from one place to another

men/women use the same brain structures differently.

results

4   Larry Cahill, a neurobiologist at the University of California, Irvine, has found evidence that, in some circumstances, people of different sexes use the same brain structures differently. In brain-imaging experiments, he asked groups of men and women to remember images they had been shown earlier. These images were chosen because they produce a strong emotional reaction. Both men and women consistently used the amygdala to complete the task. However, the men used the right side of the amygdala, while the women used the left side. What's more, each group remembered different aspects of the image. The men remembered the gist of the situation, whereas the women concentrated on the details. This suggests men and women process information from emotional events in very different ways.

Researchers only know little. More discoveries to be made

5   These studies are still in their early days, and there is much to be learned. Neurobiologists don't really have a clear overall picture yet. Large pieces of the puzzle are missing, in part because imaging techniques are still rather basic. For researchers to see the brain in action, test subjects need to lie down inside a scanner or be wired up to a PET machine, which is very different from a real world situation. One possible solution is to attach a miniature MRI scanner to subjects' heads. Then researchers would be able to see what happens as people go about their everyday lives.

Conclusion: Research is important for better health.

6   This area of research has some important uses. Working out exactly how brains are different could explain some mysteries, such as why men and women tend to have different mental health problems and why some drugs work well for one sex but have little effect on the other. Finding the reasons for this could lead to more effective treatments and better ways to prevent illness. This would be a very positive result.

Sources: Adapted from: Hoag, H. (2008). Sex on the brain. *New Scientist, Australasian Edition, 2665*, 28–31.
Marsa, L. (2007). He thinks, she thinks. *Discover Magazine*. Retrieved August 14, 2008, from http://discovermagazine.com.

2. *Cover the text. Make notes to complete the chart. Then compare your chart with a partner's and discuss any differences*

Location in the Text	Main Ideas
Introduction (paragraph 1)	• •
Middle (paragraphs 2 and 3)	• •
End (paragraphs 4–6)	• • •

3. *Work with the same partner. Discuss the questions.*

   1. Which strategies from the skill box on page 6 did you use to complete the chart?

   2. Which of the strategies you used were most useful? Why?

   3. Which strategies will you use again?

Focused Reading

Scanning: Finding Specific Information Quickly

Scanning is reading quickly to find specific information, such as words, ideas, numbers, names, places, and dates. Specific information is often found in the supporting details. These could be definitions, examples, and explanations.

As with skimming, you don't read every word when you scan.

Here are some strategies to help you scan:

- Look for capital letters if you are scanning for a place or a name.
- Look for numbers if you are looking for answers to questions about dates, times, etc.
- Find a key word in the question and search for the key word, or a synonym of *different work with similar meaning* the key word, in the text.
- Skim the text when you first see it. Then, when you need to scan, you will know which part of the text to look at first.

1. *The words in the chart have been discussed in the article on pages 6–8. As quickly as you can, scan the text to find these words. Then fill in the second column of the chart with the location of each word in the article. If the word is mentioned in a paragraph, write the paragraph number. If it is mentioned in the diagram, write diagram. Raise your hand when you finish.*

Word	Location in the Article (Paragraph Number and/or Diagram)
hormones	Par. 1
hypothalamus	3
frontal lobe	Diagram 3
limbic cortex	4 3
hippocampus	3 D
parietal cortex	3 P
amygdala	3, 4 D

detail oriented - pay attention to details.

2. *Read in detail the text around the words you identified by scanning in Exercise 1. Match the parts on the left with the situations they are used in on the right. Some parts might match more than one situation. Discuss your answers with a partner.*

	Part		**Situation**
a	1. amygdala	a.	feeling stressed because of a problem at work
b	2. frontal lobe	b.	deciding on a solution to a problem at work
d	3. hippocampus	c.	feeling hungry
f	4. hormones	d.	remembering something that was said two minutes earlier
c	5. hypothalamus	e.	finding the way to a favorite restaurant
c	6. limbic cortex	f.	sending messages around the body
g, e	7. parietal cortex	g.	imagining complex shapes

Which item from the list is the odd one out? Why?

3. *Scan the article again to answer the questions. Circle the strategy you used to find the answers.*

1. What part of the brain gives people a feeling of hunger?

   Answer: _hypothalamus_

   Strategy:
   a. scan for capital letters for names   b. scan for numbers or dates
   (c.) scan for key words or synonyms   d. skim first to find most likely paragraph

2. Who suggested that differences in sizes of structures suggest different functional organization?

   Answer: _Jill Goldstein_

   Strategy:
   (a.) scan for capital letters for names   b. scan for numbers or dates
   c. scan for key words or synonyms   d. skim first to find most likely paragraph

3. When was Jill Goldstein's study conducted?

   Answer: _2001_

   Strategy:
   a. scan for capital letters for names   (b.) scan for numbers or dates
   c. scan for key words or synonyms   d. skim first to find most likely paragraph

4. What is the limbic cortex responsible for?

   Answer: _Control emotions_

   Strategy:
   (a.) scan for capital letters for names   b. scan for numbers or dates
   c. scan for key words or synonyms   d. skim first to find most likely paragraph

5. What structures in the brain show male-female differences?

Answer: _amygdala_

Strategy:

    a. scan for capital letters for names   b. scan for numbers or dates

    c. scan for key words or synonyms   (d.) skim first to find most likely paragraph

6. Which area of your brain would you use to find a solution to a puzzle?

Answer: _frontal lobe_

Strategy:

    a. scan for capital letters for names   b. scan for numbers or dates

    c. scan for key words or synonyms   (d.) skim first to find most likely paragraph

Identifying Supporting Details

As we saw earlier, details that support the main idea can be of several kinds, including the following:

- solutions to problems
- reasons
- consequences
- examples

Often, **logical connectives** can help you notice which kind of supporting details are used. Logical connectives are words that show the relationship between ideas. For example, *because* shows us that there is a reason given. Sometimes ordinary verbs and nouns also provide clues about the kind of supporting idea. *Caused by* and *reason*, for instance, also show that a reason is provided. Here are some other logical connectives:

Type of support	Logical connectives and other words
reasons	*because, for these reasons, in order to*
consequences	*therefore, thus, so, this suggests that*
solutions	*solve, prevent the problem*
examples	*for instance, such as*

Logical connectives that link items in a list (such as *and, also, further, in addition*) also often separate examples.

Figuring out the kind of supporting detail quickly by skimming can often help you to answer questions. For example, if a question begins with *why*, you will want to look for reasons.

4. *Complete the chart on the next page. In the middle column, fill in the blanks with correct words to identify the types of supporting details (reason/s, example/s, consequence/s, or solution/s). In the third column, write the supporting details from the article on pages 6–8.*

(continued on next page)

Main Idea	Question	Supporting Detail(s)
Men and women are different.	What are the three ___reasons___ that researchers give for this difference?	• *social pressures* • •
Neuroscientists are worried.	What is the _____ that neuroscientists are worried?	•
Differences in male and female brain structure are now becoming clear.	What are three _____ of differences?	• • •
Males and females sometimes use the same structure differently.	What is an _____ of this?	•
	What is a _____ of this?	•
This research is still in early stages.	What is a _____ for this?	•
	What is a possible _____ to this?	•
There are important uses for this research.	What are two _____ of this?	• •

5. *Work with a partner. Answer the questions.*

1. What did you find most surprising about the information in the reading?

2. What did you find most interesting?

Checkpoint 1   PEARSON LONGMAN myacademicconnectionslab

Before You Listen

Preparing to Listen

Before you go to a lecture, it is a good idea to think about what the lecture will be about. If you prepare well, the lecture will be easier to understand. Here are some tips:

- **Find out what the topic is.** Often, your lecturer will tell you at the end of one lecture what the next lecture will be about. Also, at the beginning of a semester, many professors give students a course summary, which tells them the topics that the course will cover.

- **Think about what you already know about the topic.** Have you read about it in a newspaper? Chatted with a friend about it? What vocabulary about the topic do you know?

- **Speculate (make guesses) about the topic.** What might the professor say about it?

- **Find as much information as you can about the topic before you listen.** Some professors will give you something to read that matches the lecture topic. Alternatively, you can use online resources to find some information.

Remember that it's easier to understand something you know a little about than something you know nothing about. And it's easier to understand a lecture if you've already thought a little about the topic.

1. 🎧 *Listen to the end of a lecture—the one before this unit's main lecture—and answer the questions. Share your answers in small groups.*

1. What are the main topics of the lecture just finished?
   Modern brain imaging techniques have helped us understand brain
2. What are the main topics of the coming lecture?
   pain + mental health.
3. What, if anything, do you already know about the topic of the coming lecture?

4. What vocabulary related to this topic do you know?

3
Building Academic Listening Skills

In this section, you will practice some strategies that will help you identify main ideas and details in lectures.
For online assignments, go to

PEARSON LONGMAN
myacademicconnectionslab

Key Words

antidepressant *n* a drug used for treating depression

circuit *n* the complete path that an electric current travels around, usually including the source of electric energy

depression *n* a medical condition that makes you feel extremely unhappy, so that it is difficult to live a normal life; **depress** *v*

mental health *n, adj* health of the mind

suppress *v* to prevent something from growing, developing, or working effectively; **suppression** *n*

2. *Read the excerpt from a biology textbook. Fill in the blanks with the key words. Remember to use plural forms where necessary.*

A good example of a natural brain chemical is serotonin. It is a neurotransmitter, which means that it carries messages around the brain. The many functions of serotonin include controlling emotions such as anger and aggression, as well as regulating mood and body temperature. Quite a number of problems can happen to serotonin systems, including problems that (1) __suppresses__ serotonin levels, which in turn leads to low activation of certain brain (2) __circuit__. These can cause a range of (3) __mental health__ problems, one of which is (4) __depression__. Some of the best-known (5) __antidepressant__ work on the serotonin system.

3. *Work with a partner. Discuss the questions.*

1. Which mental health problem do you think will be mentioned in the forthcoming lecture?

2. What kind of brain chemicals might be mentioned in the lecture?

Global Listening

Getting the Gist: Understanding a Speaker's Main Ideas

Getting the **gist** means listening for the **main ideas** and **general information**. Listening for the gist is similar to skimming in reading. When listening for the gist, don't pay attention to details.

Here are some strategies that will help you listen for the gist of a lecture:

- Listen carefully to the introduction. Lecturers often state the main ideas toward the end of the introduction.
- Listen for signals that mark main ideas:

  Some of the points we'll cover are . . .

  In today's lecture, we will look at . . .

  In addition to that, another important point is . . .

- Listen carefully to the end of the lecture. You will often hear a summary of the main ideas at that time.

1. 🎧 Listen to the introduction of the lecture. What is the topic, and what are the main ideas? Write them in the chart. You don't need to complete the general information yet.

Topic of lecture: _Male & female brain differences_ **and their implications for** _medicine_

Main idea 1: _Pain_

General information:

- Women perhaps experience _more pain_ than men
- Research suggests that _males & females use different circuits to block pain._
- Some painkillers have _different effects in male & female._

- In the future, _we might have to create more effective medicine for women_

Main idea 2: _Mental Health_

General information:

- Women perhaps experience _depression twice as often as men._
- Serotonin works differently in _male & female brains_
- Males have other _problems that affect brain systems._
- New _research_ may help _both genders_

2. 🎧 Listen to the whole lecture. Complete the rest of the chart with general information. Listen for the signals of main ideas and the information in the summary of the lecture to help you.

3. Compare your chart with a partner's. Explain your notes. Discuss any differences.

Focused Listening

We saw in previous sections that supporting details in written English are sometimes marked by logical connectives and other words, and that these words often show which kind of supporting idea is used. The same is true in listening. So, listen carefully for words and expressions like *for instance* and *because* to indicate examples and reasons.

A second strategy to find the supporting details is just to use your sense of logic. Sometimes, it is clear that one idea supports another, and there is no need to mark it with a logical connective. For example, if the professor mentions a researcher, the researcher's university, the date of the research, and the research result, it is clear that the research result is the main idea, and the rest of the information will be the supporting details.

1. ⌒ *Work in two groups: Group A and Group B. Group A students will focus on pain. Group B students will focus on mental health. Listen to the lecture again and fill in the chart for your group.*

Group A

Main Idea: Pain	
General Information	Supporting Details
Women perhaps experience more pain than men.	*A lot of research suggests this.*
Research suggests that males and females use different circuits to block pain.	
Some painkillers have different effects on females and males.	• Nalbuphine: • Other painkillers:
In the future, there may be more effective painkillers for women.	

Group B

Main Idea: Mental Health	
General Information	Supporting Details
Women perhaps experience more depression than men.	*Women appear to suffer from depression twice as often.*
Serotonin works differently in females.	
Males have other mental health problems.	
New medicines for one gender may help males.	

2. *Work in pairs of one student from Group A and one from Group B. Explain your notes to your partner. Then complete the chart for your partner's group.*

3. *Read the statements. Decide if they are true or false. Write **T** (true) or **F** (false). Correct the false statements. Use the charts in Exercise 1 to help you. Then compare your answers with a partner's. Discuss the differences.*

_____ 1. Anne Murphy did her research in Canada.

_____ 2. Painkilling drugs are usually tested only on men.

_____ 3. Nalbuphine reduces pain in women.

_____ 4. Nalbuphine also reduces pain in men.

_____ 5. There will definitely be painkillers designed especially for women in the future.

_____ 6. Men usually produce twice as much serotonin as women.

_____ 7. It appears that women respond better to drugs that work on neurotransmitters other than serotonin.

🎧 *Listen to the lecture again to check your answers.*

4. *One criticism of the research described in the article and lecture is that it could lead to stereotyping. Work in small groups. Discuss the questions.*

1. How do you think this research might lead to stereotyping?

2. What could be the problems with stereotyping—for example, in school or at work?

3. Do you think such research should be stopped because of the danger of stereotyping? Explain.

Checkpoint 2   PEARSON LONGMAN myacademicconnectionslab

4
Building Academic Writing Skills

In this section, you will look at how to write effective introductions and how to make writing easier by planning. Then you will write a short essay about the implications of the differences between male and female brains for the development of medicine. You will use information from this unit to complete the writing assignment.

For online assignments, go to

PEARSON LONGMAN
myacademicconnectionslab

Single underline: general statement

Double underline: thesis

Squiggly line: scope

Before You Write

Understanding Essay Introductions and Their Relationship to the Body of the Essay

An essay has one main idea (a thesis) and some major points that support it. These are usually given in the introduction.

The following are typical stages in introductions:

- The **general statement** introduces the topic. It may also include definitions of important concepts, if necessary.
- The **thesis** states the main idea or opinion that the author discusses, argues for, or explains. In other words, this is the central idea of the essay. Everything else supports the thesis in some way.
- The **scope** gives some major points that support the thesis and will be discussed in the body of the essay. The scope might list the main ideas, or it might be a statement that includes the main ideas.

Each body paragraph begins with a **topic sentence**, which gives the main idea of the paragraph. There should be a clear connection between the scope and the topic sentences.

1. *Look at the example of an introduction to a student's essay, with the different sections underlined. Work with a partner. From the list below, choose two sentences that could make appropriate topic sentences for the body paragraphs of the essay.*

New technologies such as fMRI and PET scans are making it easier than ever before to study the living brain. Research that would have been impossible just a few years ago is now commonplace. Several areas of scientific research have benefited greatly from this. Two of these are medicine and psychology.

Possible Topic Sentences
- fMRI scans are different from PET scans.
- Several areas of medicine have advanced rapidly due to the ability to produce images of the brain in action.
- Cognitive psychologists greatly appreciate what fMRI and PET can do.
- Studying the living brain is easier than ever before.

2. *Read the introduction to another student's essay. Underline the general statement once. Underline the thesis twice. Underline the scope with a squiggly line. Then compare your answers with a partner's.*

With new technology such as PET and fMRI scans, more and more is being learned about the human brain. It is becoming clear that different people's brains work in different ways. For example, it has recently been discovered that there are small differences in the brains of males and females. This is a very important discovery for neuroscience. For one thing, it could lead to solutions to many long-standing mysteries. Also, it is likely to lead to differences in how research is carried out. For society, one benefit is likely to be that medicines will become better suited to the biology of females than they are now.

3. *Write two topic sentences for the body paragraphs of the essay in Exercise 2.*

_____

_____

_____

_____

Focused Writing

1. *Read about two ways of imaging the brain in action. Complete the chart. Write* **yes** *or* **no**. *Then compare your chart with a partner's.*

Key Words

injection *n* the use of a special needle to put a liquid, such as a drug, into your body through the skin; **inject** *v*

oxygen *n* the gas in the air that most living things need to live; its chemical symbol is O_2

radioactive *adj* producing a type of energy (in the form of heat or light sent out as waves) that can be dangerous; an atomic bomb is very radioactive; **radiation** *n*

sensor *n* a piece of equipment used to detect light, heat, movement, etc; **sense** *v*

To produce a PET scan, first, the person must have an injection of a slightly radioactive substance. This substance is carried in the blood to the brain, where it collects in the areas that are most active. Later, when the person is in the machine, sensors detect radiation—particles called positrons—from the injected substance. The result is a single two-dimensional or three-dimensional color image. The different colors show different amounts of mental activity. By looking at images produced while the person does different activities, researchers can see which parts of the brain are used.

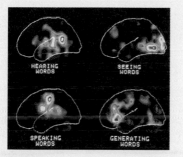

A PET (positron emission tomography) scan of a normal brain during different tasks

Neurons in the brain need oxygen; this is carried by the blood to the neurons. Blood flow increases to areas of the brain that are most active. Such changes can be measured due to an interesting property: Blood without oxygen responds differently to a magnetic field than blood that is carrying a lot of oxygen. fMRI scanners can measure this difference. Different amounts of activity are usually shown by different colors. Typically, fMRI scans can show activity in a two-millimeter to four-millimeter cube every one to four seconds; thus, films can be produced.

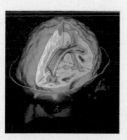

fMRI (functional magnetic resonance imaging) scan of a brain during speech activity

	PET Scan	fMRI Scan
Injection necessary?		
Uses radioactive substance?		
Color images?		
Motion pictures?		

2. *Discuss the questions with a partner.*

1. How would you feel about having a PET scan compared with having an fMRI scan?

2. Which type of scan would you prefer? Why?

3. What other advantages and disadvantages of each type of scan can you think of?

Planning for Writing: Thesis, Major Points, and Supporting Details

It is a good idea to write a short plan before each written assignment. An essay plan can help you to:

• organize your ideas
• check that your supporting details really do support your thesis strongly

Both of these processes are much easier to achieve in a plan than after you start writing—it's much quicker to change notes than to change sentences and paragraphs you have already spent time on.

Choose a clear format for your plan. The format suggested below will help you to see the connections between the thesis and the major points that support the thesis.

Remember that you can always adjust your plan as your ideas develop. Thus, it's a good idea to use a pencil, not a pen.

Here is a sample format of an essay plan.

Thesis
  • Main idea 1 to support the thesis
    * Supporting detail 1 for main idea 1
    * Supporting detail 2 for main idea 1
  • Main idea 2 to support the thesis
    * Supporting detail 1 for main idea 2
    * Supporting detail 2 for main idea 2

---

3. *Plan a short essay that compares how images of the brain at work are produced. Use the suggested format, as well as information about PET and fMRI scans on page 19. Write in your notebook or on a separate piece of paper.*

Thesis: How Images of the Brain are Produced

Main idea 1:

Supporting details:

Main idea 2:

Supporting details:

---

4. *Work with a partner. Compare your plans. Discuss any differences. After comparing, you can adjust your plan if you like.*

5. *Write your essay that compares how images of the brain at work are produced. Use your plan and the information about writing introductions and topic sentences on page 18.*

Integrated Writing Task

You have read and listened to information about the differences between male and female brains and the implications these differences have for medicine. You will now use your knowledge of the unit content, vocabulary, and skills to write a short essay in response to this question: **How similar or different are the brains of men and women? How do we know? What implications do any differences have for the development of medicine?**

Follow the steps to write your essay.

Step 1: Think about the essay questions. Then review the readings, lecture, and information in the unit. What similarities and differences between male and female brains did you learn about? What are they? How can they be seen and studied? What aspects of modern medicine will they affect?

Step 2: Plan your essay. Choose one main idea—a thesis—and some major points to support the thesis.

Step 3: Write your introduction, which should include:
- a general statement that introduces the topic
- a thesis that states the important points you will discuss in your essay
- a scope that states the main ideas in support of the thesis

Step 4: Write the body of your essay.
- Your essay should have a separate paragraph for each main point.
- Remember that the first sentence of each paragraph—the topic sentence—should state the main point of that paragraph clearly.
- Include supporting details in each paragraph.

Step 5: Write a conclusion, summarizing the main ideas.

Step 6: Show your essay to another student. Comment on each other's essays. Use the checklist on the next page. Discuss how you might improve your essays.

Step 7: Based on your discussion with your partner, write a second draft of your essay and hand it in.

Does the essay have. . .	Yes
a general statement that introduces the topic of the essay and leads nicely to the thesis?	
a clear thesis, giving the central point or opinion of the essay?	
a scope that covers the main ideas in the body of the essay?	
a topic sentence for each body paragraph that follows from the scope?	
clear supporting details in each paragraph, supporting the main idea?	
a conclusion that summarizes the main ideas?	

UNIT

2

Business

Pricing

Unit Description

Content: This course is designed to familiarize the student with concepts in marketing and pricing strategies.

Skills: Organizational Structure

- Recognizing relationships between parts of a lecture
- Recognizing detailed relationships between ideas in lectures
- Note-taking
- Recognizing organization and purpose of written texts
- Recognizing relationships within a written text
- Showing relationships between ideas
- Using notes to assist speaking

Unit Requirements

Lecture: "Pricing"

Reading: "Pricing Considerations" (from *Marketing: An Introduction*, 8th Edition, G. Armstrong and P. Kotler, Pearson Prentice Hall)

Listening: "Psychological Pricing Strategies" (a radio broadcast)

Integrated Speaking Task: Choosing pricing strategies

Assignments: www.MyAcademicConnectionsLab.com

Key Words

brand *n* a type of product made by a particular company

brand name *n* the name a company gives to the products it has made; Coca-Cola is a brand name.

consumer *n* someone who buys or uses goods and services

influence *v* to change the way people think; **influence** *n*

loss *n* if a business takes a loss, it spends more than it earns

marketer *n* a person who is responsible for company strategies for selling things

pricing *n* choosing the price for something a company sells

product *n* something (a thing or service) that a company sells

profit *n* the amount of money a company makes after paying its costs (opposite of loss); **make a profit** *exp*

purchase *n* something you buy; **purchase** *v*

strategy *n* a plan for achieving something

Previewing the Academic Content

When you walk though a shopping mall or go online to make a purchase, the price of what you see may strongly influence which product you buy—or whether you buy anything at all. Marketers know this, and they are very careful about how they price their products. The right strategy can mean success for the product and bigger profits for the company; the wrong strategy could lead to losses and failure for the product or, in some cases, it could even lead to jail!

In this unit, we will look at various pricing strategies that companies use. This will help you, as a consumer, to understand the tricks that some companies use. If you ever go on to manage any kind of company, these pricing strategies could be very useful to you.

1. *Look at the advertisement and photograph. Work with a partner. Discuss the questions.*

1. In your opinion, are these items cheap or expensive? Why do you think so?

2. Do you think the handbag would be a bargain at $3,000 or the car at $100,000?

2. *Work with a partner to sort the key words into categories in the chart. Some words might belong to more than one category.*

Money	People	Intangible Things (Things You Can't See or Touch)	Tangible Things
profit pricing. loss purchase	Consumer marketer	*profit* brand influence loss pricing strategy.	product purchase brand name

3. *Discuss the questions with your partner. Use words from the box.*

1. What are the reasons for your answers in Exercise 1?

2. If someone you knew bought one of the items in Exercise 1, how would it influence your opinion of the person?

3. Why do you think people pay more for products such as these, when there are much cheaper handbags and cars?

This unit will help you recognize organizational patterns in readings and lectures. You will also develop and effectively use organizational patterns in speaking.

Previewing the Academic Skills Focus

Organizational Structure

When you read academic texts or listen to lectures, you will notice that they are organized in certain patterns. This pattern of organization in a reading or lecture is called **organizational structure**. Some of the typical patterns of organization are explanation, process, argument, and discussion. These patterns are closely linked to the purpose of the text or lecture.

Purpose	Pattern of Organization
To say what something is or looks like	Description
To say why or how something happens	Explanation
To argue for an opinion, perhaps by showing how the advantages of one idea are stronger than its disadvantages	Argument
To discuss aspects of an issue, such as advantages and disadvantages of different ideas or theories, and come to a conclusion about which one is stronger	Discussion

Recognizing the organizational structure of a text is useful because it can help you predict what you will read or listen to. This, in turn, will help you read faster and listen more easily.

1. *Read the introductions. Decide which pattern of organization from the box each full text will follow.*

A.

There are many different strategies that businesses can use to price their products. Which one they choose will depend on their circumstances. In this section, we will examine three different pricing strategies. We will look at how each works and explore the reasons that business might choose them.

Pattern of organization: *explanation*

B.

Pricing is tricky for businesses. The wrong price can lead to low profits or even losses. So, a company must be very careful to choose the right strategy for setting prices. In this lecture, we'll look at two possible strategies—called *value-based pricing* and *cost-based pricing*. We'll examine the advantages and disadvantages of these two strategies, and then we'll draw some conclusions about when each might be appropriate.

Pattern of organization: _____Discussion_____

C.

There are many factors that influence people's purchasing decisions. In some circumstances, people buy mainly based on the price of the product. In other situations, the quality of the product may be a stronger factor, and people may pay a higher price for it. For some products, and for some consumers, the brand name is more important than any of these factors. Good marketers need to have a clear understanding of all of these factors, and several more.

Pattern of organization: _____explanation / argument_____

D.

Value-based pricing is one of several pricing strategies that a business can employ. There are several steps involved in value-based pricing. We will briefly look at each step and explain its importance in the whole process of successfully pricing a product.

Pattern of organization: _____explanation_____

E.

Canikon today announced the release of the DX3-AC compact still and video camera. The DX3-AC features several major new developments that make this camera different from all others.

Pattern of organization: _____description_____

F.

When setting prices, most people's natural tendency is to go low. It is tempting to think that a price lower than that of similar products will encourage people to buy, thus leading to greater profit. But higher prices also have advantages. For one thing, the profit on each item is higher. For another, higher prices often give the impression of quality, which may make the item more desirable. In some cases, higher prices have resulted in more products being sold. In this section, we'll discuss different pricing strategies—high and low—in detail.

Pattern of organization: _____Discussion_____

G.

Clearly profit is important, and once a product has been selling for some time, it's often tempting to reduce prices quickly. People think this will lead to higher sales, and then greater profit. However, there is an alternative. That is to persuade consumers that, really, the product is worth a higher price. The remainder of this paper will present evidence that this is usually the best strategy.

Pattern of organization: ___explanation_____

2. Compare your answers with a partner's. What are the reasons for your choices?

Before You Listen

1. Imagine that you are shopping for a digital camera. What factors are important to you when deciding which one to buy? Circle the appropriate number on the scale. Add other factors if you think of them. Then compare and discuss your choices with a partner.

	Not important	Somewhat important	Important	Very important
THE CAMERA				
Brand	1	2	3	4
Price	1	2	3	4
Quality	1	2	3	4
Style	1	2	3	4
Another factor: _____	1	2	3	4
Another factor: _____	1	2	3	4
THE STORE				
Brand	1	2	3	4
Convenient location	1	2	3	4
Customer service	1	2	3	4
Appearance	1	2	3	4
Another factor: _____	1	2	3	4
Another factor: _____	1	2	3	4

2
Building Academic Listening Skills

In this section, you will listen to a lecture and find out how to recognize the organizational structure of a lecture. For online assignments, go to

PEARSON LONGMAN
myacademicconnectionslab

associate (with) v
to make a mental
connection between
two things

competitor n a
company offering
products and services
similar to those of
another company;
compete v

(profit) margin n the
difference between
what something costs
a business and what
they sell it for

market n in business,
all the people who
might be interested
in buying a particular
product

market research n
research about what
people buy and why
they buy it

project an image exp
to try to give other
people a particular
idea about you. For
example: project a
smart, professional
image.

2. *Work with a partner. Discuss which pricing level you think would work for each type of product listed. More than one pricing level is possible for some products.*

Type of Product

_____ 1. A basic product with only common features

_____ 2. A product with special new features. Your company has found through market research that consumers want these features. Your competitors' products don't have them.

_____ 3. A product made of high-quality materials designed to project a high-quality image

_____ 4. A product that your company's management wants to sell to the widest possible market

_____ 5. A product that your company is going to associate, through advertising, with very successful people

Pricing Level

a. lower than your competitors' products

b. same as your competitors' products

c. higher than your competitors' products

3. *Work with another pair. Explain the reasons for your answers in Exercise 2. What other factors would you also consider when pricing these products?*

Global Listening

1. *Each section of a lecture has a different purpose. Look at the list of purposes of different sections of the lecture you are going to listen to. Work with a partner. What logical order would you suggest for these sections? Number them from 1 to 9 in the middle column in the chart. You will complete the right-hand column later.*

Purpose	Suggested Order	Actual Order
To show or explain one approach to the topic		
To give the disadvantages of one approach to the topic		
To show the disadvantages of the other approach		
To introduce the lecture	*1*	
To show the importance of the topic		
To summarize		
To explain a different approach to the topic		
To give the advantages of one approach to the topic		
To show the advantages of the other approach		

2. 🎧 *Listen to the lecture and complete the right-hand column in the chart with the actual order of the sections. Is the actual order the same as your suggested order? Compare answers with your partner's. Discuss any differences.*

Recognizing Relationships between Parts of a Lecture

Most academic lectures (as well as written texts) are organized in a similar way—they have an introduction, a body, and a conclusion.

In the **introduction**, the instructor may:

- review the information from a previous lecture
- introduce a new topic

The introduction can be short, but it is very important for understanding the organization of the lecture. We saw in Unit 1 that the introduction often mentions the main ideas of the lecture; these can help you figure out the organizational structure.

In the **body**, the instructor will provide more detailed information about the topic. The pattern and type of this information depends on the organizational structure.

In the **conclusion**, the instructor may:

- summarize or repeat the main point
- give the topic of the next lecture

This table summarizes how different parts of the lecture are related.

Pattern of organization	Focus	Introduction	Body	Conclusion
description	facts	names the thing to be described	lists different features of the thing	(optional) mentions the thing described again
explanation	facts	gives the idea to be explained	lists different aspects of (or reasons for) the idea	(optional) repeats the idea
argument	one side of an opinion	gives the opinion (thesis)	gives arguments, explanations, and reasons for the opinion	briefly summarizes the arguments and repeats the thesis
discussion	two or more sides of an opinion	gives the issue to be discussed	gives each side of the issue or advantages and disadvantages	repeats the issue, briefly summarizes all sides; may also say which side of the issue is stronger

Understanding these relationships between parts of the lecture will help you recognize the parts, even when the lecturer does not state the relationships clearly. However, to help you more, most lecturers use various signals, including the following:

- In the introduction, to show which idea is the main idea: *the main point/thing/ focus is . . . , the most important . . . , our focus today is . . .*
- In the body, to introduce a main idea: *first, let's move on to . . . , however, but*
- To start the conclusion: *in summary, to conclude, let's wrap up today's lecture*

Note: As we saw in Unit 1 and will see later in this unit, some of these words also mark smaller ideas such as supporting ideas.

3. *Work with a partner. Answer the questions.*

1. What is the organizational structure of this unit's lecture?

2. What is the reason for your answer to question 1?

4. 🎧 *Listen to the lecture again. Pay attention to the signals the lecturer uses. Circle the correct answers.*

1. In the introduction, to show which idea is the main idea, the lecturer says _____.
   a. "Our focus today is . . ."
   b. "The most important point in this lecture is . . ."
   c. "The main thing we'll do today is . . ."

2. To introduce the first point in the body, the lecturer says _____.
   a. "Let's start with . . ."
   b. "So, first of all, . . ."
   c. no signal, just mentions a main idea

3. To introduce the next point (cost-based pricing), the lecturer says _____.
   a. "Now for the next point. . . . Let's look first at . . ."
   b. "Let's move on now to . . . The first we'll consider is . . ."
   c. "Next, we'll consider . . ."

4. To introduce the disadvantages (of cost-based pricing), the lecturer says _____.
   a. " . . . though . . ."
   b. "On the other hand . . ."
   c. "However, . . ."

5. To introduce the final point (value-based pricing), the lecturer says _____.
   a. "Finally, . . ."
   b. "So, we come now to the final point, . . ."
   c. "But . . . alternative approach . . ."

6. To introduce the conclusion, the lecturer says _____.
   a. "So, in conclusion, . . ."
   b. "Now, let's wrap up."
   c. "Finally, to sum up, . . ."

Focused Listening

Recognizing Detailed Relationships between Ideas in Lectures

We saw earlier that various signals are used to mark the different stages in a lecture and to show the relationships between them. The same applies within each stage.

These logical connectives are common within sections of a lecture:

- To add a similar point, idea, argument, or reason: *in addition, also, furthermore, another*
- To show differences between ideas: *however, but, although, in contrast*
- To show stages in a process: *first, then, next, after that, finally*

In Unit 1 (page 11), we saw some of the words used to mark reasons, consequences, solutions, and examples.

1. *Listen to the excerpts from the lecture. For each excerpt, fill in the blanks with the logical connectives you hear. Then decide what relationship each connective signals.*

⌒ Excerpt One

. . . some managers see pricing as a big headache. _____,

clever managers use pricing as a key tool.

Relationship: _____

⌒ Excerpt Two

Price plays an important role in how much value customers see in a product—

higher prices often send the message that quality is higher, even if it isn't. It

_____ plays a role in building customer relationships . . .

Relationship: _____

⌒ Excerpt Three

In cost-based pricing, _____, a company designs a product.

_____ it works out how much each item costs to make, plus all

the other costs, such as delivery, packaging, and design. _____,

a margin is added, to produce the profit.

Relationship: _____

⌒ Excerpt Four

With a value-based strategy, you can be more certain that people will be

happy to pay for your product. _____, you have a good idea in

advance whether a product is going to turn a profit.

Relationship: _____

2. *Discuss your answers with a partner. Listen to the lecture again if necessary to confirm your answers.*

Taking notes is very important during lectures. It not only helps you to study later, but also helps to focus your thoughts while listening.

You can use these tools to take notes:

- charts
- outlines
- diagrams

Your choice of the appropriate note-taking tools may depend on the organizational structure of the lecture.

3. *Work with a partner. Write the most appropriate organizational structure next to each note-taking tool. More than one note-taking tool is possible for some of the organizational structures.*

Organizational Structure—Sections of a Lecture that:

- give different features of a product (description)
- give reasons why something happens (explanation)
- give steps in a process that repeats (explanation)
- support an opinion with reasons and evidence (argument)
- examine similarities and differences (discussion)
- give advantages and disadvantages, or strengths and weaknesses (discussion)

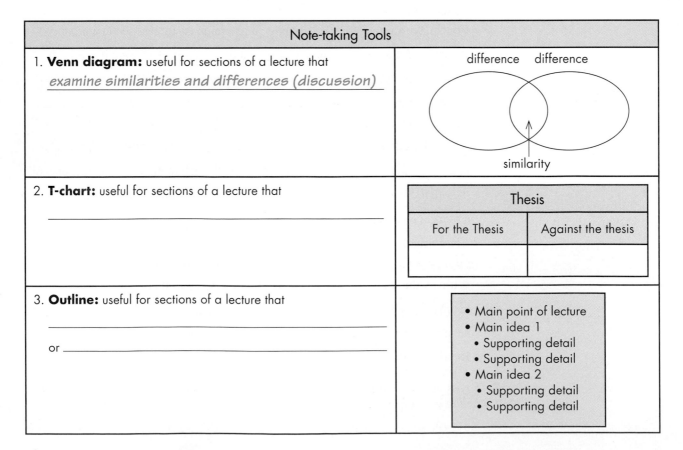

Note-taking Tools
1. **Venn diagram:** useful for sections of a lecture that *examine similarities and differences (discussion)*
2. **T-chart:** useful for sections of a lecture that
3. **Outline:** useful for sections of a lecture that ___ or ___

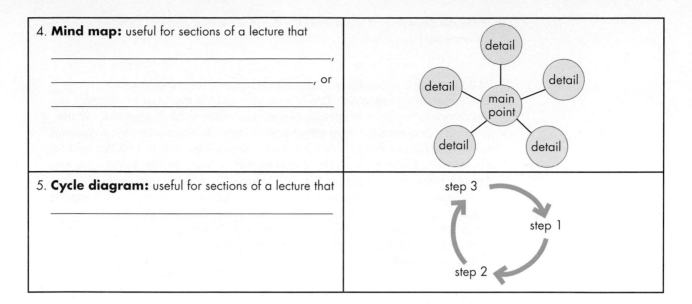

| 4. **Mind map:** useful for sections of a lecture that _____, _____, or _____ | |
| 5. **Cycle diagram:** useful for sections of a lecture that _____ | |

4. Work with a partner. How would you design a note-taking tool for this unit's lecture? Draw the tool on a separate piece of paper. Make sure it is big enough to use for taking notes.

5. 🎧 Listen to the lecture again. Take notes in the note-taking tools you drew in Exercise 4. Then compare your notes with a partner's. Discuss any differences.

6. Work with a partner to answer the questions. You may use your notes.

In the lecturer's opinion:

1. Who would be the best managers? Why?
   a. those who see pricing as complicated and difficult
   b. those who see pricing as an opportunity

2. Which is "good value"? Why?
   a. a $200 handbag that is strong and looks OK, but is nothing special
   b. a $2,000 handbag that projects the same image as one costing $3,000

3. Which pricing strategy has the greatest focus on the market? How do you know?
   a. cost-based pricing
   b. value-based pricing

4. Which pricing strategy considers the greatest number of factors? How do you know?
   a. cost-based pricing
   b. value-based pricing

5. Which pricing strategy is easier to use?
   a. cost-based pricing
   b. value-based pricing

6. Which pricing strategy is more effective?
   a. cost-based pricing
   b. value-based pricing

7. *Read the case study. Then discuss the questions with a partner. Refer to your notes as necessary.*

P&G is a large U.S. company, selling a wide range of consumer goods and famous for its marketing skill. One of their successes is the Crest SpinBrush®. The company usually sets prices quite high compared to its competitors, but the SpinBrush designers came up with the new idea while walking through a discount store. They noticed that other electric toothbrushes were all over $50, but held only a small fraction of the overall toothbrush market. A cheap electric toothbrush, they thought, could have a huge market. They decided on a target price of just $5—only $1 more expensive than the most expensive traditional toothbrush—and designed a brush they could sell at a small profit at that price. The Crest SpinBrush became one of P&G's most successful new products ever. It is now the nation's best-selling toothbrush—traditional or electric—with a more than 40 percent share of the electric toothbrush market.

Source: Armstrong, G., & Kotler, P. (2007). *Marketing: An Introduction* (8th ed.). Upper Saddle River, NJ: Pearson Prentice Hall.

1. Which pricing strategy did the company use? How do you know?

2. Why do you think the other pricing strategy wouldn't work in this case?

Checkpoint 1 PEARSON LONGMAN **myacademicconnectionslab**

3

Building Academic Reading Skills

In this section you will practice identifying organizational patterns in longer texts and recognizing the relationships between parts of a text.
For online assignments, go to

myacademicconnectionslab

Before You Read

1. *Work with a partner. Complete the scenarios with key words on the next page.*

1. You buy a product that's cheap. Later, when you want to buy a(n) _____ for it, you find they are quite expensive.

2. You find it difficult to compare products from different companies because the way they _____ their prices is very different from each other.

3. A company has invented a _____ product that you are very excited about. However, it is the only company making the product, and it's very expensive.

4. An advertisement for a great product _____ you to visit a _____ store. However, when you get there, the product is not available. The store does have other, more expensive products, though.

5. The product you want to buy is only slightly more expensive if you buy it in a _____ with another product.

accessory *n* an extra item that can make something more attractive, more useful, or more functional

bundle *n* a group of things; **bundle** *v*

calculate *v* to find out how much something will cost, how long something will take, etc, by using numbers; **calculation** *n*

retail *n* selling goods to the public, not to other businesses; **retail** *v*

supplies *n* things that get used up and have to be replaced

tempt *v* to make someone want to do something or have something by making it seem attractive; **temptation** *n*; **tempting** *adj*

unique *adj* the only one of its kind; special

volume *n* the number or amount of something; this word is used especially for large numbers or amounts

6. A shop sells something in large _____.

7. You go to a store to buy something. The salesperson tries very hard to sell you an extra _____ for it.

Which scenarios are you familiar with? Tell a partner.

2. *Mingle with other students in your class. Find people who have experienced each of the scenarios in Exercise 1. Which product was involved? Find out as much as you can about the situation. Try to find at least two or three products for each scenario. Complete the chart.*

Scenario	Product
1.	• • •
2.	• • •
3.	• • •
4.	• • •
5.	• • •
6.	• • •
7.	• • •

3. *Share what you found out with a partner. Explain the situations that you noted in the chart.*

Global Reading

Just like lectures, written texts have an organizational structure with an introduction, body, and conclusion. A text's organization follows very similar patterns, each with a purpose:

- **Description**, focusing on facts, listing features of things
- **Explanation**, also focusing on facts, but saying how or why something happens
- **Argument**, giving points to support an opinion about an issue
- **Discussion**, giving two sides of an issue, and perhaps deciding which side is strongest

As with lectures, understanding and following the organizational structure will help you understand the text.

The main difference between lectures and written texts involves style. While lectures often use conversational signals (for example, *now, we'll move on to the next topic*), written English tends to use more formal signals (for example, *The next topic is . . .*).

1. Work with a partner. Imagine that each of the questions is answered by a text, such as an essay or a section of a textbook. Which organizational structure (description, explanation, argument or discussion) fits best with each question? Why?

1. Why do many companies use value-based pricing?

2. How are various pricing strategies used to set prices?

3. What is the best pricing strategy?

4. What is value-based pricing?

5. What are the advantages and disadvantages of cost-based pricing?

2. Read the introduction to an excerpt from a business textbook. Then answer the questions.

> So far, we've looked at the two main price-setting strategies: cost-based pricing and value-based pricing. As we'll see, there are different kinds of value-based pricing. This section will first look at how some of them work. Then it will show how to avoid some pricing problems.

1. Which of the questions in Exercise 1 will this text answer?

2. What other question does the text answer?

3. Skim the whole text on pages 37–38 and answer the questions.

1. How many pricing strategies are covered?

2. How many possible problems are mentioned?

Pricing Considerations

1 So far, we've looked at the two main price-setting strategies: cost-based pricing and value-based pricing. As we'll see, there are different kinds of value-based pricing. This section will first look at how some of them work. Then it will show how to avoid some pricing problems.

Value-based pricing strategies

2 **Market-skimming pricing.** Many companies that invent new products set high initial prices to "skim" profits from the market layer by layer. In this way, the company skims the maximum amount of profit from the various segments of the market.

3 Market skimming makes sense only under certain conditions. First, the product must interest consumers enough for them to pay a higher price. Also, it helps if there is something unique or unusual about the product. Third, the cost of producing a smaller volume cannot be too high; otherwise it would cancel the advantage of charging more. Finally, competitors should not be able to enter the market easily and undercut the price.

4 **Market-penetration pricing.** In this type of pricing, companies set a low price initially in order to quickly attract a large number of buyers and win a large share of the market. The high sales volume results in falling costs, allowing the company to cut its prices even further.

5 Several conditions must be met for this low-price strategy to work. First, the market must be very sensitive to price so that the low price brings in as many buyers as possible. In addition, production and distribution costs must fall as sales increase. Also, the low price must help keep out the competition, and the product must maintain its low price—otherwise, the price advantage may be only temporary.

6 **Captive product pricing.** Companies that make products that must be used along with another product often use this technique. Examples include razor blades, video games, and printer cartridges. Producers of the main

product (for example, the printer) often price it very low, but sell the supplies (for example, the printer cartridges) at a high margin.

7 **Product bundle pricing.** Sellers often combine several of their products and offer the bundle at a reduced price. For example, fast food restaurants bundle a burger, fries, and a soft drink at "combo" prices. Price bundling can promote the sales of products consumers might not otherwise buy, but the combined price must be low enough to get them to buy the bundle.

8 **Optional-product pricing.** Companies may tempt customers into the store with low prices, but make most of their profit on optional extras, upgrades, and accessories that they try to sell to the customer. For example, a computer buyer may choose to order extra memory and a larger hard drive. Companies have to be careful with this strategy, as it can lead to a reputation for misleading customers

(continued on next page)

if the main product has too few features to be useful.

9 An extreme form of this strategy, called bait and switch, is illegal in many countries. In this strategy, the advertised product is simply not available. The advertisements are designed to attract people into the store, where many will eventually buy a higher-margin product.

Other issues

10 Marketers should be careful about two things. One is consumer backlash, which happens when consumers feel that a company is taking advantage of them. The other is the law. There are several ways in which a company's pricing strategy could be illegal, depending on the countries in which the company is doing business.

11 One act that is against the law in many countries is price fixing. This is when two companies work together to set prices.

In 2004, four executives from a German company were sentenced to between four and six months in prison by U.S. authorities as a result of their participation in a price-fixing scandal involving computer memory. This incident led to consumers' paying millions of dollars more than necessary.

12 Sellers are also often prohibited from using predatory pricing—selling below cost to put competitors out of business. This can get particularly nasty when large, powerful companies try to put small ones out of business.

13 One strategy that may be deceptive, if not actually illegal, is price confusion. This happens when the way a company calculates the price of a product is difficult for consumers to understand. As a result, consumers find it impossible to understand exactly what price they can expect to pay, or to compare products from different companies.

Source: Armstrong, G., & Kotler, P. (2007). *Marketing: An Introduction* (8th ed.). Upper Saddle River, NJ: Pearson Prentice Hall.

Focused Reading

1. *Carefully read the text on pages 37–38 and the list of points below. Which strategy does each point best summarize?*

1. Set a very low price to make it impossible for other companies to compete in the market.

    predatory pricing
    _____

2. Sell the basic item at a low price, perhaps below cost, but make money on optional items and accessories.

    _____

3. Set prices jointly with another company that would normally be a competitor.

    _____

4. Advertise a product that doesn't exist, so that more people come to the store; then try to sell them something similar that has a higher margin and higher price.

    _____

5. Sell as many items as possible by selling them cheaply.

_____

6. Sell the main item at a low price, but set a high price for the supplies.

_____

7. Introduce a new product at a high price and sell it just to the top level of the market. Then steadily reduce the price, selling to a lower level of the market each time.

_____

8. Sell several items in one package.

_____

2. *What are three examples of the strategies that, according to the writer, might cause problems in some countries. Check (✓) your answers.*

_____ bait and switch

_____ price confusion

_____ captive product pricing

_____ market skimming

_____ predatory pricing

_____ market penetration

_____ price fixing

Recognizing Relationships within a Written Text

We have seen that, in spoken texts such as lectures, logical connectives and signals are used to make the organizational structure clear, and also to make the relationships between ideas clear. The same applies to written texts.

Here are some examples of logical connectives and other expressions used in written texts:

- to add a similar point, example, idea, or reason: *first, third, similarly, additionally*
- to add examples: *for instance, such as*
- to show reasons: *in order to, because*
- to show consequences: *as a result, consequently, one effect is, leads to*

As with spoken texts, the types of logical connectives often reflect the type of organizational structure. For example, an explanation essay might use many logical connectives and grammatical structures expressing reasons (for example, *because, so, thus*). A discussion essay may have a number of logical connectives showing opposing ideas (for example, *however, on the other hand, in contrast*).

3. Circle the type of supporting detail each question is asking for. Compare your answers with a partner's.

1. What are the three qualities a product must have for market-skimming pricing to work?

   a. reason   b. consequence   c. example   d. list of similar points

2. In market-penetration pricing, why is a low price set to begin with?

   a. reason   b. consequence   c. example   d. list of similar points

3. In market-penetration pricing, how does the increasing sales volume affect production costs?

   a. reason   b. consequence   c. example   d. list of similar points

4. What are three examples of captive product pricing?

   a. reason   b. consequence   c. example   d. list of similar points

5. Why should companies be careful with optional-product pricing?

   a. reason   b. consequence   c. example   d. list of similar points

6. What are two other issues that marketers should be careful about?

   a. reason   b. consequence   c. example   d. list of similar points

7. What were two results of the price-fixing scandal involving computer memory?

   a. reason   b. consequence   c. example   d. list of similar points

8. How might consumers be affected by complicated pricing systems?

   a. reason   b. consequence   c. example   d. list of similar points

4. Read the questions in Exercise 3 again. Find answers to these questions by scanning the text on pages 37–38 for markers indicating the type of supporting detail.

1. a. _____
   b. _____
   c. _____
2. _____
3. _____
4. a. _____
   b. _____
   c. _____
5. _____
6. a. _____
   b. _____
7. a. _____
   b. _____
8. a. _____
   b. _____

5. *Work in two groups, Group A and Group B. Follow the instructions.*

1. Some examples that illustrate the different pricing strategies are missing from the reading on pages 37–38. They are listed below and on the next page. Read only the examples listed for your group.

2. Discuss the examples with your group. Decide what pricing strategy each example illustrates.

3. Decide which paragraph of the reading each example belongs in. Then write the number of the example in the appropriate place in the paragraph you identified. How did you decide where each example belongs in the paragraph? How do you know if each example is the only one in the paragraph or if it is followed or preceded by another example?

4. Work with one student from the other group. Take turns explaining your answers. Do you agree on the placement of the examples?

Group A's Examples

1. GM is a good example. The company often advertised basic models of its cars at low prices. However, showrooms were full of cars with lots of tempting extras at higher prices. The basic model had so few features that many people rejected it. Now, however, GM follows the lead of many Japanese and German car companies, and includes many desirable features in its base models.

   Pricing strategy: _____

   Paragraph: _____

2. For example, cell phone companies often have such different combinations of fixed and per-minute fees that it can be very difficult for consumers to figure out in advance how much they are likely to pay, thus making it difficult to choose a plan.

   Pricing strategy: _____

   Paragraph: _____

3. Cell phone companies use a similar technique. They often charge a flat rate for a basic plan and then charge high prices for minutes over the plan's limit.

   Pricing strategy: _____

   Paragraph: _____

4. Additionally, transport companies and sports teams sell multi-journey tickets or season tickets at less than the cost of single tickets.

   Pricing strategy: _____

   Paragraph: _____

Group B's Examples

5. For example, Dell used this technique to enter the personal computer market, selling computers directly to customers. Its sales soared when IBM, Apple, and other competitors selling through retail stores could not match its prices.

   Pricing strategy: _____

   Paragraph: _____

6. One example is Wal-Mart. This company has been sued[1] by dozens of small competitors, who claimed that Wal-Mart lowered prices in their specific areas to steal their customers.

   Pricing strategy: _____

   Paragraph: _____

7. Also, travel agents sell vacation packages that include airfare, accommodation, meals, and entertainment. And computer makers include attractive software packages with their personal computers.

   Pricing strategy: _____

   Paragraph: _____

8. For instance, Sony frequently uses this strategy. When it introduced the world's first high-definition television (HDTV) to the Japanese market in 1990, the price was $43,000. Sony rapidly reduced the price over the next few years to attract new buyers. By 2001, a Japanese consumer could buy a 40-inch HDTV for about $2,000, a price that many people could afford. An HDTV set now costs under $1,000 in the United States, and prices continue to fall.

   Pricing strategy: _____

   Paragraph: _____

   _____

   [1]**sue** *v* to claim money from someone through the legal system because they have done something wrong to you

6. *Work with a partner. Think again about the products you talked about in Exercise 2 on page 35. Discuss the questions.*

  1. Were any of the products you talked about on page 35 mentioned in the examples in Exercise 5? If so, what are they?

  2. For the other products, which pricing strategy fits them best?

  3. Can you now think of any other examples involving the pricing strategies described in the reading?

7. *Work in small groups. Discuss the questions.*

  1. Which pricing strategy is most likely to influence you, personally, to buy? Why?

2. For what kinds of products would you be an early adopter (someone who buys a new product when it's new, before the price comes down)? Why?

3. Which of the main pricing strategies listed in the reading (except the ones mentioned as having negative influence) do you think consumers dislike most? Why?

4. The reading mentions four strategies in a negative light (bait and switch, price fixing, predatory pricing, and price confusion). Which strategies do you think are the worst? Which ones (if any) do you think should be illegal? Why?

5. Do you think that the punishment given to the German executives for price fixing was too light, fair, or too heavy? Why?

Checkpoint 2 PEARSON LONGMAN myacademicconnectionslab

Before You Speak

1. 🎧 *Listen to the first part of a short student presentation. (You will give a short presentation like this later.) Answer the questions.*

1. What did the presenter want to buy?

2. Why did it take longer than expected at the store?

3. Did the presenter buy the item she first wanted?

4. Which pricing strategy, from this unit's reading, is the closest to the one used here?

2. 🎧 *Now listen to the end of the presentation. Check your answer to question 4 in Exercise 1.*

3. 🎧 *Listen to the presentation again. In the chart, write down the logical connectives you hear that have the listed functions. Then compare your answers with a partner's.*

Function	Logical Connective/Signal
State the main point of the talk	*In this talk, I'm going to . . .*
Show time order	
Introduce a different/opposite idea	
Consequence	
Reason	

4
Building Academic Speaking Skills

In this section, you will practice showing relationships between ideas and taking notes to prepare for a presentation. Then you will work in groups to choose the best strategy to price a product.
For online assignments, go to

PEARSON LONGMAN
myacademicconnectionslab

We have examined how logical connectives and other signals are used to express relationships between ideas. This is important to remember in speaking as well, especially when giving an oral presentation. By using connectives, you can help the listener to follow the pattern of ideas in your talk and to see the relationships between your ideas.

Be aware that there are some differences between spoken English and written English, and between levels of formality. By using some of the spoken-style logical connectives, this can help you to avoid sounding as if you're reading from your notes.

4. *Using your instinct and previous knowledge, place the logical connectives/signals from the box in the chart according to whether they are most commonly used in speaking, in writing, or in both.*

additionally	first of all	next
after that	furthermore	Our focus today is . . .
also	however	so
although	in addition	the main point/thing/ focus
another	in contrast	
because	in summary	the most important
but	In this talk, I'm going to . . .	then
finally	Let's move on to . . .	thus
first	Let's wrap up . . .	to conclude

← —— More Formal ———————————————— Less Formal —— →		
More Common in Written English	Common in Both Written and Spoken English	More Common in Spoken English

← More Formal		Less Formal →
More Common in Written English	Common in Both Written and Spoken English	More Common in Spoken English

5. Compare your chart with a partner's. Discuss any differences.

Focused Speaking

1. Read the key words and listen as your teacher pronounces them.

2. 🎧 Listen to the excerpt from a consumer affairs radio program about pricing. Take notes.

3. Work with a partner. Use your notes to answer the questions.

1. What is the name for the pricing strategies mentioned in the radio program?

2. Which three variations on this strategy are mentioned? List them.

_____

_____

_____

Key Words

psychological *adj* relating to the way people's minds work and the way that affects their behavior; **psychology** *n*

subtle *adj* very smart in noticing and understanding things

tricky *adj* likely to mislead; deceptive

up-market *adj* associated with people who have lots of money

We looked earlier at note-taking during lectures. Notes can also be useful to help with speaking. It is important that the ideas in your presentations be well organized. Making notes as a preparation step can help you a lot with organization.

You can use any of the note-taking tools mentioned on pages 32–33: Venn diagrams, T-charts, outlines, mind maps, cycle diagrams, or any other tools. Here are some tips:

- Use a tool that goes well with the organizational structure of your talk, and that you are comfortable using.
- Make sure your notes are easy to follow while speaking. If you use a mind map, for example, the ideas might be numbered and flow in a clockwise direction.
- Highlight the main ideas using a colored highlighter, so that they are easy to see during your talk.

The introductions of oral presentations usually have the same structure you learned for essay introductions in Unit 1:

- general statement that introduces the topic
- main point (or thesis if the main point is an opinion)
- scope, to give a preview of the main ideas

Put these points at the top of your notes to make them easy to see.

During your presentation, try to look at the audience more than at your notes. It is important that you make eye contact with as many people as possible. This will make the audience feel closer to you and more interested in what you say. Try not to just read from your notes. It will take lots of practice!

4. *Prepare a short presentation, like the one you heard on page 43. You should talk about a time when you came across one of the pricing strategies described in the radio program or in this unit's reading.*

1. Talk informally with a partner about your incident.
   - Describe the situation.
   - Say whether you actually wanted to purchase something, and why.
   - Talk about what happened during the incident.
   - Say whether you bought anything in the end.
   - Name the pricing strategy used.
   - Explain why the company might have used that strategy.

2. Prepare your presentation. Use a note-taking tool that works for your presentation. Make sure you are prepared for all the points listed in the checklist on the next page.

Does the presenter . . .		Yes
Introduction	introduce the topic with a general statement?	
	make the main point of the talk clear?	
	mention the main points to be covered in the body?	
Body	introduce the main ideas, clearly using logical connectives?	
	show the relationships between supporting details by using logical connectives?	
Conclusion	summarize the main point?	
General points	make eye contact?	
	use style that is appropriate for spoken English?	

3. Practice your presentation with a different partner. Your partner should complete the checklist.

4. Discuss your presentation with the person who listened to it. What improvements can you make?

Integrated Speaking Task

You have read and listened to information about different strategies marketers use to price their products. You will now work in small groups to decide on the best value-based and psychological pricing strategies for a product of your choice. Then you will present your choices and reasons for them to the class.

Follow the steps to prepare for your presentation.

Step 1: In your group of three or four students, choose one product from the list, or use your own idea (check with your teacher first).

- Mobile phone plan
- Fashionable clothing, such as jeans
- Exotic vacation package
- Internet service
- Your own idea: _____

Step 2: In your group, discuss the pricing strategies you learned about in this unit. Which strategies (value-based and psychological) do you think will work best for your product?

Step 3: Prepare a presentation in which you describe your product and give reasons why the pricing strategies you have chosen are the best ones for your product.
- Choose the organizational structure for your talk.
- Choose an appropriate note-taking tool to organize your notes.
- Make sure that each student in your group has a speaking part.
- Write your notes.

Step 4: Practice your presentation. Use logical connectives to make the organizational structure clear to your audience. As you practice the presentation, use the checklist in Step 5 to make sure the presentation includes all the important points.

Step 5: Give your presentation to the class. While listening to the other groups' presentations, complete the checklist. After each presentation, discuss as a class what the best features of the presentation were.

Does the presenter . . .		Yes
Introduction	introduce the topic with a general statement?	
	make the main point of the talk clear?	
	mention the main points to be covered in the body?	
Body	introduce the main ideas clearly, using logical connectives?	
	show the relationships between supporting details by using logical connectives?	
Conclusion	summarize the main point?	
General points	make eye contact?	
	use style that is appropriate for spoken English?	
Content	give clear reasons for using value-based pricing?	
	give a value-based pricing strategy, with clear reasons?	
	give one or more psychological pricing strategies, with clear reasons?	

Social Psychology
Conformity

Unit Description

Content: This course is designed to familiarize the student with concepts in social psychology.

Skills: Coherence and Cohesion

- Understanding coherence and cohesion
- Recognizing cohesion
- Recognizing speech markers that build coherence in lectures
- Writing body paragraphs and connecting ideas

Unit Requirements

Readings: "The Asch Effect" (from *Psychology*, 9th Edition, C. Wade & C. Tavris, Pearson Prentice Hall and *Psychology: The AP Edition*, P. Zimbardo et al., Pearson Allyn & Bacon)

"Business Decision Making" (a blog entry)

Lecture: "Groupthink"

Integrated Writing Task: Writing an essay about the dangers of the group influencing an individual's opinions

Assignments: www.MyAcademicConnectionsLab.com

1
Preview

For online assignments, go to

PEARSON LONGMAN
myacademicconnectionslab

conformist *n* someone who behaves or thinks like everyone else because he or she does not want to be different. This word is often used in a negative way; **conform** *v*; **conformity** *n*; **conformist** *adj*

conscience *n* the part of your mind that tells you whether your behavior is morally right or wrong

dissent *v* to disagree with an opinion or decision that most people accept; **dissent** *n*

get along with (someone) *v* to have a friendly relationship with another person

majority *n* most of the people or things in a group

pressure *n* a feeling that you should do something because other people want you to; sometimes this feeling is stressful; **pressure** *v*

Previewing the Academic Content

Imagine that you're in a meeting. The chairperson of the meeting is an important person—you need to get along well with her. You also know that two or three other people in the meeting always say "yes" to the chairperson, and she seems to appreciate them for agreeing with her.

However, there is a catch. The idea that is getting the most attention in the meeting is the chairperson's idea, but you don't like the idea at all. You think it will cause many problems.

The discussion is turning more and more to the chairperson's idea. People seem generally in favor of it. The time for the vote is coming. You have to make the decision: Do you choose to be faithful to your opinion? Or do you go against your conscience, decide that your relationships with the group are more important, and vote for the idea you dislike so much?

In this unit, we will look from a psychological point of view at the pressures people face in this kind of situation, and how these pressures often lead to bad decisions. We will also look at some ways to avoid these pressures.

1. *Work with a partner. Answer the questions. Try to use the key words in your answers.*

1. In the imaginary scenario described above, are you a conformist or a non-conformist?

2. Whose view does the majority agree with, yours or the chairperson's?

3. How comfortable do you think conformity feels? How about dissent?

4. What are the advantages of being a conformist in this situation? What are the disadvantages?

5. What might the other people in the meeting be thinking?

2. *Think of a similar situation you have experienced. Discuss the questions in small groups. Try to use the key words.*

1. Describe the situation. What happened?

2. Describe the pressures you felt. What were they? How strong did they feel?

3. Did you try to resist the pressure? If so, how?

4. What did you do in the end?

5. How did you feel afterward?

This unit will help you recognize coherence and cohesion in readings and lectures. It will also show you how to create coherence and cohesion in your own writing.

Previewing the Academic Skills Focus

Understanding Coherence and Cohesion

A text has **coherence** if it makes sense—that is, if all the clauses together convey an overall message. A text is coherent when:

- all ideas are related to the main idea
- the order of ideas makes sense

If a text has coherence, we can say it is **coherent**.

Cohesion, on the other hand, is about the connections between ideas in the text. A cohesive text uses words and expressions that connect ideas within and between sentences. Words and expressions might include the following:

- pronouns and possessive adjectives, to avoid repeating phrases when you need to mention them again. For example: *The manager was a powerful person. She influenced many people.*
- logical connectives, to show the relationship between ideas. For example: *The manager was a powerful person. However, not everyone liked her.*

If a text has cohesion, we can say it is **cohesive**.

Understanding coherence and cohesion will help you follow readings and lectures. Using techniques for cohesion will make your writing and speaking effective and clear.

Read the two paragraphs. Notice how they are different. Then complete the tasks on the next page.

Paragraph A

Human beings are social creatures—we live with others, work with others, and play with others. Our everyday contact with other people provides many opportunities for others to directly or indirectly influence our behavior, feelings, and thoughts. This process is called social influence. There are many forms of social influence. For instance, we might speak to a coworker in order to persuade him or her to follow our own opinion, even when our coworker might not want to. Alternatively, sometimes a person can influence other people just by being near them. For example, a boss may make a worker nervous, and as a result the worker might not be able to perform effectively.

Paragraph B

Human beings are social creatures—we live with others, work with others, and play with others. We had a difficult day today. The Canikon DX3-AC is a superb camera. It ended very suddenly, with a flash. Like the horse, the cow can also digest grass. Red meat often has a high fat content. I knew the answer yesterday, I'm sure, but I seem to have forgotten it today. Social contact is important for child development. That's a big one, isn't it? There's a slight chance of rain tomorrow. My friend is afraid of her boss. Sometimes she is so nervous that her boss is watching her that she can't finish her project on time.

1. Underline the topic sentence of each paragraph, if there is one. In which paragraph are all ideas related to the main idea?

2. In the other paragraph, are there any sentences that don't relate to or support the main idea? Draw a line through them.

3. Which paragraph is coherent?

4. In the coherent paragraph, mark the following:
   - the logical connectives with a <u>single line</u>
   - the words that mean "human beings" with a <u>double line</u>.
   - the words that mean "another coworker" with a <u>squiggly</u> line.
   - the word that means "someone" with a dotted line.

Before You Read

Recognizing Cohesion

There are several ways that writers and speakers give cohesion to a text. Here are a few tools of cohesion:

- In **reference**, various words, such as pronouns and possessive adjectives, can be used to refer to a previous idea. There are many different pronouns—for example, *he, she, his, her, which, who, that, it, they, them,* and *those.* Possessive adjectives include *my, your, her, its, his, our,* and *their.*

  Example

  Social psychologists are interested in how individual people affect each other. They use many techniques for this, including experiments.

- Lexical cohesion occurs when words with connected meanings are used. This reduces repetition. One word may name a group of which the other is a member, or the two words may be synonyms.

  Example

  Social psychologists have carried out some very interesting experiments. In one study, researchers asked people to make a judgment.

- **Substitution** allows the writer to replace words in order to avoid repetition.

  Example

  Social psychology looks at the effect of other people on individuals. Sociology does [looks at the effect of other people on individuals] too. (*does too* replaces a phrase in the previous sentence)

- **Ellipsis** allows the author to omit some words in order to avoid repetition.

  Example

  Several academic disciplines look at how people influence each other. One [of these academic disciplines] is social psychology. Another [of these academic disciplines] is sociology.

- **Logical connectives**, covered in Unit 2, are also a form of cohesion.

  Example

  While both social psychology and sociology look at how people influence each other, social psychology focuses on the individual, whereas sociology focuses on the group.

2

Building Academic Reading Skills

In this section, you will look at the tools that effective writers use to create cohesion.

For online assignments, go to

PEARSON LONGMAN
myacademicconnectionslab

As you can see, some types of cohesion have a second function. As well as linking ideas, they allow the writer or speaker to avoid repetition and to add variety. This makes the writing or speaking more interesting. So, watch out for different ways a speaker or writer mentions the same person or idea.

1. *Read the paragraph. Then work with a partner. Complete the tasks.*

> Decision makers such as government and business leaders have to be very careful about the advice they receive. Sometimes their advisors and subordinates may only tell them what they think their bosses want to hear, perhaps because they think this will help them get promoted or gain favor with their superior. However, this can mean that the boss doesn't get impartial information. What can the leader do to avoid this situation? We will find some answers later in this unit.

1. Write the words from the text (*they, their, them*) that do the following:
   a. refer to decision makers such as "government and business leaders"

   Line 2: <u>they</u>, _____

   Line 3: _____

   b. refer to "their advisors and subordinates"

   Line 3: _____, _____, _____

   Line 4: _____, _____

2. Write words or expressions that are synonyms of the following:
   a. "government and business leaders"

   Line 3: _____

   Line 4: _____

   Line 5: _____, _____

   b. "advice"

   Line 5: _____

3. Find an example of ellipsis. Rewrite the sentence, adding the part that was omitted in the paragraph.

   _____

   _____

4. List at least two logical connectives used in the paragraph.

   _____

2. *Work with a partner. Discuss some ideas for how leaders can avoid the problem described in the paragraph. Then share your ideas with the class.*

3. Read the situations and think about your answers to the questions. Then discuss your answers and ideas with a partner.

1. Think back to a school you went to and the different groups of friends there.
   - How much did clothing and hairstyles vary within each group? Between groups?
   - How different or similar were your friends' clothes and their parents' clothes?
   - What do you think are the reasons for people's decisions about what clothes to wear?

2. Choose a job or a workplace that you know something about—perhaps a job that a family member does or a job you have had. Do not choose a job that requires a uniform.
   - Think about the people who do the job. How similarly or differently do they dress at work?
   - How similar or different are their work clothes to the clothes they wear outside work?
   - If people wore clothes that are <u>very</u> different from those of their coworkers, what would be the consequence?
   - How strong is the social influence on what people wear?

Global Reading

1. In this unit, you will read an excerpt from a psychology textbook. Read the introduction to the excerpt. Then complete the task.

© 2000 Ted Goff

"GOSH, ACKERMAN, DIDN'T ANY-ONE IN PERSONNEL TELL YOU ABOUT OUR CORPORATE CULTURE?"

Social pressure is more powerful than many people think. What are you wearing now? What are your classmates wearing? How similar do they look? Now think about a typical office. What do people usually wear? We can see the effects of social pressure in people's clothing styles, moods, and leisure activities (Totterdell, 2000; Totterdell et al, 1998). So, pressure to obey social norms[1] is strong. But can it be strong enough to make people change their minds, to express an opinion that is clearly completely wrong? One related phenomenon[2] that psychologists have identified is the Asch effect.

[1] **social norms** *n* the usual ways of doing things in a particular society
[2] **phenomenon** *n* something that happens or exists in society, science, or nature (especially something that academic researchers study)

Work with a partner. Which of the questions do you think the rest of the excerpt will answer? Circle them.

1. Can we see the effects of social pressure in people's clothing styles, moods, and leisure activities?

2. Is pressure to obey social norms strong?

3. Can social pressure be strong enough to make a person express an opinion that is clearly completely wrong?

4. What is the Asch effect?

THE ASCH EFFECT

1   Social pressure is more powerful than many people think. What are you wearing now? What are your classmates wearing? How similar do they look? Now think about a
5 typical office. What do people usually wear? We can see the effects of social pressure in people's clothing styles, moods, and leisure activities (Totterdell, 2000; Totterdell et al, 1998). So, pressure to obey social norms is
10 strong. But can it be strong enough to make people change their minds, to express an opinion that is clearly completely wrong? One phenomenon that psychologists have identified in this area is the Asch effect.

2   Solomon Asch carried out one of the most famous experiments in psychology (Asch, 1940, 1956). College students were told they would be participating in research about
5 visual perception. They were shown cards with three lines of different lengths and asked to indicate which was the same length as another, standard line (see Figure 3.1). The correct answer was very clear. But when the
10 students were put in a group of people who all

gave the wrong answer, the results were rather surprising.

3   In each experiment, a number of trials were held. In each trial, the confederates[1] (people who knew the real purpose of the experiment) gave their answers first. The only real subject
5 of the experiment was always one of the last. In the first three trials, everyone agreed on the correct answer. But in the fourth, the first person to speak gave a response that

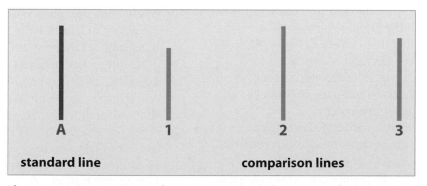

standard line   **comparison lines**

Figure 3.1 Participants in Asch's experiment were shown a standard line. They were also shown cards, each of which had three comparison lines. *Source: Based on Asch (1956).*

---

[1]**confederates** *n* this word has a technical social psychology meaning here

was obviously incorrect, reporting that two
10 lines were of the same length when actually
they were clearly different. The next person
said the same thing—and the next, and so
on, until all group members except the real
participant had unanimously agreed on an
15 incorrect judgment. The real participant then
had to decide whether to conform or to remain
independent and believe the evidence of his or
her own eyes.

4   What did the participants in this position
finally do? As you might expect, nearly
everyone showed signs of disbelief and
discomfort when faced with a majority who
5 saw the world so differently from how they did.
As one participant later said, "I felt disturbed,
puzzled, separated, like an outcast from the
rest." But despite the participants' distress, the
group pressure usually won. Three-quarters of
10 those subjected to group pressure conformed
to the false judgment of the group one or
more times, while only a quarter remained
completely independent on all trials. In
various related studies, between 50 and 80
15 percent conformed with the majority's wrong
judgment at least once; one-third gave in to the
majority's incorrect judgments on half or more
of the trials.

5   This effect—the tendency for people
to follow what the group says, even if it
contradicts what they can see or know—is
called the Asch effect. It prevents good
5 decision making in all walks of life, from
family discussions to company decision
making and government debates.

6   However, the Asch effect doesn't affect
everyone. Conformity researchers do regularly
find "independents." These are people who are
uncomfortable with going against the majority,
5 but who still point out mistakes when they see
them even if the other group members dislike
them for not being "team players."

7   In further experiments, Asch identified
three factors that influence whether people
give in to group pressure: (1) the size of the
majority, (2) the presence of a partner who
5 dissented from the majority, and (3) the size
of the difference between the correct answer
and the majority's position. He found that
individuals tended to conform if as few as
three people went with the false answer, but
10 not if they faced only one or two. However,
even in a large group, giving the person
one ally[2] who dissented from the majority
opinion sharply reduced conformity (as
shown in Figure 3.2). With such a "partner,"
15 nearly all subjects resisted the pressure
to conform. Remarkably, however, some
individuals continued to give in to the group
even with a partner present. All who gave
in underestimated the influence of social
20 pressure and the frequency of their conformity.
A few even said that they really had seen
the lines as the majority had claimed. They
claimed they were reporting accurately what
they were seeing (Asch, 1956).

8   Numerous studies have revealed additional
factors that influence conformity. Specifically,
a person is more likely to conform under the
following circumstances:

- When a judgment task is difficult or unclear
  (Deutsch & Gerard, 1955; Lott & Lott, 1961;
  Saltzstein & Sandberg, 1979).
- When the group members are seen as
  especially skilled or knowledgeable.
- When responses are given publicly rather
  than privately.
- When the group majority is unanimous—
  but once that unanimity is broken, the rate
  of conformity drops dramatically (Allen &
  Levine, 1969; Morris & Miller, 1975).

---

[2]**ally** *n* someone who helps and supports you when others are against you

Figure 3.2 This graph illustrates conformity across 12 trials, when individuals were grouped with a unanimous majority or had the support of a single dissenting partner. Note that a lower percentage of correct estimates means a greater degree of conformity with the group's false judgment.

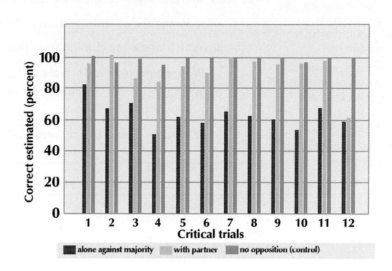

REFERENCES

Allen, V. S., & Levine, J. M. (1969). Consensus and conformity. *Journal of Experimental Social Psychology, 5*, 389–399.

Asch, S. E. (1940). Studies in the principles of judgments and attitudes: II. Determination of judgments by group and by ego standards. *Journal of Social Psychology, 12*, 433–465.

Asch, S. E. (1956). Studies of independence and conformity: A minority of one against a unanimous majority. *Psychological Monographs, 70* (9, Whole No. 416).

Deutsch, M., & Gerard, H. B. (1955). A study of normative and informational social influence upon individual judgment. *Journal of Abnormal and Social Psychology, 51*, 629–636.

Lott, A. J., & Lott, B. E. (1961). Group cohesiveness, communicational level and conformity. *Journal of Abnormal and Social Psychology, 62*, 408–412.

Morris, W. N., & Miller, R. S. (1975). The effects of consensus-breaking and consensus-preempting partners on reduction of conformity. *Journal of Experimental Social Psychology, 11*, 215–223.

Saltzstein, H. D., & Sandberg, L. (1979). Indirect social influence: Change in judgmental processor anticipatory conformity. *Journal of Experimental Social Psychology, 15*, 209–216.

Totterdell, P. (2000). Catching moods and hitting runs: Mood linkage and subjective performance in professional sport. *Journal of Applied Psychology, 85*, 848–859.

Totterdell, P., Kellett, S., Briner, R. B., & Teuchmann, K. (1998). Evidence of mood linkage in work groups. *Journal of Personality and Social Psychology, 74*, 1504–1515.

3. *Skim the text again. Write the number of the paragraph(s) that give(s) you the following information.*

1. Whether conformity applies to everyone: Paragraph(s) _____

2. Results of the experiment: Paragraph(s) _____

3. The circumstances under which Asch found that conformity happens: Paragraph(s) _____

4. How the experiment worked: Paragraph(s) _____

5. A definition of the Asch effect: Paragraph(s) _____

Compare your answers with a partner's. Explain the clues you used to find the answers.

Focused Reading

participant *n* someone who takes part in an activity, such as an experiment

subject *n* a person or animal that is used in a test or experiment; **subject** *v*

trial *n* a test to see if a particular phenomenon happens

unanimous *adj* a unanimous decision, vote, etc. is one on which everyone agrees; **unanimity** *n*; **unanimously** *adv*

underestimate *v* to guess that something is smaller than it really is

1. *Work with a partner. Complete the tasks. Note that the symbol ¶ means "paragraph."*

1. Read Paragraphs 1 and 2 and answer the questions.

   a. Which words are ellipsed from line 7? (¶1) Add it to the sentence.

   What do people usually wear <u>*in a typical office*</u> ?

   b. What is the "area" mentioned in line 14? (¶1)

   _____

   c. What does "they" in line 3 refer to? (¶2)

   _____

   d. Which words are ellipsed from lines 6–12? (¶2) Add them to the sentences.

   . . . and _____ asked to indicate which

   _____ was the same length as another, standard, line. The

   correct answer _____ was very clear. But . . . the results

   _____ were rather surprising.

2. Read Paragraphs 3 and 4 and answer the questions.

   a. What words are ellipsed from lines 4–5? (¶3) Add them to the sentence.

   The only real subject of the experiment was always one of the last

   _____.

   b. Which phrase earlier in the paragraph has the same meaning as "real participant" in lines 13–14? (¶3)

   _____

   c. Which two words in Paragraph 3 are used to avoid repetition of "answer"?

   (line 8) _____ (line 15) _____

   d. What words does "did" in line 5 substitute for? (¶4)

   _____

   e. Which words are ellipsed from lines 13–16? (¶4) Add them to the sentence.

   In various related studies, between 50 and 80 percent _____ conformed with the majority's wrong judgment at least once.

3. Read Paragraphs 5 to 8 and answer the questions.

   a. What does "it" in line 4 refer to? (¶5)

   _____

   b. Which two words in Paragraph 5 are used to avoid repetition of "discussions"?

   _____ _____

c. Which words in paragraph 6 refer to "independents"?

_____   _____   _____

_____   _____

d. Which word in Paragraph 7 is used to avoid repetition of "people" (line 8)?

_____

e. Which word in Paragraph 7 is used to avoid repetition of "ally" (line 14)?

_____

2. *Read the text again and answer the questions. Then discuss the questions in small groups.*

The Experiments

1. Were the researchers honest with the real participants before the experiment started? Explain.

_____

_____

2. What did the group members have to compare?

_____

_____

3. Who gave the last answers in each trial?

_____

_____

4. In the first three trials, did the researcher's confederates give a correct or incorrect answer?

_____

_____

5. What was different about the third trial in each experiment?

_____

_____

6. How did the real participant feel when the majority held a different opinion?

_____

_____

The Results

1. What proportion of real participants was influenced by the majority in at least one trial?

_____

_____

2. How was this different in related studies?

_____

_____

Conclusions and Inferences

1. How does the Asch effect usually influence decision making?

_____

_____

2. Does the Asch effect apply only in some circumstances? Explain.

_____

_____

3. How does the Asch effect influence "independents"?

_____

_____

Key Words

diverse *adj* if things are diverse, they are very different from each other; **diversity** *n*

expert *n* someone who has special skill or knowledge about a subject; **expertise** *n*

3. *Work with a partner. Do you think the situations in the chart will encourage conformity or encourage diverse views? Check (✓) the appropriate column. What evidence from the text did you use to find your answers?*

	Encourages Conformity	Encourages Diverse Views
1. Giving everyone lots of complicated information just before a meeting		
2. Putting a few outside experts on the committee		
3. Taking votes by marking pieces of paper rather than raising hands		
4. Discussing issues that you know many in the group agree with		
5. Giving no time to think about the issues before the meeting		
6. Encouraging someone to be a "devil's advocate"—that is, to disagree with everything even if they really agree		

4. *Work with a partner. How do you think you would respond if you were the subject of Asch's experiment? Would you be an "independent"? Give an example from your own experience to support your answer.*

Checkpoint 1   PEARSON LONGMAN myacademicconnectionslab⛵

In this section you will
practice following the
ways that effective
speakers create cohesion.
For online assignments,
go to

PEARSON LONGMAN
myacademicconnectionslab

Key Words

attitude *n* the way
someone generally
thinks, feels, and
behaves

cohesive *adj*
connected together to
make a united whole;
cohesiveness *n*

consensus *n* an
opinion that everyone
in a group agrees with

external *adj* from
outside

impartial *adj* able
to give a fair opinion
or advice, due to not
supporting one side
more than the other;
neutral

invulnerability *n*
freedom from harm or
damage; **invulnerable**
adj

isolate *v* to separate
from other people or
things; **isolated** *adj*;
isolation *n*

*(continued on
next page)*

Before You Listen

1. *Work with a partner. Complete the tasks.*

1. Imagine two groups. In one group, everyone gets along very well, comes from
   a similar social background, holds similar values, and feels in tune with each
   other. In the other group, people are very diverse, often disagree, and have
   different attitudes. Discuss the questions.
   a. Which group would you prefer to be a member of? Why?
   b. Which group do you think works best together?
   c. Which group do you think is likely to be more cohesive?
   d. Which group do you think is most likely to reach a consensus easily?
   e. Which group do you think makes the best decisions?

2. Think about conformity within organizations. Discuss the questions.
   a. What are some advantages of conformity?
   b. What are some disadvantages of conformity?

2. *Read the information about Company A and Company B. Work with a partner.
Complete the paragraphs with words from the box. For the verbs, remember to
adjust the tense if necessary. You will not use all the words.*

attitude	external	invulnerability	open-minded
cohesive	impartial	isolated	social background
consensus	in tune	isolation	values

In Company A, there was a very strong culture of making money no matter what
the consequences were. Everything the company did followed this aim. On the
surface, the company was very successful. Profits appeared high, and the share
price increased sharply. Many considered the company to be one of the most
successful in the United States. But there were problems. Top management

developed a sense of (1) _____—they felt that everything they

did was right. No one was allowed to question the company's way of doing

things; people who did so were often fired. Managers (2) _____

themselves from (3) _____ external advice. As a result, there was

little discussion.

In Company B, debate is encouraged. Before reaching a (4) _____,
managers are expected to gather a diverse range of opinions from as many people
as possible. They are expected to involve all members of their team in the decision-
making process, and to encourage debate. Data is used as much as possible, to
help figure out which options are most likely to succeed. Managers are seen as

(continued on next page)

open-minded *adj*
willing to consider and
accept a diverse range
of opinions and ideas

social background *n* a
person's position in his
or her society, family,
and groups of friends

in tune (with) *exp*
thinking in the same
way as someone
else; understanding
someone else easily

values *n* ideas about
what is right or wrong
and what is important
in life

collectors of viewpoints, which differs from the traditional view of a manager as a quick, decisive decision maker working independently. No one works in

(5) _____. Managers stay (6) _____ with their

colleagues, and being (7) _____ is one of the company

(8) _____. All of this is reflected in one of the company mottos:

"many are smarter than the few."

3. *The paragraphs in Exercise 2 describe two companies—Google and Enron Corporation. Read the statements. Which do you think describes Company A, and which do you think describes Company B?*

1. Google is one of the most successful existing information technology (IT) companies.

   Company _____

2. Enron Corporation collapsed spectacularly in 2001.

   Company _____

4. *Look again at the questions in Exercise 1 on page 61. After reading the paragraphs in Exercise 2, will you change your mind about any of your answers?*

Global Listening

Recognizing Speech Markers that Build Coherence in Lectures

As we saw in Unit 2, lecturers use speech markers to make the stages in the lecture clear to their audiences. These markers can be logical connectives or other phrases, sentences, and questions that show (for example) that a new main idea is being introduced.

1. *Work with a partner. Match the speech markers from the box to their most likely functions. Write them in the correct places in the chart on the next page.*

In summary, . . .	So, now it's time to wrap up.
First, we'll look at . . . Then, we'll move on to . . .	The main point we'll cover today is . . .
As we'll see throughout the rest of this lecture, . . .	There are two main reasons for this. First, . . . Also, . . .
Now, let's move on to . . .	Today, we'll be talking about . . .
So, how do we . . . ?	

Stage	Function	Speech Marker
Introduction	• to indicate the main point of the lecture	
	• to say what will be covered in the body	
Body	• to introduce a new topic/ main idea	
Conclusion	• to introduce the conclusion	

2. The lecture in this unit is about a phenomenon called groupthink. Work with a partner. In your notebook, write down as many questions as you can that you might want to ask about a new phenomenon such as groupthink.

Example

What is groupthink?

3. 🎧 Listen to the introduction of the lecture. Check (✓) the questions you wrote in Exercise 2 that the lecturer will answer. Write down any other questions the lecturer will answer. Then compare your questions with a partner's.

4. 🎧 Copy the questions from Exercise 3 to the chart. Then listen to the whole lecture and write the signals that introduce the part of the lecture that answers each question.

Question	Signals Introducing the Answer

5. 🎧 *Listen to the lecture again. Circle the best answer to complete each statement.*

According to the Lecturer, . . .

1. conformity is _____.
   a. positive
   b. negative
   c. both negative and positive

2. groupthink occurs in _____.
   a. cohesive groups
   b. diverse groups
   c. U.S. government groups

3. people change their opinions because _____.
   a. decisions are made more quickly
   b. they're lazy
   c. conformity is comfortable

4. there are _____ circumstances in which groupthink happens.
   a. three
   b. six
   c. nine

5. examples of problems caused by groupthink include _____.
   a. decisions by children to take risks
   b. company collapses
   c. traffic accidents

6. in groupthink, the majority feels _____ and dissenters feel _____.
   a. comfortable; comfortable
   b. uncomfortable; uncomfortable
   c. comfortable; uncomfortable

7. to avoid groupthink, it's good to hear _____ ideas.
   a. focused
   b. diverse
   c. strong

Focused Listening

1. *Listen to the excerpts from the listening. Answer the questions. Then compare your answers with a partner's.*

🎧 **Excerpt One**

Which two words in the excerpt refer to "groupthink"?

_____   _____

🎧 **Excerpt Two**

Which word in the excerpt refers to "conform their opinions to the consensus of the group"?

_____

⌒ Excerpt Three

1. Which word in the excerpt is ellipsed after *some*?

   _____

2. Which word in the excerpt substitutes for *change their opinion*?

   _____

⌒ Excerpt Four

What is the relationship between the ideas in the excerpt? Circle one.

reason   example   items in a list

2. ⌒ *Read the lists of items. The lecturer agreed with some of these points, but not all of them. Listen to the lecture again. Check (✓) ideas that she agrees with. Place an **X** next to the ideas that she doesn't agree with or ideas that are not mentioned. Then compare your answers with a partner's.*

Circumstances: Groupthink is most likely to happen when. . .

_____ 1. groups are very cohesive.

_____ 2. members have a lot in common with each other.

_____ 3. there is little contact with similar groups.

_____ 4. members dislike making decisions.

_____ 5. the leader expects subordinates to follow.

_____ 6. there is strong pressure from outside.

_____ 7. circumstances make decisions difficult.

Symptoms: Groupthink might be happening when. . .

_____ 1. team members are sure they will never make mistakes.

_____ 2. there is excitement.

_____ 3. no one disagrees.

_____ 4. everyone is quiet.

_____ 5. only a few ideas are discussed.

_____ 6. the leader makes doubters feel uncomfortable.

Groupthink Avoidance Strategies: Ways to avoid groupthink include. . .

_____ 1. thanking people for dissent.

_____ 2. asking for various opinions.

_____ 3. keeping meetings short.

_____ 4. including external people.

_____ 5. telling people they are problem solvers.

_____ 6. telling people to defend their opinions.

3. *Work with a partner. Read the scenarios. Identify the circumstances and/or symptoms of groupthink, and any groupthink avoidance strategies. Then complete the chart on the next page.*

Scenario 1

A group of teenagers, 14 and 15 years old, is playing soccer in a park. They are all from the same part of town, and they go to the same local school. They get along very well and have played together for a number of years. Suddenly, one of them accidentally kicks the ball to the other side of a river. There is a bridge, but it is a ten-minute walk away. There is also a pipe across the river, with a warning sign saying that walking on it is dangerous. A fence makes it difficult to reach the pipe. The children talk about what to do. One says that the bridge is safer. Another, who is often the leader, laughs at him and tells him not to be silly, because he has walked across the pipe many times before and nothing happened. The dissenter stays quiet after that. The other teenagers decide that one of them should climb the fence, walk across the pipe, and get the ball.

Scenario 2

Abraham Lincoln was one of the most respected presidents of the United States. One of the first things he did upon becoming president was to bring four people from the opposite side of politics, who had been his competitors during the election, into his government. He made sure they knew he was happy to hear their true opinions, even if they were very different from his. These people took part in many of the discussions that led to some of the important decisions of Lincoln's presidency.

Scenario 3

A government agency, charged with an important research project, has been told that the government wants to see results quickly. The government has spent a very large amount of money on the project. The project is complex and is taking longer than expected. A panel of external expert engineers is providing advice. They have found some problems with the agency's latest piece of equipment, and they recommend a further delay while the problems are solved. However, instead of acting on the recommendation, senior management has removed five of the panel's members and is refusing to change the project's schedule.

Scenario	Circumstance, Symptom, or Groupthink Avoidance Strategy	Evidence from the Scenario	Is Groupthink Likely?
1.	• *group is very cohesive* • •	• *the children get along very well, have played together for years* • •	
2.	• • • •	• • • •	
3.	• • • •	• • • •	

4. *Compare your answers with another pair's. Did you come to the same or different conclusions? Did you use the same evidence or different evidence?*

5. *Work in small groups. Discuss the questions.*

1. What are some similarities between groupthink and the Asch effect?

2. What are some differences between groupthink and the Asch effect?

3. Go back to the scenario you talked about on page 50. After reading about the Asch effect and groupthink, how would you deal with a similar situation differently in the future?

4. Which ideas from this unit will be most useful in your life? How will they be useful? Why do you think so?

Checkpoint 2   PEARSON LONGMAN myacademicconnectionslab

Building Academic Writing Skills

In this section, you will practice writing body paragraphs and connecting ideas. Then you will write an essay about the dangers of a group influencing an individual's opinions. For online assignments, go to

PEARSON LONGMAN
myacademicconnectionslab

Before You Write

1. *Read the short student essay. In the introduction,*
- underline the general statement once
- underline the thesis twice
- underline the scope with a squiggly line

Then compare your answers with a partner's.

In all walks of life—in companies, government, and even families—effective decision making is important. The right decision can lead to success, while the wrong one can cause disaster. Organizations must consider a range of ideas and choose the best from these. An excellent way to ensure that the widest possible range of ideas is considered is to consult with people outside the organization. This is because different people have different experiences, all of which may help in dealing with the issue. Also, consulting with external people helps to avoid groupthink.

A common expression in English is "two heads are better than one," meaning that two people's minds working together can think of better ideas than just one person. This is especially true when it comes to decision making. The more people who are consulted, the more experiences will be considered, and thus the more likely it is that the best idea will be found. Further, running the ideas by more people will mean that the ideas are examined more carefully. Thus, it is more likely that possible problems can be predicted in advance and solutions can be found. So, in short, the more heads, the better.

There is another reason to consult with others. That is to avoid the danger of groupthink. Groupthink occurs when people who get along well and know each other well reinforce each other's ideas rather than questioning them. This can reduce the level of critical thinking and lead to bad decisions. Someone from outside brings in new ideas, especially if that person is encouraged to freely express them. And that person will not allow old habits of the organization to prevent questioning of old ideas.

In conclusion, fresh ideas from outside an organization can greatly assist in decision making. Thus, it is important for organizations to consult with others whenever possible.

A body paragraph in an essay has one main idea and some details that support the main idea. As you saw in Unit 1, the last stage of the introduction—the scope—gives us clues about what the main ideas of the body paragraphs will be.

As we saw in Unit 2, the purpose of the body paragraph depends on the organizational structure:

- Description essays: Body paragraphs list different features of the thing being described.
- Explanation essays: Body paragraphs list different features of the idea being explained, such as different reasons or support for it.
- Argument essays: Body paragraphs give arguments, explanations, and reasons for the opinion—in other words, evidence.
- Discussion essays: Body paragraphs give evidence for each side of the issue, or advantages and disadvantages.

Each body paragraph in an essay usually has two essential stages, and may have up to two optional stages:

- **A transition from a previous paragraph** (optional). If used, this comes first. It could be a sentence or just a single logical connective such as *however*.
- **A topic sentence giving the main idea of the paragraph** (essential). Actually, a topic sentence could be just a single clause, or it could be longer than a sentence. Topic sentences are usually at the beginning of paragraphs, but they could also be at the end.
- **Supporting details** (essential). Most of the sentences in the paragraph are usually supporting details. They give further information about the main idea. For example, in an argument essay, they give the detailed evidence. In an explanation essay, they may give the detailed reasons for the phenomenon being explained.
- **A summary sentence** (optional). If used, this comes last and repeats the main idea.

Body paragraphs often use several logical connectives to help the reader see the relationships between the ideas.

2. *Read the student essay in Exercise 1 again. Mark the two body paragraphs of the essay as follows:*

- underline any <u>transitions once</u>
- underline the <u>topic sentence twice</u>
- underline the supporting details with a squiggly line
- underline any summary sentences with a dotted line

Compare your answers with a partner's. Discuss any differences.

Focused Writing

1. Read the blog entry from a business management advice website. The ideas mentioned in this blog entry can be applied to other situations as well, not just business.

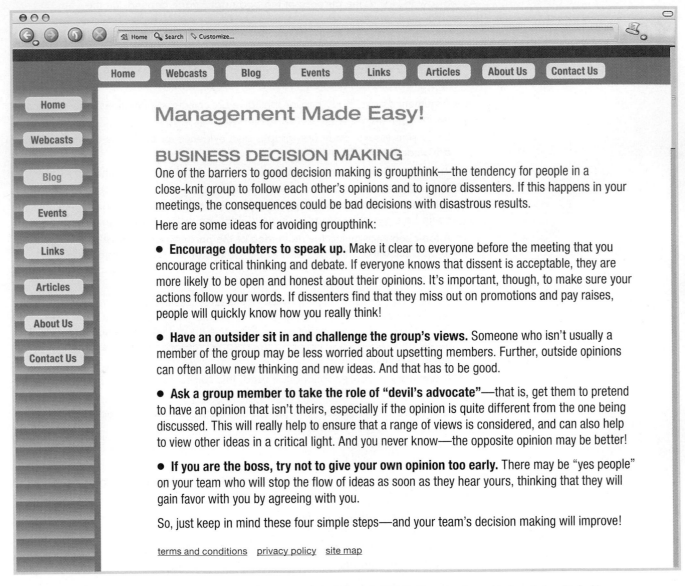

Management Made Easy!

BUSINESS DECISION MAKING

One of the barriers to good decision making is groupthink—the tendency for people in a close-knit group to follow each other's opinions and to ignore dissenters. If this happens in your meetings, the consequences could be bad decisions with disastrous results.

Here are some ideas for avoiding groupthink:

- **Encourage doubters to speak up.** Make it clear to everyone before the meeting that you encourage critical thinking and debate. If everyone knows that dissent is acceptable, they are more likely to be open and honest about their opinions. It's important, though, to make sure your actions follow your words. If dissenters find that they miss out on promotions and pay raises, people will quickly know how you really think!

- **Have an outsider sit in and challenge the group's views.** Someone who isn't usually a member of the group may be less worried about upsetting members. Further, outside opinions can often allow new thinking and new ideas. And that has to be good.

- **Ask a group member to take the role of "devil's advocate"**—that is, get them to pretend to have an opinion that isn't theirs, especially if the opinion is quite different from the one being discussed. This will really help to ensure that a range of views is considered, and can also help to view other ideas in a critical light. And you never know—the opposite opinion may be better!

- **If you are the boss, try not to give your own opinion too early.** There may be "yes people" on your team who will stop the flow of ideas as soon as they hear yours, thinking that they will gain favor with you by agreeing with you.

So, just keep in mind these four simple steps—and your team's decision making will improve!

terms and conditions   privacy policy   site map

Source: Based on Wood, S.E., Wood, G., & Boyd, D. (2006). *Mastering the world of psychology* (2nd ed.). Boston: Pearson Allyn & Bacon.

2. *Work with another student. Using context, match the key words and phrases from the blog entry with their meanings.*

Key Words

actions follow (your)
words *exp*

barrier *n*

ignore *v*

outsider *n*

pretend *v*

tendency *n*

upset *v*

yes person *n*

_____ make someone feel unhappy or worried

_____ behave as if something is true when actually it isn't true

_____ deliberately pay no attention to something, or to imagine it doesn't exist

_____ someone who always agrees with his or her superior, in order to gain an advantage or to make the superior like him or her

_____ do what you say you will do

_____ a rule or problem that makes it difficult to do something

_____ an external person

_____ a habit; a likelihood of doing something

3. *Think back to the situation you discussed at the beginning of the unit (page 50). Decide which pieces of advice (bullet points) from the blog would have been most useful in that situation. Mark them with these symbols:*

u useful in the situation

~ perhaps useful, perhaps not

n not useful in the situation

Discuss your ideas with a partner. Explain why you think the ideas would or would not have been useful in the situation.

4. *Choose one of the ideas listed below. Write body paragraphs for the idea of your choice. Include a topic sentence and supporting details in each paragraph, and include at least one transition and one summary sentence. Use logical connectives to make the relationships between ideas clear. Use the checklist on the next page to make sure you include all the important elements. When done, work with a partner and exchange paragraphs. Comment on each other's paragraph using the checklist.*

1. What are some things you can do to avoid the situation you talked about at the beginning of the unit? (explanation)

2. Why is it important to encourage doubters to speak up in meetings? (explanation or argument)

3. Why is it useful to ask a group member to take the role of "devil's advocate" during the decision-making process? (explanation or argument)

4. Why is it best if the boss doesn't give his or her opinion too early in decision-making meetings? (explanation or argument)

5. Your own idea: _____

Do the body paragraphs . . .	Yes
show types of ideas appropriate to the organizational structure?	
have a clear topic sentence, giving the main idea of each paragraph?	
have clear supporting details, supporting the main idea of each paragraph?	
have logical connectives that make the relationships between ideas clear?	
have transitions between them, where appropriate?	
have summary sentences, where appropriate?	

Integrated Writing Task

You have read about and listened to ideas about how groups can influence the actions, opinions, and thoughts of an individual and how to avoid groupthink. You will now use your knowledge of the content, vocabulary, and techniques to create coherence and cohesion to write an academic essay in response to this question: **In what circumstances does a group influence an individual's opinion? What are the dangers of this? How can the dangers be avoided? Use what you know about the Asch effect and groupthink in your answer.**

Follow the steps to write your essay.

Step 1: Think about the essay question. Then review the readings, lecture, and blog entry in this unit.

Step 2: Plan your essay. Choose one main idea (a thesis) and some major points to support the thesis (the main ideas of the body paragraphs).

Step 3: Write your essay. Use the checklist in Step 4 to help you.

Step 4: Show your essay to another student. Discuss each other's essays. Use the checklist below. Based on your discussion, write a second draft of your essay and hand it in.

Does the essay have . . .	Yes
clear stages in the introduction: general statement, thesis, and scope?	
supporting ideas appropriate to the organizational structure?	
a topic sentence for each body paragraph that follows from the scope?	
clear supporting details in each paragraph, supporting the main idea?	
logical connectives, making the relationships between ideas clear?	
transitions between body paragraphs, where appropriate?	
summary sentences at the end of body paragraphs, where appropriate?	
a conclusion that summarizes the main ideas?	

UNIT 4

Architecture
Aesthetics

Unit Description

Content: This course is designed to familiarize the student with concepts in architecture.

Skills: Summarizing

- Distinguishing major from minor points and essential from non-essential information
- Identifying non-essential information, including digressions and asides
- Recognizing summary statements and conclusions
- Distinguishing essential from non-essential information in written texts
- Paraphrasing
- Preparing spoken summaries

Unit Requirements

Lecture: "Architecture for the People: Emotional Responses"

Readings: "What Makes a Building Attractive? Some Ideas through the Ages" (an excerpt from an architecture textbook)

"Money is the Overriding Problem with Architecture Today" (a newspaper opinion article)

Integrated Speaking Task: Discussing the aesthetics of buildings and summarizing the main points of the discussion

Assignments: www.MyAcademicConnectionsLab.com

1
Preview

For online assignments, go to

Previewing the Academic Content

Buildings surround us and are an important part of our lives. People have strong opinions about them. For example, many say that modern architecture is boring and ugly and that the buildings of the past were far more attractive. Others claim that modern buildings are far more varied and interesting than what was previously possible.

In this unit, we will explore, from an architectural viewpoint, some ideas about what makes a building a good building, with an emphasis on aesthetics.

Pompidou Center,
Paris, France

Taj Mahal, India

Hundertwasser Apartments,
Vienna, Austria

Key Words

aesthetics *n* the study of beauty, especially beauty in art; **aesthetic** *adj*; **aesthetically pleasing** *exp*

form *n* the shape of something

ornamentation *n* decoration on an object; **ornamental** *adj*

scale *n* the size or level of something, when compared to the things around it

Look at the pictures of the three buildings. Then discuss the questions in small groups.

1. Which of these buildings have you seen pictures of or heard about?

2. What do you know about these buildings?

3. What do you like about each of the buildings? What do you dislike?

4. Overall, do you think these buildings are attractive? For each, circle a number on the scale from one to six to express your opinion. Explain your opinion.

	Very aesthetically pleasing				Not at all attractive	
Pompidou Center	1	2	3	4	5	6
Taj Mahal	1	2	3	4	5	6
Hundertwasser Apartments	1	2	3	4	5	6

5. Choose at least one other building that you like. Tell your partner about it. You can draw a rough sketch if you think it will help with your description. Use a dictionary for any vocabulary you need.

6. How important do you think it is for buildings to be attractive? Why?

7. What do you think makes a building attractive? Brainstorm for ideas using a mind map like the one below. Write in your notebook. Add as many words to the mind map as you can.

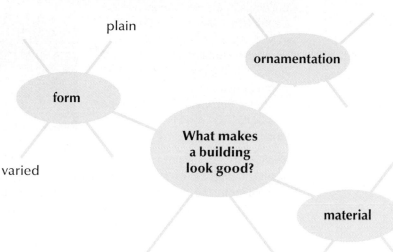

8. Which of the factors you listed are the most important? Which ones are the least important?

Previewing the Academic Skills Focus

In this unit, you will practice distinguishing essential from non-essential information. You will also practice preparing written and spoken summaries.

Summarizing

A summary is a short piece of text or speech that contains the most important ideas from a longer text.

You will find summaries at the ends of essays, at the ends of sections or chapters of a textbook, at the ends of lectures, and at the ends of explanations that are parts of lectures. You might have to give a summary as part of a presentation. You will often write a summary at the end of an essay.

When reading and listening, noticing the summaries can help you find the main ideas quickly. In writing and speaking, summarizing can help you emphasize the main ideas for your audience.

A good summary:

- is much shorter than the original text
- includes <u>all</u> the important ideas
- <u>only</u> includes important ideas
- leaves out detailed information such as numbers and dates, unless they are very important
- does not (usually) include the opinions of the summary writer
- uses the summary writer's own words—does not usually repeat words from the original (unless a short quotation makes the conclusion stronger)

1. *Read the excerpt from an architecture textbook. As you read, pay attention to the main ideas.*

One of the most extraordinary buildings in the world must surely be the Great Mosque[1] at Djenné in Mali, Africa. It is of a style completely unfamiliar outside West Africa. It is the largest building built of mud brick (otherwise known as adobe) in the world. It has been part of a UNESCO World Heritage Site since 1988.

The Great Mosque's exact origins are unknown as no written records were kept, but it is thought to be at least 700 years old. It is an excellent example of the use of local materials. It is built on a platform about 245 feet (75 meters) square, raised 9 feet (3 meters) above the surrounding ground. The walls are made from sun-dried mud bricks coated with a mud plaster. Numerous sticks cut from palm trees stick out from the surface of the walls. Every year, some of the plaster is washed away during the rainy season and cracks appear in the wall due to the heat of the dry season. For this reason there is an annual repair ceremony, during which the whole town helps to repair the surface. It is an incredible sight—hundreds of people scrambling over this impressive structure.

---
[1]**mosque** *n* a religious building in which Muslims worship

2. *Read three summaries of the excerpt. In the chart, check (✓) the features that each summary has.*
   A. The Great Mosque of Djenné is one of the most impressive buildings in the world. It is of a style completely unfamiliar outside West Africa.
   B. The Great Mosque of Djenné, the largest mud brick building in the world, is remarkable. It is hundreds of years old, yet it is still in use.
   C. The Great Mosque of Djenné, a UNESCO World Heritage Site that is about 245 square feet, is a remarkable building. You should visit it!

Feature of Summaries	A	B	C
Much shorter than the original text	✓	✓	✓
Includes all the important ideas			
Only includes important ideas			
Leaves out detailed information such as numbers and dates, unless they are very important			
Does not include the opinions of the summary writer			
Uses the summary writer's own words, rather than repeating words from the original			

3. *Which is the best summary? What problems do the other two summaries have? Discuss with the class.*

2
Building Academic Listening Skills

In this section, you will practice distinguishing between major and minor points and between essential and non-essential information in a lecture.
For online assignments, go to

PEARSON LONGMAN
myacademicconnectionslab

Before You Listen

1. *Work in small groups. Look at the photographs and information about the buildings that the professor will discuss in the lecture. Then read the* Claim to Fame *statements. These statements describe features of the buildings that made them famous. Decide which building each* Claim to Fame *statement describes. Write the statement in the correct places in the chart.*

Claim to Fame

A. It is still the largest wooden building in the world.

B. The curved shape of the concrete roof is uniquely elegant.

C. It is said by UNESCO to be the largest and most perfect example of its style of architecture.

D. It was the world's tallest reinforced concrete office building when it was built.

E. It was the world's tallest building for just 11 months after construction; it is still the world's tallest brick building.

F. It was built in memory of an emperor's wife.

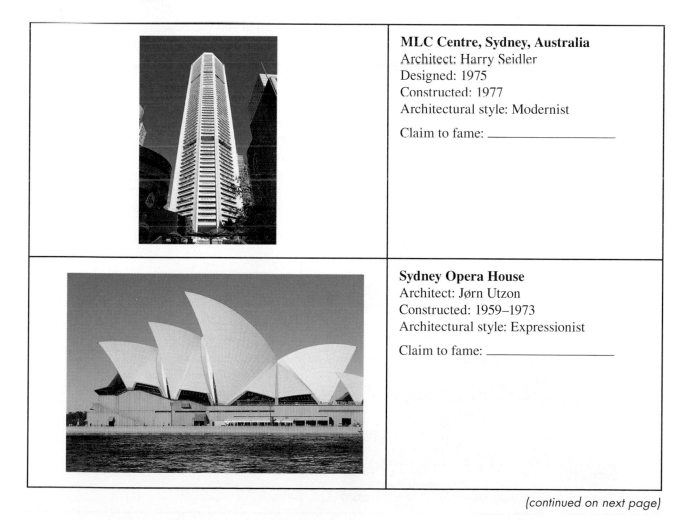

MLC Centre, Sydney, Australia
Architect: Harry Seidler
Designed: 1975
Constructed: 1977
Architectural style: Modernist

Claim to fame: _____

Sydney Opera House
Architect: Jørn Utzon
Constructed: 1959–1973
Architectural style: Expressionist

Claim to fame: _____

(continued on next page)

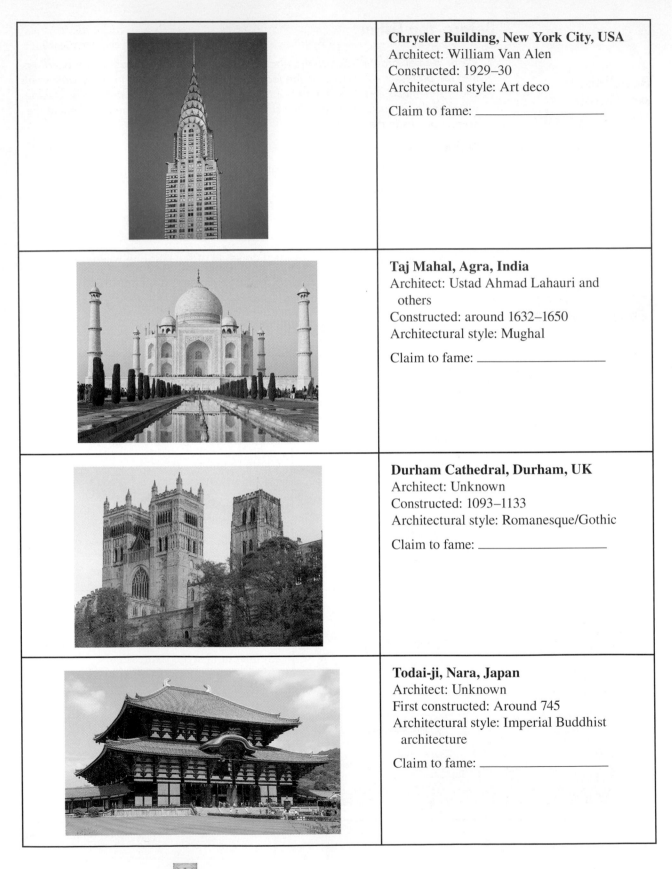

Chrysler Building, New York City, USA
Architect: William Van Alen
Constructed: 1929–30
Architectural style: Art deco

Claim to fame: _____

Taj Mahal, Agra, India
Architect: Ustad Ahmad Lahauri and
  others
Constructed: around 1632–1650
Architectural style: Mughal

Claim to fame: _____

Durham Cathedral, Durham, UK
Architect: Unknown
Constructed: 1093–1133
Architectural style: Romanesque/Gothic

Claim to fame: _____

Todai-ji, Nara, Japan
Architect: Unknown
First constructed: Around 745
Architectural style: Imperial Buddhist
  architecture

Claim to fame: _____

Key Words

brick *n* a building material, usually red, consisting of small pieces of the same size

cathedral *n* a large and important religious building in which Christians worship

concrete *n* a building material, usually grey or cream colored, made from water, a powder, small stones, and sand

curve *n* a line that follows the edge of a circle; it isn't straight; **curve** *v*; **curved** *adj*

elegant *adj* beautiful, attractive, pleasant, and usually having curves

energetic *adj* having a lot of energy

inspire *v* to make someone have a particular feeling or react in a particular way

monotonous *adj* boring because of always being the same

rectangle *n* a shape that has four sides at 90° to each other; two of the sides are usually longer than the other two; **rectangular** *adj*

reinforced *adj* made stronger; for example, reinforced concrete has steel bars running through it

repetition *n* something that happens again and again; **repetitive** *adj*; **repeat** *v*

rich *adj* having lots of interesting details

(continued on next page)

2. *Read the key words on this page and on the next page. Decide which relate to a form, material, or type of building, and which is an adjective that describes a building. Organize the words in the chart.*

Form	Material	Type of Building	Adjective

3. *Work with a partner. What is your emotional response to the buildings you discussed in Exercise 1? Which adjectives would you choose to describe each of the buildings? Use the adjectives from the chart in Exercise 2 and add some of your own. Discuss your choices. Do you agree with each other's choices?*

- MLC Centre: _____

  _____

- Sydney Opera House: _____

  _____

- Chrysler Building: _____

  _____

- Taj Mahal: _____

  _____

- Durham Cathedral: _____

  _____

- Todai-ji: _____

  _____

4. *Work with the same partner. Which of these buildings do you like? Which don't you like? Explain.*

Unit 4 ■ Aesthetics **79**

Global Listening

Distinguishing Major from Minor Points and Essential from Non-essential Information

Major points are main ideas and supporting details that are necessary for understanding—the essential information. These include evidence and explanations. **Minor points** are additional details or information that add interest to the lecture but are not necessary for understanding—non-essential information. These often include examples.

Noticing the difference between major and minor points is important because it will make your note-taking and study more efficient—you only need to focus on the essential information. Also, in summarizing, only major points should be used.

You have already learned about some ways to identify main ideas:

- Think about the focus of the lecture beforehand. The major points will support the focus.

- Listen carefully to the introduction. The thesis will state the main point or opinion of the lecture, and the scope will give the main ideas to be covered.

- Listen for logical connectives and certain phrases that often introduce main ideas and supporting details, for example:

    Let's begin with . . .
    Most importantly, . . .
    One of the main reasons is . . .

Here are some other ways to identify main ideas:

- Sometimes a lecturer also gives emphasis to a point <u>after</u> saying it. Notice that in the following sentences, *this* and *that* refer to the previous idea.

    I believe this is a key point.
    I think that goes a long way to explaining why . . .

- Pay attention to <u>how</u> the lecturer is talking about major points. Ideas that the lecturer emphasizes—perhaps by speaking more slowly, more clearly, more loudly, or more quietly—and ideas that the lecturer repeats are most likely the major points.

As a check, ask yourself these questions:

- Is this information important for me to understand the purpose of the lecture?

- Is it an important detail that supports the main idea (such as an explanation or reason)?

1. *Professors often post course notes on their websites. Look at the overview of the lecture you will listen to. Work in pairs. Think of at least three questions that you think may be answered in the lecture. Write them on the next page.*

www.architecture101.com/spring

Lecture 4: In this lecture, we'll look at three techniques that architects use to inspire an emotional response to their buildings. We'll see that, perhaps, modern architects can learn at least one lesson from the architects of the past.

Question 1: _____

Question 2: _____

Question 3: _____

2. ⌒ *Listen to the introduction of the lecture. Answer the questions.*

1. What is the lecturer's main opinion (thesis)?

   _____

2. Which three main ideas will the lecturer talk about to support the thesis?

   a. _____

   b. _____

   c. _____

3. ⌒ *Copy the main ideas from question 2 in Exercise 2 onto the first column of the chart. Then listen to the whole lecture. How does the lecturer indicate the main ideas? Check (✓) all that apply. Then compare your chart with a partner's.*

Main Idea	Ways the Lecturer Indicates the Main Idea		
	Signals the point before explaining it (e.g., let's move on to)	Gives emphasis to the point after mentioning it	Changes how he talks

4. ⌒ *Listen to the lecture again. Complete the chart on the next page. Then compare your answers with a partner's. Discuss any differences.*

Main Idea	Major Point about the Main Idea	Building Used as Example (Check All that Apply)	
Form	• plain rectangular forms → *negative or neutral emotions* • interesting, varied shapes with meaning →	MLC Centre Sydney Opera House Chrysler Building Durham Cathedral Todai-ji Taj Mahal	☐ ☐ ☐ ☐ ☐ ☐
Texture	• texture comes from • • •	MLC Centre Sydney Opera House Chrysler Building Durham Cathedral Todai-ji Taj Mahal	☐ ☐ ☐ ☐ ☐ ☐
Scale	• •	MLC Centre Sydney Opera House Chrysler Building Durham Cathedral Todai-ji Taj Mahal	☐ ☐ ☐ ☐ ☐ ☐

5. *Use your notes to answer the questions.*

1. What is the effect of variety on both form and texture?

2. Why, according to the lecturer, do older buildings look better than modern ones?

6. *Look back at the questions you wrote in Exercise 1 on the previous page. Which of those questions were actually answered by the lecturer?*

Focused Listening

Lecturers often try to make their lectures sound interesting, lively, and friendly. One way they do this is by telling personal stories, giving personal opinions, or mentioning other points that might be interesting but are not essential to the lecture. These short trips into different (but related) topics are called **digressions** and **asides**.

Here is how to recognize digressions and asides:

- Try to notice if the lecturer is talking about a personal story, or if the topic is quite different from the main ideas.
- Try to notice whether facts mentioned are relevant—that is, whether they support the main idea.
- Pay attention to the words and phrases that the lecturer uses. Digressions and asides are often introduced with phrases such as *by the way, incidentally,* and *while we're on the subject.*

1. *Listen to the excerpts from the lecture. Make notes about the non-essential information.*

⌒ Excerpt One

Non-essential information: _____

_____

⌒ Excerpt Two

Non-essential information: _____

_____

⌒ Excerpt Three

Non-essential information: _____

_____

⌒ Excerpt Four

Non-essential information: _____

_____

2. ⌒ *In addition to course notes, professors often post slides on their websites. You can download these notes or slides and bring them to the lecture. Usually, the notes or slides will include only the main ideas, and you will need to fill in the supporting details. Listen to the lecture again. Then fill in the missing details in the slides on pages 84–85. Don't take notes about any digressions, asides, or non-essential information.*

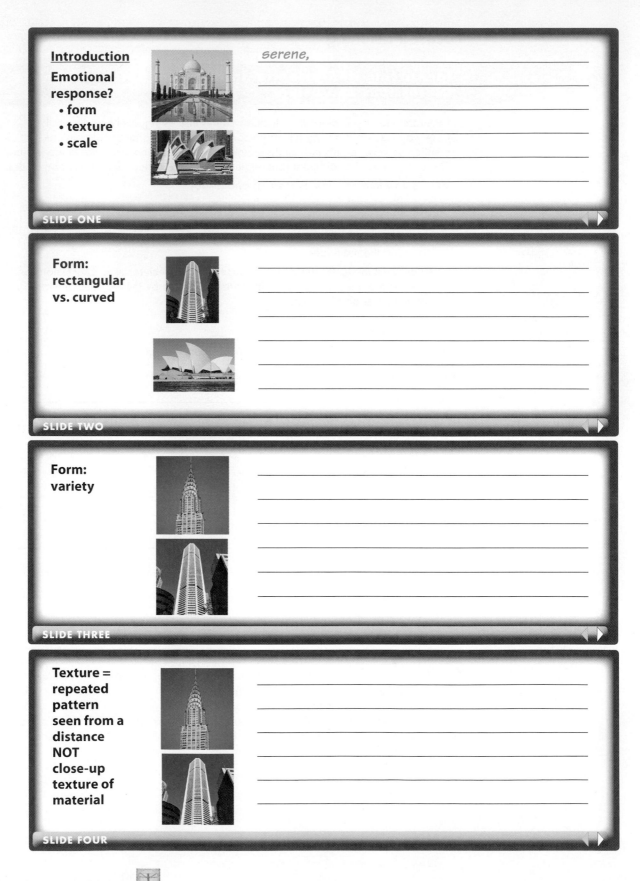

Introduction

Emotional response?
- **form**
- **texture**
- **scale**

serene,

SLIDE ONE

Form: rectangular vs. curved

SLIDE TWO

Form: variety

SLIDE THREE

Texture = repeated pattern seen from a distance NOT close-up texture of material

SLIDE FOUR

**Texture:
old vs. new**

SLIDE FIVE

Scale

SLIDE SIX

Conclusion

**Emotional
response:**
 • **form**
 • **texture**
 • **scale**

SLIDE SEVEN

3. *Work with a partner. Use your notes to answer the questions.*

1. Which building does the lecturer not like? Why?

2. What inspired the shape of the Sydney Opera House's roofs?

3. What is more important for the type of texture the lecturer describes: materials, or patterns such as patterns of windows?

4. Does the lecturer think there is any repetition on the Chrysler Building?

5. What is generally the difference between the texture of old and new buildings?

6. Which key point have modern architects forgotten, according to the lecturer?

(continued on next page)

7. Does the lecturer think that bigger is better?

8. How can architects design buildings people like?

4. *Work with a partner to summarize the lecture. Follow the steps.*

1. Review the skills for summarizing on page 75.

2. Review the notes you made in the slides in Exercise 2. Underline the points that are most important for your summary, and ignore details that are unimportant in a summary.

3. Prepare and practice your summary together. You can use these expressions:
   The lecture talks about . . .
   The first/second/third point . . .
   An important example of this . . .

4. Find a new partner. Give your summary, and listen to your partner's summary. Whose summary was shorter? Did either of you leave out any important information?

5. *Work with your partner from Exercises 3 and 4 on page 79. Answer the questions.*

1. Did the lecturer use the same adjectives as you did to describe the buildings?

2. Did the lecturer like the same buildings as you did?

Checkpoint 1 PEARSON LONGMAN myacademicconnectionslab

3
Building Academic Reading Skills

In this section, you will practice recognizing summary statements and conclusions in texts. For online assignments, go to

PEARSON LONGMAN myacademicconnectionslab

Before You Read

Wainwright Building, St. Louis, USA. Completed 1891. Architect: Louis Sullivan.

Parthenon, Athens, Greece. Completed 431 BCE.

Macquarie University, Sydney, Australia. Completed 1978.

1. *Work with a partner. Look at the photos. Discuss the questions.*

1. What type of building do you think each is?

2. Which building has the most elaborate ornamentation?

3. Which building has the most pleasing proportions?

4. Which building do you think has the greatest evidence of durability?

2. *What would the lecturer in Section 2 think of these buildings? Work with a partner to complete the chart.*

Key Words

durability *n* the ability to stay in good condition for a long time; **durable** *adj*

elaboration *n* the supply of extra details; **elaborate** *adj*

proportions *n* relationships between length, width, height, and depth; good proportions are aesthetically pleasing

	Wainwright Building	Parthenon	Macquarie University
Form			
Texture			
Scale (for example, compared with local area)			

Key Words

arch *n* a shape or structure with a curved top and straight sides; **arched** *adj*

column *n* a tall, vertical structure used to support a roof, or as decoration

dome *n* a shape that is like a ball cut in half

façade *n* the front of a building, especially a large and important one

pediment *n* a flat, triangular shape, often above the entrance to buildings

sculpture *n* a three-dimensional work of art

3. *The text you are going to read introduces a lot of vocabulary related to architecture. Work with a partner. Label the elements in the photograph with as many key words as possible.*

Global Reading

In written texts, just as with lectures, explanations of major points often finish with a summary of the point. We saw in the writing section of Unit 3 that paragraphs often have a summary statement. These aren't difficult to recognize in reading—they are usually at the end of a paragraph or series of paragraphs.

Statements at the ends of paragraphs give a sense of closure in other ways, too. For example, they may give an opinion about the point or show the significance of the point.

These statements, whether they summarize, give an opinion, or show the significance, are evidence that the point is a major one. This is why, when skimming, it helps to read the last sentence of each paragraph, as well as the topic sentence.

There is also often a summary at the end of the text (or the book section), which may be part of a conclusion. Such summaries are often signaled with a logical connective, such as *In conclusion, . . .* , *In summary, . . .* , *To sum up, . . .* , or *To summarize, ...*

Skim the excerpt from an architecture textbook. Then complete the tasks on page 90.

WHAT MAKES A BUILDING ATTRACTIVE?
Some Ideas through the Ages

1   People like attractive buildings. However, exactly what it is that makes a building attractive is difficult to identify. People have thought about this throughout history, and ideas have varied from culture to culture. Here, we will explore some important concepts in aesthetics.

2   Our exploration will begin in ancient Greece, around 2,500 years ago, with the Parthenon in Athens. Its façade is famous for having proportions that are very well balanced. With the limited technology of the time, how did the architects achieve this? Did the ancient Greeks simply have a strong sense of proportion, or were there some consistent design principles behind it? The real answer is that we don't know—no records exist. But people do speculate. The lines on Figure 4.1 suggest an explanation.

3   The white lines on the diagram show some interesting proportions. All the vertical and horizontal lines have the same ratio. This is called the golden ratio. No one can explain why, but across cultures, people find objects with this ratio very pleasing to the eye. This ratio was certainly a concept that ancient Greeks knew about. (Wilson, 1995) Artists through the ages have also used the same concept, or something similar called the rule of thirds. This rule says that objects placed on lines drawn a third of the way from each edge will look good. You can

Figure 4.1 Parthenon, Athens

see for yourself the next time you go to an art gallery.

4   Architects in other cultures have also used the golden ratio. The Great Mosque of Kairouan in North Africa is one such example—the golden ratio is used in the building's floor plan. (Boussora & Mazouz, 2004)

5   One of the best-known early writers about aesthetic principles in architecture was Vitruvius, who lived about 2,000 years ago during Roman times. He said that a good building should satisfy three requirements. First, durability. It should stay in good condition for a long time. Second, utility. The building should achieve its purpose and perform its function well. And lastly, beauty. He claimed that a building should delight people and raise their spirits. (Vitruvius, nd/1960) Vitruvius's principles have stood the test of time and are still learned by architects today.

6   About 1,400 years later, Europe was emerging from a long period of little development. The arts, including architecture, experienced a renaissance—in fact, this period is called the Renaissance. At this time, Leone Battista Alberti from Florence wrote that beauty is mainly about

Figure 4.2   Great Mosque of Kairouan (also known as Mosque of Uqba)

proportion, but ornamentation is somewhat important as well. (Alberti, 1485/1988) Not surprisingly for someone who valued proportion, Alberti was also a fan of the golden ratio, thus resurrecting another old idea. Since then, Greek and Roman themes have held a prominent position in western architecture, coming and going in and out of fashion. Characteristic Greek elements include rectangular plans, columns, low triangular pediments filled with sculptures, and, above all, pleasing proportions. The Romans added arches and domes (which are really three-dimensional arches).

7   If you look at modern buildings, however, you see very few (if any) of these aesthetic features. Instead, such buildings tend to be boxes, with little elaboration other than patterns generated by their construction materials or windows. So, what happened? We have to go back to the 1870s to find out. By that time, larger buildings were needed as cities were becoming crowded due to industrialization. And there was a real mood for change in the western world—a feeling that rather than re-inventing ideas from the past, as architects had been doing for centuries, society was ready for new ideas. With perfect timing, new materials such as steel were becoming cheaper. Thus, conditions were ideal for steel-framed skyscrapers, which changed architecture forever. Modernism was born.

8   One of the first proponents of this style, Louis Sullivan, popularized an important saying: Form follows function. (Sullivan, 1896) What he meant was that a building's

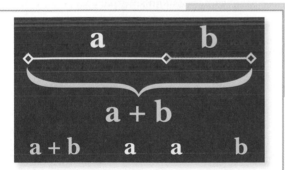

Figure 4.3   Golden ratio

THE GOLDEN RATIO is a unique number that fascinates mathematicians and artists alike. This diagram illustrates the golden ratio. Looking at the line, we call the long part *a* and the short part *b*. So the total length is a + b. If the ratio of the total length to *a* is the same as the ratio of *a* to *b*, then we have the golden ratio. A rectangle with one side length *a* and the other side length *b* is said by many people to be well proportioned and aesthetically pleasing.

function, its purpose, should be the first thing an architect thinks about, and appearance should be secondary to this. Gone was the idea of creating a building primarily for its looks; ostentation[1] and excess decoration were on the way out. Sullivan himself allowed some decoration, but the writing was on the wall. Architecture was changed forever.

9   Sullivan's ideas, though, were just the start of a trend. In the early 1900s, Austrian architect Adolf Loos stated that ornamentation was criminal. (Cox & Minaham, 2005) The Brutalist movement, popular from the mid-1950s to the mid-1970s, took these ideas further. Large, flat, angular, raw, rough concrete surfaces were the Brutalist style's characteristic feature. Nowadays, ideas from modernism predominate, and there has not yet been a return to the ornamentation of previous periods.

10   In summary, we've seen how aesthetic principles in architecture have changed through history. It's interesting to speculate what the future will bring!

---

[1]ostentation *n* extra, unnecessary decoration, often used to draw people's attention to something and to demonstrate wealth

REFERENCES

Alberti, L. B. (1988). *De re aedificatoria. On the art of building in ten books.* (J. Rykwert, N. Leach, & R. Tavernor, Trans.) Cambridge, MA: MIT Press.

Boussora, K., & Mazouz, S. (2004). The use of the golden section in the Great Mosque of Kairouan. *Nexus Network Journal, 6*(1).

Cox, J. W., & Minaham, S. (2005). Organization, Decoration. *Organization, 12*(4), 531.

Sullivan, L. (1896, March). The tall office building artistically considered. *Lippincott's Magazine.*

Virtuvius, P. (1960). *The ten books on architecture.* (M. H. Morgan, Trans.) New York: Dover Publications.

Wilson, A. M. (1995). *The infinite in the finite.* Oxford: Oxford University Press.

1. What is the thesis of the reading selection?

2. Which body paragraphs in the text do these points best summarize? Write the paragraph number next to each summary. (One point summarizes two paragraphs.) Then underline the topic sentences and summary sentences in the reading that helped you.

   a. Renaissance ideas about architecture   Paragraph(s): _____

   b. Effect of modernism on current architecture   Paragraph(s): _____

   c. Sullivan's effect on architecture   Paragraph(s): _____

   d. Ancient Greek buildings often had good proportion.   Paragraph(s): _____

   e. Vitruvius's principles   Paragraph(s): _____

   f. Golden ratio in another culture   Paragraph(s): _____

   g. The origins of modernism   Paragraph(s): _____

3. Compare your answers with a partner's. Discuss any differences.

4. With your partner, decide whether each summary sentence. . .
   • just summarizes
   • gives an opinion
   • shows the significance of the point

Focused Reading

1. *Read the list of ideas, styles, and features. With whom are they associated? Scan the text, and write the name from the box next to each idea. For some ideas, more than one answer is possible. Then compare your answers with another student's.*

Alberti	Sullivan	the Romans
Loos	the ancient Greeks	Vitruvius

1. modernism _____
2. arches _____
3. ornamentation _____
4. durability _____
5. columns _____
6. "form follows function" _____

7. against ornamentation _____
8. beauty _____
9. proportion _____
10. utility _____
11. golden ratio _____

2. *Work with a partner. The words and expressions in the box are all in the text. Use context to help you match the terms with their meanings.*

characteristic
excess
ideal
on the way out
popularize
predominate
~~principle~~
proponent
ratio
raise (their) spirits
renaissance
stand the test of time
the writing is on the wall
trend
utility

___*principle*___ *n*   a basic idea that something is based on

_____ *n*   a new interest in something, especially in a particular form of art, music, etc., that has not been popular for a long time

_____ *adj* a feature of something that is typical and makes it easy to recognize

_____ *n*   a general tendency in the way a situation is changing or developing

_____ *exp* to show that something can work well for a long period, usually many years

_____ *n*   a number showing the relationship between two amounts, sizes, etc.

_____ *adj* the best that something could be

_____ *exp* there is a sign that something will happen in the future

_____ *exp* going out of fashion

_____ *n*   a larger amount of something than is useful or needed

_____ *v*   to be greater in number or amount than any others

_____ *exp* to make people happy or optimistic

_____ *v*   to make something well known

_____ *n*   someone who supports an idea or persuades people to do something

_____ *n*   being useful; having usefulness

Just like lecturers, writers of material such as textbooks, course notes, and websites (but not academic essays, articles, or reports) often add interesting but non-essential information.

In writing, this information sometimes appears in a sidebar (a separate part of a text where additional information is given) or footnote. Other times, though, it is not signaled. If you are reading for an academic purpose, you can often ignore information that is not important to your purpose for reading.

Quickly identifying the important points as you read will help you to read more efficiently. You can read more quickly if you can identify which points (the non-essential points) you do not have to spend time on or think about.

3. *Read the excerpts from the reading. Imagine that you are reading the excerpts to gather information for an academic assignment about what makes a building attractive. For each excerpt, discuss with a partner which information is most essential for your purpose. Underline this information. What are the reasons for your choices?*

Excerpt One

> This is called the golden ratio. No one can explain why, but across cultures, people find objects with this ratio to be very pleasing to the eye. This ratio was certainly a concept that ancient Greeks knew about. Artists through the ages have also used the same concept, or something similar called the rule of thirds. This rule says that objects placed on lines drawn a third of the way from each edge will look good. You can see for yourself the next time you go to an art gallery.

Excerpt Two

> Since then, Greek and Roman themes have held a prominent position in western architecture, coming and going in and out of fashion. Characteristic Greek elements include rectangular plans, columns, low triangular pediments filled with sculptures, and, above all, pleasing proportions. The Romans added arches and domes (which are really three-dimensional arches).

4. *Do you think the sidebar in the reading on pages 88–90 is essential or non-essential information for the main purpose? Why?*

5. *Read the text on pages 88–90 again. Then work with a partner. Discuss the questions.*

1. What would the following people think of the buildings described in the lecture and slides on pages 84–85?
   - Vitruvius (durability, utility, beauty)
   - Alberti (proportion, ornamentation)
   - Sullivan (form follows function)
   - Loos (ornamentation is criminal)

2. Who do you think would like each building the most? The least?

3. Where would the lecturer and the people mentioned in the reading agree and disagree? What evidence supports your answer?

Checkpoint 2   PEARSON LONGMAN **myacademicconnectionslab**

Before You Speak

1. Read the newspaper opinion article. Underline the author's opinions.

4
Building Academic Speaking Skills

In this section, you will practice summarizing and paraphrasing. You will discuss whether certain buildings are examples of good architecture using examples from the lecture and readings in this unit. Finally, you will summarize the points made in your discussion to another student.
For online assignments, go to

PEARSON LONGMAN **myacademicconnectionslab**

Money Is the Overriding Problem with Architecture Today

When we think of great architecture, we often think of the spectacular buildings of the past, those great buildings present in most cultures around the world—cathedrals, castles, temples, palaces, and seats of government. But in most cases, they're old. Few of the famous ones were built in the twentieth century, never mind the twenty-first.

So what happened? Is it just that we're running out of skill? Probably not. The evidence points to another factor: money. For one thing, there is the cost of building. Flat slabs of concrete are cheaper than sculpted stone. Prefabricated[1] materials, which lead to boring, repetitive patterns, are cheaper to design, make, and put together. Buildings are designed nowadays to maximize profit. Profit first, aesthetics last. Greater floor space means more income from tenants, while open space means wasted dollars in many developers' eyes. Maximizing floor plans allows less flexibility to develop style and inspire feeling. This leads to plain, monotonous architecture.

Will we ever have the flamboyant[2] buildings of yesteryear? Will we ever again see anything like the cathedrals of Europe, with their masses of ornament, sculpture, and detail, or the intricate[3] woodwork of traditional East Asian temples? I suspect not. I expect that the power of profit and greed will win.

---

[1]**prefabricated** *adj* made from parts that are made in standard sizes at a place away from where they will be used in a building
[2]**flamboyant** *adj* confident and exciting in a way that attracts attention
[3]**intricate** *adj* containing many small parts and details that all fit together

2. Work in small groups. Answer the questions.

1. Which points in the article do you agree with? Which ones do you disagree with? Give reasons.

2. Which opinions do you think the author of the reading on pages 88-90 will agree and disagree with?

3. What counter-arguments can you think of?

Paraphrasing

In your assignments and presentations it is important to mention other people's ideas, theories, and facts that you have read or heard about—and to discuss what you think about them. But you have to be careful not to use someone else's exact words as your own. Presenting other people's ideas as your own or copying another person's words without putting them in quotation marks is called **plagiarism**.

In order to avoid plagiarism, you can paraphrase the information. **Paraphrasing** is expressing other people's ideas in your own words.

A good paraphrase:

- uses few words from the original (if possible, none)
- has the same meaning as the original
- includes neither more nor a lot less information than the original

You can use the following techniques to help you paraphrase:

- Cover the original text and then write from memory.
- Put the ideas of the original in a different order.
- Use synonyms or near-synonyms.
- Change word forms—for example, turn a noun into a verb.
- Use a different grammatical form. For example, you might write in the active voice to paraphrase something in the passive voice.
- Use one sentence to paraphrase several sentences, or several sentences to paraphrase one sentence.

You could use a combination of these techniques.

3. Read the paraphrases of the final paragraph of the newspaper article on the previous page. Then answer the questions on the next page. Compare your answers with a partner's.

Paraphrase 1: I don't think we'll ever see new buildings like the flamboyant buildings of the past, such as the cathedrals of Europe or the traditional East Asian temples with their intricate woodwork.

Paraphrase 2: The buildings of the past had far more ornamentation than modern buildings do.

Paraphrase 3: I don't think we'll ever see new buildings that are as detailed and ornate as many of the buildings from the past.

Paraphrase 4: Buildings with the detail and ornamentation of the famous buildings of the past may never be seen again, I believe.

1. Which paraphrase is the best?
2. Why are the others not good paraphrases?
3. Which techniques from the skill box on page 94 might have been used to form the good paraphrase?

4. *Paraphrase these points from the article.*

1. When we think of great architecture, we often think of the spectacular buildings of the past, those great buildings present in most cultures around the world—cathedrals, castles, temples, palaces, and seats of government.

   _____

   _____

   _____

   _____

2. So what happened? Is it just that we're running out of skill? Probably not. The evidence points to another factor: money.

   _____

   _____

   _____

   _____

3. For one thing, there is the cost of building. Flat slabs of concrete are cheaper than sculpted stone. Prefabricated materials, which lead to boring, repetitive patterns, are cheaper to design, make, and put together.

   _____

   _____

   _____

   _____

4. Maximizing floor plans allows less flexibility to develop style and inspire feeling. This leads to plain, monotonous architecture.

   _____

   _____

   _____

   _____

5. *Work with a partner. Check each other's paraphrases using the list of features of good paraphrases in the skills box on page 94. Then work together to improve the paraphrases where you think improvement might be possible.*

Focused Speaking

You will often have to prepare spoken summaries in college. For example, you might be asked to give a summary of some articles you have read during a class. Or, you may have to include a summary at the end of an oral presentation.

A summary is a kind of paraphrase, in that it uses your own words and has the same meaning as the original.

Follow these steps to prepare a spoken summary:

1. Take notes while reading source texts or listening to lectures.
2. Close the source texts and cover your notes.
3. Make a list of main points.
4. Check the main points against your notes and, if necessary, the source texts. Adjust the list if necessary.
5. Cover your notes again.
6. Think about what you're going to say, and practice it in your mind.
7. Practice your summary with a partner.

Write a summary of the article on page 93. Follow the steps.

1. Follow steps 1–4 in the skills box.

2. Compare your notes with a partner's. Explain the reasons for your choices of main points, and discuss any differences.

3. Adjust your list of main points if necessary.

4. Follow steps 5–7 in the same skills box. At step 7, your partner will use the checklist.

Is/Does the summary. . .	Yes
short?	
include only important ideas?	
leave out detailed information such as numbers and dates, unless they are important?	
avoid including the personal opinions of the speaker?	
use the speaker's own words?	
have a conclusion that summarizes the main ideas?	

5. Listen to your partner's summary. Use the checklist to give feedback to your partner. Then discuss the results.

Integrated Speaking Task

You have listened to and read about ideas of what makes buildings examples of good architecture. You will now use your knowledge of the concepts, ideas, key vocabulary, and skills from this unit to choose a building and discuss this question: **Is the building you have chosen an example of good architecture?** Following your discussion, you will present a summary of the discussion to other students.

Follow the steps to prepare for the discussion.

Step 1: Work with a partner. Choose a building that you both know about and like. Together, come up with reasons why it is an example of good architecture. Use the chart to help you. Remember that you will need to justify your answer. You can use paraphrases of ideas from the texts.

Example

Let's think about Alberti's idea—you know, that a building's good looks come from its proportions and ornamentation.

	Idea about the Building
Proportions: subjective (your own impressions)	
Proportions appropriate? (for example, golden ratio)	
Durability	
Utility	
Beauty	
Ornamentation	
Does form follow function?	
Form	
Texture	
Scale	
Emotional response	
Profit?	
Spectacular and/or inspiring?	

Step 2: Find a new partner who has chosen a different building. Have a discussion with that person. Justify why your building is a good example of architecture. Who has the most evidence that his or her building is an example of good architecture? Who has the strongest evidence?

Step 3: Together, list the main points you made during your discussion. Then prepare a summary of your discussion. Practice giving the summary together. Use the checklist in Step 4 to help you.

Step 4: Form new groups with people you haven't yet worked with in this task. Take turns presenting your summaries. While listening, use the checklist. Who has the best summary? Why?

Is/Does the summary. . .	Your Summary	Speaker 1	Speaker 2
short?			
include only important ideas?			
leave out detailed information such as numbers and dates, unless they are important?			
avoid including the personal opinions of the speaker?			
use the speaker's own words?			
have a conclusion that summarizes the main ideas?			

UNIT
5
Transportation Engineering
Managing Traffic Flow

Unit Description

Content: This course is designed to familiarize the student with concepts in traffic management.

Skills: Synthesizing Information

- Recognizing the relationship between abstract concepts and concrete information
- Recognizing relationships between two spoken sources
- Recognizing the relationship between abstract concepts and concrete information in reading
- Elaborating on information from sources
- Synthesizing information

Unit Requirements

Lecture: "Transportation Challenges"

Readings: "Intelligent Transportation Systems" (from *Fundamentals of Transportation Engineering: A Multimodal Systems Approach*, J.D. Fricker & R.K. Whitford, Pearson Prentice Hall)

"Traffic Congestion in Markdale" (a report)

Integrated Writing Task: Writing a conclusion to a report about a traffic challenge in the city of Markdale

Assignments: www.MyAcademicConnectionsLab.com

1
Preview

For online assignments, go to

myacademicconnectionslab

For online assignments, go to

Key Words

high-occupancy vehicle lanes *exp* lanes on a busy highway that are reserved for cars with two or more people in them

highway capacity *exp* the maximum number of vehicles that a highway was designed to carry

lane *n* one of two or more parallel areas on a road divided by painted lines to keep traffic apart

rush hour *exp* the time of day when the roads, buses, trains, subways, etc. are most crowded because people are traveling to or from work

traffic congestion *exp* vehicle overcrowding that results in slow traffic (*informal synonym* **traffic jam**)

vehicle *n* a machine with an engine used for transportation (includes cars, buses, trucks)

Previewing the Academic Content

We have all experienced sitting in traffic, waiting for the roads to clear so we can continue to our destination. With recent increases in population, numbers of drivers, and distance traveled per vehicle, it is not surprising that traffic congestion is becoming worse. To eliminate traffic problems, conventional wisdom suggests that we build more roads for more cars. However, concerns about cost and the environment suggest that we should look for alternative solutions. Intelligent transportation systems (ITS) apply communications technology to the field of transportation. Is it possible to use advanced technology to solve traffic congestion? What kinds of technology would be most efficient, least costly, and best for our environment?

1. *Look at the graph showing the number of vehicles per hour on a typical highway. What problem can you see here?*

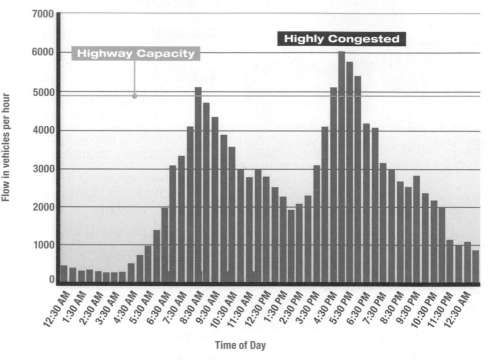

Typical daily traffic pattern showing periods of high congestion

Source: Fricker, J.D., & Whitford, R.K. (2004). *Fundamentals of transportation engineering: A multimodal systems approach.* Upper Saddle River, NJ: Pearson Prentice Hall.

2. *Work in a small group to discuss the questions. Use as many key words as possible. Then share your answers with the class.*

1. What would this highway look like between the hours of 4:30 and 6:30 P.M.?

2. What is the best solution to the traffic problem shown in the graph?

3. What actions could transportation engineers take to reduce traffic congestion without building more or bigger roads?

This unit will help you distinguish between abstract concepts and concrete information. This skill will help you to better understand what you read and hear in academic English.

Previewing the Academic Skills Focus

Recognizing the Relationship between Abstract Concepts and Concrete Information

When you read or listen to academic texts, you should notice the difference between abstract concepts and concrete information. Abstract concepts are general ideas or principles, rather than something real that you can see or touch. Here is an example of an abstract concept:

True trip speed is really not the speed of a given vehicle; it is the distance traveled divided by the total trip time, including stops, delays, and vehicle changes from origin to destination.

Concrete information describes what exists, or what is real. It is definite and specific. Here is an example of concrete information:

Railroad trains in Europe (the French TGV and the German ICE) are operating at speeds in excess of 400 kilometers per hour, but passenger rail speeds in other countries are limited to 100–160 kph, depending on track conditions.

Often abstract concepts and concrete information are presented at the same time. It is common for professors and textbooks to introduce an abstract concept first, followed by concrete information. Sometimes transition words (such as *for example* or *for instance*) are used to show the move from abstract to concrete, but not always.

Concrete information can either **support** or **contradict** the abstract concept. Here is an example of an abstract concept followed by supporting concrete information:

All forms of ground transportation have limited speed. Even race cars have a limit of approximately 320 kph, and safe travel on our road systems occurs at speeds less than 100 kph.

Here is an example of an abstract concept followed by contradicting concrete information. Notice the transition word *however*, which points out this relationship for the reader.

For airplanes, faster speeds should be possible with supersonic transport (SST). However, the ticket cost of $500 or more, and the time cost of two to three hours for security clearance, reduce the overall trip speed and efficiency for air travelers.

Examples from: Fricker, J.D., & Whitford, R.K. (2004). *Fundamentals of transportation engineering: A multimodal systems approach.* Upper Saddle River, NJ: Pearson Prentice Hall.

Read the text on the next page. Mark each paragraph as follows:
- Circle the sentences that state an abstract concept.
- Underline the sentences that state concrete information (if any).
- Highlight transition words or phrases that show the move from abstract to concrete.
- Write in the margin whether the concrete information supports or contradicts the abstract concepts.

Location, Time, and Cost Utility of Transportation

1   The function of transportation is to provide for the movement of people and products from one place to another safely and efficiently, with minimum negative impact on the environment. The demand for transportation is based on the demand for an activity or product. When no particular demand for a specific activity or product exists, then no transportation will occur. This could happen because people do not want to travel to a certain place or because the cost of transport exceeds the value placed on it by the traveler. When viewed as a system, transportation has three main requirements for it to be effective: location utility, time utility, and cost utility.

Location Utility

2   The demand for most vehicle transportation is to provide access from an origin, such as a residence, to a destination, such as an industry, commercial center, or public place. Therefore, transportation is closely tied to how land and space are used. For instance, Ottawa, the capital city of Canada, has many urban streets on which people drive, walk, or ride buses to get from their homes to work or to school. It has major highways that connect it to the neighboring cities of Toronto and Montreal. It has an airport that permits its residents to travel long distances by plane. It is also located at the meeting point of three rivers: the St. Lawrence, the Rideau, and the Gatineau. In the past, these rivers were used to move valuable trees to national and international markets. Ottawa has strong location utility.

Time Utility

3   Time utility is related to the trip speed of transportation. True trip speed is really not the speed of a vehicle; it is the distance traveled divided by the total trip time including stops, delays, and vehicle changes from origin to destination. For example, to fly from Beijing to New York, you might have to choose between two flights. The first flight with Continental Airlines leaves Beijing at 3:45 P.M. and arrives in New York at 10:54 P.M. the following night, with an overnight stay in Houston, Texas. The total trip time is 31 hours and 9 minutes. The second flight with Air China is a nonstop flight that leaves Beijing at 1:00 P.M. and arrives in New York at 1:30 P.M. the next day. The total trip time is 13 hours and 30 minutes. Clearly, the time utility of the nonstop flight with Air China is best.

Cost Utility

4   Cost-effective transportation is required for both passenger and product movement to take place. When the cost to move people from an origin to a destination is so high that the trip becomes undesirable, then the person will choose not to travel. To return to our Beijing to New York example, the nonstop Air China flight has the highest time utility, but it costs $2,673. The slower Continental Airlines flight costs just $1,141. The cost utility of the Continental Airlines flight is best.

Source: Fricker, J.D., & Whitford, R.K. (2004). *Fundamentals of transportation engineering: A multimodal systems approach.* Upper Saddle River, NJ: Pearson Prentice Hall.

2
Building Academic Listening Skills

In this section, you will practice your ability to recognize the relationship between abstract concepts and concrete information, and you will identify the relationship between two spoken sources: a lecture and student comments. For online assignments, go to

PEARSON LONGMAN
myacademicconnectionslab

Key Words

carpool *n* a group of people who agree to travel together to work or school in one car and share the cost; **carpool** *v*

public transportation *exp* buses, trains, and other vehicles that are available for everyone to use

shuttle *n* a bus, train, or plane that makes short trips between two places; **shuttle** *v*

trade-off *n* a balance between two opposing things that you are willing to accept in order to achieve something

Before You Listen

1. *Look at the picture of a crowded stadium during a sports event. This kind of event is likely to cause traffic problems. Work in small groups and talk about the traffic problems listed in the chart. Add any other traffic challenges that you can think of in the first column of the chart. In the second column, write down possible solutions to these problems. Write as many solutions as possible. The key words may be useful.*

Traffic Problems	Traffic Solutions
1. too many cars arriving at and leaving from the stadium at the same time	• *build more roads*
2. not enough places to park	
3. not enough public transit (buses)	
4. other problems:	

2. *Now work with your group to discuss which solutions are expensive, which solutions are best for the environment, and which solutions require electronic or communication technology.*

Global Listening

1. 🎧 *Listen to the introduction of the lecture. What are the four challenges presented as abstract concepts that transportation engineers must face? List the four challenges in the first column of the chart. Before listening to the whole lecture, check your answers with the class.*

Abstract Concepts: The Challenges	Transition Word	Concrete Information	Relationship between Abstract Concept and Concrete Information (Support or Contradict)
efficient			
Solutions to Transportation Challenges:			

2. 🎧 *Now listen to the whole lecture and take brief point-form notes. Complete the second and third columns in the chart. You may also want to add more information to the first column. In the final row, write down some of the solutions to these transportation challenges. You may need to listen more than once to capture the information required in the chart. After each listening, compare your notes with a partner's, and fill in any gaps you may have.*

3. *Complete the fourth column by deciding whether the concrete information supports or contradicts the abstract concept. Share your answers with the rest of the class.*

Focused Listening

As you learn about a topic, you will gather information from a variety of sources. You will certainly learn from textbooks and your own research; you will also learn from lectures and conversations with classmates. As you listen to your lectures and speak with your classmates about a topic, it is important to notice the relationships among the pieces of information that you hear. Recognizing the relationships among pieces of information will help you to understand the information more deeply and quickly.

Here are some common relationships that you might notice among pieces of information. The pieces of information might be:

- similar
- contrasting
- solutions to a problem
- reasons why something is true
- unrelated

In this activity, you will practice recognizing relationships between two spoken sources. Follow the instructions to complete the tasks.

1. Before you can recognize the relationship between two sources, you must clearly understand the first source. For this activity, the lecture will be your first source of information. In the first row of the chart, write the four main challenges for transportation engineers that you learned about in the lecture. You will complete the rest of the chart later. Listen to the lecture again if necessary.

Four Main Transportation Challenges:	
Student Opinions	**Relationship between Student Opinion and Main Lecture** (*similar, contrasting, solutions to a problem, reasons why something is true, unrelated*)
Student 1:	
Student 2:	

(continued on next page)

 Unit 5 ■ Managing Traffic Flow **105**

Student Opinions	Relationship between Student Opinion and Main Lecture (*similar, contrasting, solutions to a problem, reasons why something is true, unrelated*)
Student 3:	
Student 4:	
Student 5:	
Your opinion:	

2. Listen to five students discuss the lecture. Take notes about what they say in the first column of the chart. You will complete the last row of the chart later.

3. Identify the relationship of the students' statements to the information in the lecture. Write the relationship in the second column of the chart.

4. In the last row of the chart, add your own statement about the lecture. Then identify the relationship of your own statement to the lecture information.

Checkpoint 1 PEARSON LONGMAN **myacademicconnectionslab**

Before You Read

3

Building Academic Reading Skills

In this section, you will practice recognizing the relationships among pieces of information and the differences between abstract concepts and concrete information. For online assignments, go to

1. Group the words from the box into the best columns to complete the chart on the next page. Then compare your answers with a classmate's.

carpooling	heavy traffic flow	public transit	traffic gridlock
expressway	high-occupancy vehicle lanes	road	~~traffic jam~~
fare payment	highway networks	shuttles	traffic lights
~~freeway~~	lane	toll collection	traffic signals

Synonyms for Highways and Highway Systems	Synonyms for Traffic Congestion	Words for Collection of Money from Drivers	Cheap Solutions for Traffic Problems	Words Related to Streets
freeway	*traffic jam*			

2. Work with a partner. Use as many of the words from the chart as you can in sentences that describe the picture. You can say or write your sentences. Put your best sentences on the board.

Global Reading

1. *Match the technical words on the left with their descriptions on the right. Then compare your answers with another student's, check with your teacher, or check a dictionary.*

Technology Vocabulary   **Description**

__c__ 1. **road sensors** *n*   a. a large electronic sign, usually above a freeway, whose message can be changed when necessary

____ 2. **dispatcher** *n*   b. an electronic system that receives information from a variety of sources and sends letters requesting payment

____ 3. **variable message sign** *n*   c. metal plates installed under the road that sense traffic flow

____ 4. **intersection** *n*   d. a sum of money that is paid to allow a driver to travel on a specific road

____ 5. **peak periods** *n*   e. a sign of letters and numbers that is on the front and back of vehicles

____ 6. **central billing system** *n*   f. someone whose job is to send out vehicles such as taxis or ambulances to places where they are needed

____ 7. **vehicle license plate** *n*   g. the time when the greatest number of people are using the same service at the same time

____ 8. **toll** *n*   h. equipment that sends electronic information from a vehicle to a central computer

____ 9. **transponder** *n*   i. a place where two roads meet

____ 10. **ramp** *n*   j. a short road for driving onto or off of a highway; on-ramp, off-ramp

2. *Study the questions. Then read the text on pages 109–110 and answer the questions. Compare your answers with two other classmates'.*

1. What are intelligent transportation systems (ITS)? What kinds of technology do they use?

2. Why is it difficult to argue that adding new lanes is the best solution for rush hour traffic congestion?

3. What are the three alternatives open to traffic engineers trying to solve rush hour traffic congestion? Which alternative leads to ITS?

4. How are road sensors and smart traffic lights used to control traffic flow?

5. Why are freeway management systems built?

6. What are the benefits of controlling traffic flow entering a freeway?

7. Can you think of other examples of ITS that you have seen?

INTELLIGENT TRANSPORTATION SYSTEMS

1   Intelligent transportation systems—or ITS—use current communication technologies to improve the efficiency of existing transportation systems. Electronic devices such as road sensors, smart traffic signals, and variable message signs can provide valuable information to drivers, dispatchers, and police.

2   Efficiency is a constant challenge for transportation engineers because transportation demand varies by time of day. Almost all daily congestion occurs during peak periods; however, in most cities, it lasts only a few hours. Therefore, it is difficult to argue that building more roads is the most cost-effective way to eliminate traffic problems, especially if something else can be done. Three alternatives are possible:

  a. Do nothing. Some people believe that traffic control in cities is now effectively accomplished by the congestion. Adding more vehicle capacity would only encourage more traffic.

  b. Increase the cost of using the highway during peak periods. City governments could collect tolls or increase downtown parking prices to discourage use of the highway.

  c. Use all the technology possible to encourage drivers to use the highway when it is less crowded. Communications technologies can help drivers make better decisions about when and where to travel.

3   The development of intelligent transportation systems (ITS) is a result of the third alternative. ITS are designed to improve existing road systems. This helps transportation engineers overcome the efficiency, cost, environmental, and safety challenges[1] they face.

TECHNOLOGY USED IN ITS

4   Road sensors are key technology for ITS. Buried under the roads, they sense heavy traffic flow at road intersections. The road sensors send a signal to "smart" traffic lights, which automatically change the signal timing to help move the vehicles more quickly through an intersection. This allows express buses to travel quickly through crowded downtowns during rush hours because all the traffic lights are green for them. If the smart traffic lights are connected to a traffic operations center, a dispatcher at the center can also control the traffic signals, allowing ambulances and police to travel quickly in an emergency situation. In Shanghai, for instance, transportation engineers have already installed road sensors and smart traffic lights near on-ramps to elevated roads. The smart light turns red shortly after an accident. This prevents other vehicles from entering the elevated roads and reduces traffic congestion.

5   Freeway management systems are another example of ITS. There are different types of freeway management systems. Some are used to collect tolls electronically. Traditionally, collecting tolls has meant that a person in a toll booth collects money from each driver, which increases the travel time of the trip. Freeway management systems that use ITS can collect tolls electronically without increasing total travel time. For example, in Toronto, Canada, many drivers who use the freeway install transponders in their vehicles, which signal a central billing system every time the driver uses the freeway. For vehicles that don't have transponders, cameras take photos of the vehicles' license plates. This identifies the drivers who should be billed. This freeway management system increases the cost of using the freeway without increasing total travel time. This reduces traffic congestion on the freeway.

---

[1]**overcome . . . challenge** *exp* to successfully solve a problem in the face of difficulties, challenges, or opposition

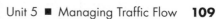

6   Other freeway management systems control the number of vehicles entering freeways. Drivers can only get onto the freeway if the traffic signal on the on-ramp is green. If the freeway is already over capacity, the driver will not be allowed to enter the freeway, and will have to wait until the traffic flow decreases. Variable message signs above the freeways are used to inform drivers of traffic and weather conditions. Figure 5.1 shows how this works. The positive outcome is improved traffic flow for those drivers already on the freeway. However, you might think that the trade-off is longer waiting times for those wishing to enter the freeway. Research shows that this is not the case.

7   In Minnesota, U.S.A., the Department of Transportation installed 430 smart traffic signals on its busiest on-ramps to create a freeway management system. Over a 6-week period, the smart signals increased the freeway capacity by 9 percent, increased average highway speed by 7 percent, and reduced highway accidents by 26 percent. They also reduced vehicle pollution by 1,160 tons and reduced highway travel times by 22 percent. Clearly, freeway management systems made a difference.

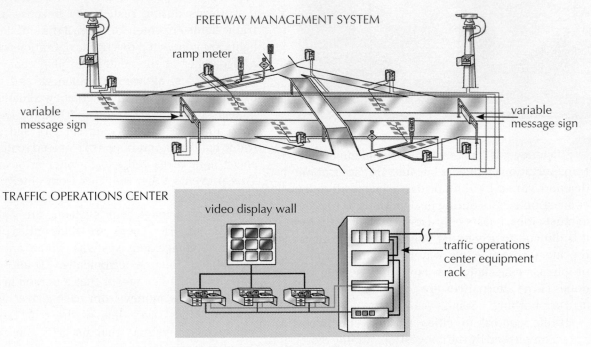

Figure 5.1 Freeway management system

Source: Fricker, J.D., & Whitford, R.K. (2004). *Fundamentals of transportation engineering: A multimodal systems approach.* Upper Saddle River, NJ: Pearson Prentice Hall.

Focused Reading

Recognizing the Relationship between Abstract Concepts and Concrete Information in Reading

As you know, abstract concepts are general ideas or principles, rather than something real that you can see or touch. Concrete information describes something that exists or is real—a specific example. It is important to recognize the difference between abstract concepts and concrete information when you read.

Answer the questions. Then compare your answers with a classmate's.

1. The reading on pages 109–110 is printed in two colors. What does each color represent? Circle the correct answer.
   a. Black = abstract concepts, and red = concrete information
   b. Red = abstract concepts, and black = concrete information

2. Where are the abstract concepts located in the reading? Why?

3. How do you know when the writer has moved from abstract concepts to concrete information?

Checkpoint 2   PEARSON LONGMAN myacademicconnectionslab

Before You Write

1. The text you are about to read is the beginning of a report that introduces a transportation challenge in the city of Markdale. It demonstrates a report writing style, with headings for each section. As you read, think about which of the proposed solutions in the report is the best.

4
Building Academic Writing Skills

In this section, you will finish writing a report about a traffic challenge in a city called Markdale. Your report must recommend the best possible solution to the traffic problem. Keep this goal in mind as you complete the tasks, which will prepare you to finish writing the report.
For online assignments, go to

PEARSON LONGMAN
myacademicconnectionslab

Report on Traffic Congestion in Markdale
Presented by The Markdale Office of Urban Planning

The Challenge

Markdale is a city of 500,000 people that is growing quickly. Highway 6 (HW6) runs east-west through the city. The highway crosses a bridge over the Beaver River, which runs north-south. HW6 carries most of the traffic heading for downtown Markdale, which is west of the river; it is also the main route through the city. Highway capacity is exceeded for five hours each day: from 7:30 to 9:30 A.M. and from 4:30 to 7:30 P.M. During rush hour, it can take drivers up to 50 minutes to cross town. Recently, taxpayers have complained about the congestion, and three significant businesses have decided not to locate in Markdale because the rush hour traffic is so bad.

Another concern is safety. The police have noted a recent increase in the number of vehicle and pedestrian accidents at intersections on the highway, especially at downtown intersections. Pedestrian fatalities occur at the rate of one to two per year.

The city has saved some money for a transportation project; there is enough money to add a single extra lane that will widen HW6 from east to west. However, there is not enough money to widen the bridge across the river. Bridge construction is much more expensive than road construction.

(continued on next page)

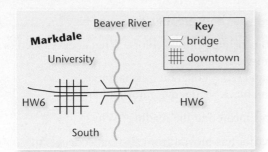

Markdale

Beaver River

University

Key
⊢⊣ bridge
▦ downtown

HW6

HW6

South

Summary of Possible Solutions

1. Land developers want to relocate HW6 to the north, so that it completely bypasses the city. To relocate the highway, the city would have to construct a new bridge across the river and purchase valuable farmland to the east, north, and west of the city. The land developers feel this solution will open up new land for them to build homes on, which will allow the city to grow.

2. Downtown merchants want the city to expand HW6 from two to four lanes in the city. Some homes, trees, and commercial property along HW6 would have to be purchased and demolished. The merchants believe this will bring more customers into the downtown area.

3. A local environmental group wants the city to offer increased public transit along the existing HW6. The group also recommends the construction of a subway from south Markdale through downtown to the university campus in the north end of the city. The city would have to purchase some land, but far less than it would have to purchase for solution 1 or 2. The environmentalists feel this solution would cause the least damage to the environment.

4. Most taxpayers favor the "do nothing" approach. These people say that increasing the highway's capacity only encourages more driving. The taxpayers know that construction of new road networks is expensive, and they do not want their taxes to increase. They want the money the city has already saved to be spent on improving the schools and health care in Markdale.

5. Markdale's transportation engineers suggest the use of intelligent transportation systems (ITS) _____

_____

_____

_____

_____

_____

Recommended Solution

_____

_____

_____

_____

_____

_____

_____

_____

_____

_____

_____

_____

_____

_____

Conclusion

_____

_____

_____

_____

_____

_____

2. *Work with a partner to complete the paragraph about the use of ITS as a possible solution for the transportation challenge in Markdale (point 5). Then share your answers with the class. You will write the recommended solution and conclusion for the report later.*

3. *Divide the class into five groups. Each group will represent one of the possible solutions. In your group, discuss the advantages and disadvantages of your possible solution. Consider the efficiency, cost effectiveness, environmental impact, and safety of the solution. As you discuss your possible solution, take notes in the chart. Then share your information with the class. Which is the best solution to overcome the transportation problem in Markdale? Is there any disagreement among the groups? Explain.*

Solution	Advantages	Disadvantages
1. Land developers: move HW6 north of Markdale		
2. City merchants: expand HW6		
3. Environmental group: increase public transit and build a subway		
4. Taxpayers: do nothing; spend money on education and health care		
5. Transportation engineers: use ITS		

Focused Writing

When you do not feel comfortable working in a language, you may try to write or say as little as possible in that language. While this may help you to avoid making mistakes, it is usually a clear sign that your language skills are weak.

To show that you are comfortable speaking or writing in your alternative language, there will be times when you will want to elaborate. Elaborating on ideas or information means giving more details or information about something. Look at the two responses to the question. Which answer demonstrates that the speaker is comfortable using his or her alternative language?

Question: *What are intelligent transportation systems (ITS)?*

Answer 1: *An ITS applies electronic and communications technology to solve transportation challenges.*

Answer 2: *An ITS uses technology, like road sensors and smart traffic signals, to sense the flow of traffic, and then it sends that information to a traffic operations center. Using this traffic flow information, dispatchers can control traffic signals to clear traffic jams and permit emergency vehicles to pass through a congested area.*

While Answer 1 is correct, it is abstract and not supported by concrete information. Also, it doesn't show the ability to work comfortably in an alternative language. Answer 2 is a more elaborate answer to the question and would demonstrate that you are a strong user of your alternative language.

1. *Work with a partner. Answer the questions either in writing or by speaking (or both), elaborating on your answers by adding concrete information. This will help your listener to understand the content, and you will demonstrate your comfort writing and speaking in English.*

1. Why is building extra highway capacity not always the best solution to rush-hour traffic?

   _____

   _____

   _____

2. What are the three alternatives that must be considered when traffic congestion causes problems?

   _____

   _____

   _____

3. What is a freeway management system?

   _____

   _____

   _____

2. *Share your written and/or spoken answers with another pair or group. Share your best answers with the class.*

Integrated Writing Task

You have listened to and read information from various sources about some transportation challenges and solutions to those challenges. You will now use your knowledge of the content, key vocabulary, and report format to complete your writing assignment: **Write a conclusion to the report that recommends the best solution to traffic congestion in Markdale.**

Synthesizing Information

When you write in an academic context, you need to combine different pieces of information into whatever you are writing—an essay, a report, a response paper, or even a lab report. This is called synthesizing information. To synthesize well, you need to identify your pieces of information, determine the relationships among the pieces of information, and express these relationships clearly in writing.

To help you synthesize the information from this unit into a **Recommended Solution** section in the report, use the chart. Write your recommended solution in the first row of the chart.

Information from the readings and the lecture has been included in the first column of the chart. In the second column, indicate the relationship of this information to your recommended solution (*similar, contrasting, solutions to a problem, reasons why something is true, unrelated*). In the third column, place a check (✓) next to information you will include in your section.

Your Recommended Solution:		
Information Sources	**Relationship to Recommended Solution** *similar, contrasting, solutions to a problem, reasons why something is true, unrelated*	**Included in the Report? (✓ or X)**
Reading: Location, Time, and Cost Utility • Location utility • Time utility • Cost utility		
Lecture: Transportation Challenges Four transportation challenges: • Inconsistent demand (efficiency) • Lack of money • Environmental concerns • Safety		

(continued on next page)

Information Sources	Relationship to Recommended Solution *similar, contrasting, solutions to a problem, reasons why something is true, unrelated*	Included in the Report? (✓ or X)
Reading: Intelligent Transportation Systems (ITS) • Smart traffic signals • Freeway management systems		

Follow the steps to complete your report.

Step 1: Write a short paragraph to complete the transportation engineers' ITS recommendation in the report on pages 111–112. This will complete the **Summary of Possible Solutions** section in the report.

Step 2: Write the **Recommended Solution** section, using the chart on pages 115–116 to help you synthesize the information from the unit readings and lecture. This section may be more than one paragraph long. Be sure to elaborate on your points.

Step 3: Write the **Conclusion** section, briefly summarizing your recommended solution and the reasons why you think it is the best one.

Step 4: When you have finished writing, ask your teacher or a classmate to review your report based on the features listed in the checklist.

Features of a Report	Yes	No
Are there three sections that form the end of the report, and does each begin with a clear heading?		
Is the report a synthesis of information from the unit? In other words, does the report contain information from the readings and the lecture?		
Is there enough elaboration, so that the points are clearly explained?		
Is the vocabulary specific to the topic of traffic engineering?		
Does the recommended solution seem reasonable?		

Step 5: Based on the information in the checklist, rewrite your report and hand it in.

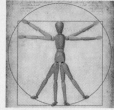

UNIT 6

Art History
Art versus Craft

Unit Description

Content: This course is designed to familiarize the student with concepts in art history.

Skills: Fact and Opinion

- Using facts to support an opinion
- Evaluating information used to support an opinion
- Recognizing degree of certainty when expressing opinions
- Distinguishing between facts and opinions
- Emphasizing important information

Faith Ringgold.
Tar Beach. 1988.
Acrylic pieced and printed fabric.

Unit Requirements

Lecture: "Collingwood's Theory of Art and Craft"

Readings: "The Blending of Art and Craft" (from *Prebles' Art Forms*, 8th Edition, P. Frank, Pearson Prentice Hall)

"Japanese Swords" (from *Japanese Crafts*, The Japan Times Ltd.)

Integrated Speaking Task: Giving an oral presentation that expresses and supports an opinion about an object

Assignments:
www.MyAcademicConnectionsLab.com

117

art *n* the use of painting, drawing, or sculpture to represent things or to express ideas

craft *n* a job or activity in which you use skills to create things with your hands

Previewing the Academic Content

For some people, there is a distinction between art and craft. They say that painting and sculpture are arts that express emotions, while rug making and quilting are crafts that are merely useful. At certain times in history, this distinction has been hotly debated. In this unit you will study the difference between art and craft, and you will decide whether this distinction is still true today. Do you believe there is a difference between art and craft? If so, how would you define the difference?

1. *Read the definitions of* art *and* craft *from a popular English dictionary. Work with a partner. Based on the dictionary definitions, decide which of the objects is art and which is craft. Circle your answers.*

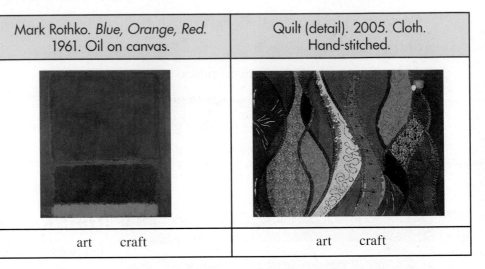

Mark Rothko. *Blue, Orange, Red.* 1961. Oil on canvas.	Quilt (detail). 2005. Cloth. Hand-stitched.
art craft	art craft

2. *Discuss your answers with the class. Why might there be disagreement among your classmates?*

3. *With your partner, try to determine your own definitions of art and craft. To do this, write each characteristic from the list in the appropriate column in the chart.*

List of Characteristics
- expresses ideas or emotions
- is useful or functional in a specific way
- is planned before it is created
- is created for a specific consumer
- demonstrates skill
- is unpredictable

Art	Craft

4. *What other characteristics of either art or craft could you add to the chart? Discuss any additional characteristics with the class.*

5. *Use the information in the chart to write sentences to create your own definitions of art and craft. Do these new definitions change your ideas about whether the objects in Exercise 1 are art or craft? Why or why not?*

_____

_____

_____

_____

_____

In this unit, you will practice distinguishing between a fact and an opinion. You will also practice recognizing a writer or speaker's degree of certainty. Finally, you will practice expressing and supporting an opinion.

Previewing the Academic Skills Focus

Fact and Opinion

As you progress in your academic work, it is important to be able to distinguish between facts and opinions. If you can do this, you will be able to quickly identify what information is known to be true and what information you can agree or disagree with.

A **fact** is a piece of information that must be accepted. It is known to be true, and you can't argue about it.

A fact can be

- common information

  Examples

  The Earth travels around the Sun.

  Water is composed of hydrogen and oxygen molecules.

- a specific idea or a statistic supported by research. For academic use, the source of this information must be referenced in a footnote.

  Example

  In the past, many paintings were attributed to the great Dutch artist Rembrandt van Rijn. Over the years, however, art historians have proven that these paintings were painted by his students and are not Rembrandt's paintings at all.[1]

An **opinion** is someone's idea or belief about a subject. An opinion is something you can question or discuss. You can agree or disagree with someone's opinions.

An opinion may be indicated by these specific phrases:

I think (that) . . .

I believe (that) . . .

I feel that . . .

In my opinion . . . / In my view . . .

I am of the opinion that . . .

It seems to me that . . .

---

[1] Davies, P. et al. (2007). *Janson's History of Art* (7th ed.). Upper Saddle River, NJ: Pearson Prentice Hall. p. 716.

(continued on next page)

A collocation is a set of words that are frequently used together. The verbs *state, give, provide,* and *express* are often used with the nouns *fact* and *opinion.*

We can state, give, or provide a fact.
We can state, give, or express an opinion.

As far as I'm concerned . . .
From my perspective . . .
I agree with . . . / I disagree with . . .

Example

It seems to me that craft is more consistently skillful than art. If a craft is not skillful, it is garbage. If art is not skillful, it is still art.

An opinion may also be provided without these specific phrases. Opinions may be difficult to recognize in these cases.

Example

Too many definitions of art are too narrow. If we consider a broader definition of art, the distinction between art and craft is eliminated.

When professors present academic information to students, they often present facts first and opinions second.

1. 🎧 *Work with a partner. Imagine that you are visiting a famous art gallery. As you walk through the gallery, you listen to the audio tour, which states facts and expresses opinions about the objects in the gallery. To show you can distinguish between fact and opinion, listen carefully to the audio tour. Then complete the tasks.*

a. *The Ardabil Carpet.* Tabriz. 1540. Wool pile on silk warps and wefts.

b. Faith Ringgold. *Tar Beach.* 1988. Acrylic pieced and printed fabric.

c. Gustave Courbet. *The Stone Breakers.* 1849. Oil on canvas.

1. State the opinion you hear about each of the objects.

a. _____

_____

_____

_____

b. _____

_____

_____

_____

c. _____

_____

_____

_____

2. *Which came first, facts or opinions? This is a common pattern in academic contexts.*

3. *What were the phrases that introduced the opinions in the audio tour? Which opinion was not introduced by a typical opinion phrase (see the skills box on pages 119–120)?*

Before You Listen

In this lecture, the art professor explains the key points of Collingwood's theory of art and craft. Your listening goal is to understand the main points of Collingwood's theory.

Before you listen, look at the pictures. These pictures will help illustrate the professor's points. Which pictures are examples of art, and which are examples of craft? Under each picture, circle either art or craft—whichever category you think the object belongs to. Discuss your answers with the class to determine if everyone agrees. If there are any differences in opinion, find out why.

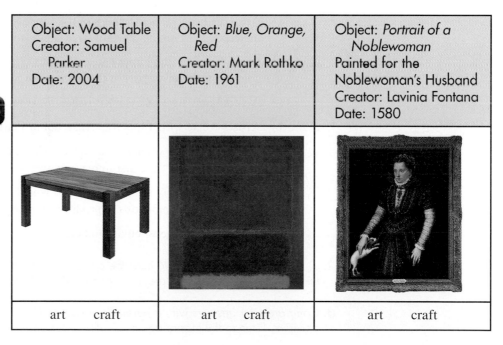

Object: Wood Table Creator: Samuel Parker Date: 2004	Object: *Blue, Orange, Red* Creator: Mark Rothko Date: 1961	Object: *Portrait of a Noblewoman* Painted for the Noblewoman's Husband Creator: Lavinia Fontana Date: 1580
art craft	art craft	art craft

2 Building Academic Listening Skills

In this section, you will learn how to evaluate information presented to support an opinion and how to recognize a speaker's degree of certainty.

For online assignments, go to

PEARSON LONGMAN
myacademicconnectionslab

Global Listing

1. *These true/false statements will help you identify the main points in the lecture. Read them before you listen to the lecture.*

_____ 1. Before 1930, people believed that the defining characteristic of art was the type of material used by the creator.

_____ 2. People thought that anything made from fabric, wood, or metal was art.

_____ 3. Craft is the skillful application of a technique to a material.

_____ 4. This definition of *craft* includes the mass production of objects.

_____ 5. The professor states that craft produces objects of no specific function; art produces functional objects.

_____ 6. Many works of art have the same characteristics of craft. Architecture is an example of an art that is like a craft: It is both skillful and useful.

_____ 7. Collingwood states that crafts are planned. Craftspeople know what they are going to make before they begin.

_____ 8. Because craftspeople plan their creations, they don't know when their creations are finished.

_____ 9. Craftspeople make their creations for a consumer or market.

_____ 10. The outcome of a craft is predictable.

_____ 11. Art is art because the creators of the art push the limits of their material. They are not certain what the results of their creation will be.

_____ 12. Because artists don't know the outcomes of their creations, they consider themselves part of the audience.

_____ 13. Artists know when they are finished creating their objects.

_____ 14. Artists create with a specific consumer or market in mind.

_____ 15. Art calls forth emotion in the viewer. The emotion may be different for each viewer, and the artist may not have predicted the emotions.

_____ 16. Collingwood's theory of art and craft is influential because it relies on the materials creators use to produce their objects.

_____ 17. The distinction between art and craft is completely clear.

2. 🎧 *Listen once to the lecture to hear the content. Then, as you listen again, decide if the statements in Exercise 1 are true or false. Write* **T** *(true) or* **F** *(false).*

3. *Compare your answers with a partner's. If you and your partner are not sure of the answers, listen to the lecture again. Confirm your answers with the class.*

4. *Rewrite each false statement to make it true.*

As you saw in the Preview, professors often use a common pattern of information presentation: facts first, opinions second. However, students are often asked to reverse this pattern in their own work.

In an academic context, students are frequently asked to take a position, or state an opinion, and explain why they hold this opinion. In this case, the pattern of information presentation changes. You must first express your opinion, or take a position, and then follow with facts that support your position.

Example

I agree with R. G. Collingwood's theory that art and craft are different. Collingwood's theory states that art is distinct from craft because artists don't plan the outcome of their creations, while craftspeople must plan the outcome.

In this case, the first sentence expresses the student's opinion. The second sentence is the fact about Collingwood's theory. Students are often asked to follow this pattern of information presentation: opinion (or position) first, facts to support the opinion second.

5. *With a partner, form an opinion about whether the examples represent art or craft. Next, determine if Collingwood's theory supports your opinion. Orally state your opinion followed by facts from Collingwood's theory that support or contradict your opinion. Use the 'opinion first, fact second' pattern.*

Example 1

A carpenter sets out to create a carving with leftover pieces of wood. He works for his own pleasure. He has no plans to sell his creation and no specific consumer. He knows his carving is complete when he believes the work will create a feeling of happiness in the viewer—himself.

Response:

I believe this is an example of art. According to Collingwood, this is an example of art because the artist does not know what his final creation will look like, and he has no specific consumer to buy his creation.

Example 2

A painter paints a landscape and displays the painting in an art show. During the show, a viewer admires the painting and asks the painter to paint a similar landscape—a landscape that is familiar to the viewer. The painter agrees. Is the second painting an example of art or craft?

Example 3

An actress is playing a character who must express anger during a play. She plans to make the audience feel angry, too. Because she's good at what she does, she succeeds in making the audience feel angry with her. This requires good technical skill.

Example 4

An actress has a complicated and difficult character to play. She is not sure how the audience will react to her character, so as she is acting, she explores the role she is playing, testing out the character's reactions to events. She is clarifying the character to herself at the same time as she is clarifying the character to the audience.

Focused Listening

Evaluating Information Used to Support an Opinion

Generally, when you are asked to state an opinion and support that opinion with facts, your professors are less concerned with your opinion than they are with how you use facts to support that opinion. This means the facts that you use to support your position are very important.

You must use *reliable* facts to support your opinions. When you plan to state your opinion, or when you are listening to other students state their opinions, you need to evaluate whether the facts are reliable. Reliable information can come from a variety of sources:

- Academic textbooks are generally reliable because you know the author and the date of publication.
- Lectures are generally reliable because your professor, an expert in his or her field, has provided the information.
- Academic journals are generally reliable because you know the author and the date of publication. Most journal articles are reviewed by experts before they are published.

Internet content, newspaper articles, or magazines may also be reliable, but be careful if the author's name or date of publication is not included. These are signs that the facts may not be reliable and should not be used to support your opinion.

1. *Discuss these sources of information with the class. Do you think these sources provide reliable facts, or should you question their reliability? Why?*

1. an audio tour of a large art gallery

2. a lecture given by your professor

3. an article on Wikipedia

4. a chapter from your textbook

5. an article from a newspaper that states the author's name and date of publication

6. a comment about art made by a friend who is a math major

7. an Internet article with no indication of the author's name or the date of posting

8. an academic journal article

People sometimes express opinions about a topic without being 100 percent sure that their opinion is well supported. In these cases, people may use one of a number of common helping (or modal) verbs, or words/expressions that show exactly how certain a speaker/writer is about her or his opinion. If you know these expressions, you will understand the speaker or writer's degree of certainty. You will find them in this chart.

Modal Verbs	Degree of Certainty
I believe that the distinctions between art and craft *will* become less important as time passes.	absolutely certain something will happen
I believe that the distinctions between art and craft *should* become less important as time passes.	mostly certain something will happen
I believe that the distinctions between art and craft *may* become less important as time passes.	possible something will happen
I believe that the distinctions between art and craft *might/could* become less important as time passes.	possible something will happen
Words/Expressions	**Degree of Certainty**
I am *certain* that art and craft will draw together.	absolutely certain something will happen
I am *almost certain* that art and craft will draw together.	mostly certain something will happen
I think it is *very probable/highly likely* that art and craft will draw together.	mostly certain something will happen
I think that it is *likely* that art and craft will draw together.	possible something will happen
I think that it is *unlikely/highly unlikely* that art and craft will draw together.	mostly certain something *won't* happen
I think that art and craft *will never* draw together.	absolutely certain something *won't* happen

2. 🎧 Listen to some people in an art gallery who are viewing works of art and expressing opinions about them. In the first column of the chart, you can see the works of art they are speaking about. Listen to their statements and check (✓) the box in the column that indicates the degree of certainty they have about their opinions.

Work of Art	Degree of Certainty (from 1 to 5)				
	1 Absolutely certain something won't happen	2 Mostly certain something won't happen	3 Possible something will happen	4 Mostly certain something will happen	5 Absolutely certain something will happen

3. *Which came first, the facts or the opinions? Listen again if necessary.*

Before You Read

1. *Work with a partner to find the collocations (frequently used multi-word groups) in the text on pages 128–129 that match the definitions in the chart. Use the paragraph references as clues to help you find the expressions quickly.*

Paragraph Number	Expression	Definition
1	*tend to*	to do something often
2		to eliminate obstacles
2		made individually, not mass produced
3		together
5		to change something to be similar to something else
5		as worthy as

3

Building Academic Reading Skills

In this section, you will practice identifying common collocations and phrasal verbs in a text and distinguishing between facts and opinions.
For online assignments, go to

PEARSON LONGMAN
myacademicconnectionslab

2. *Look at the picture of Toshiko Takaezu's bowl with a closed top. Then complete the tasks.*

1. Read what Takaezu said about her work.

"When working with clay I take pleasure from the process as well as from the finished piece. Every once in a while I am in tune with the clay, and I hear music, and it's like poetry. Those are the moments that make pottery truly beautiful for me."

Source: Coyne, J. Handcrafts. *Today's Education.* (November–December 1976):75. In Frank, P. (2006). *Prebles' artforms: An introduction to the visual arts* (8th ed., p.196). Upper Saddle River, NJ: Pearson Prentice Hall.

Toshiko Takaezu. *Makaha Blue II.* 2002. Stoneware.

2. Is Takaezu's work an art, a craft, or a blend of art and craft? Discuss your answer with the class. Present your answer as a statement of opinion followed by facts that support your opinion.

Global Reading

Study the questions about The Blending of Art and Craft, *which you are about to read. Then read the text and answer the questions.*

1. According to Westerners, what was most important: art or craft? What did Westerners see as the traditional characteristics of art and craft?

   _____

   _____

   _____

2. What was the common goal of William Morris (in the 1870s) and the Bauhaus (in 1919)?

   _____

   _____

3. Why did art and craft begin to draw together in the 1970s?

   _____

   _____

4. What is the western perception of art and craft today?

   _____

   _____

5. Peter Voulkos created pottery plates, flexed them out of shape, and scratched their surfaces. Why did this cause controversy?

   _____

   _____

controversy *n* a serious argument about something that involves a lot of people over a long time

harassment *n* unpleasant or threatening behavior

media *n* materials that are used in works of art or craft

pottery/ceramics/ stoneware *n* the art or craft of making pots, bowls, and other items from clay

typography *n* the work of preparing written material for publication

upscale *adj* relating to people from a high social and economic class

The Blending of Art and Craft

1   Ever since the Renaissance, people in the West have tended to rank the crafts a little below the arts. Westerners have generally considered craft objects to be useful things, such as dishes, blankets, or jewelry, while art (painting and sculpture) in a gallery or on a wall in someone's home is meant to be only looked at and thought about. Crafts are made with different media (clay, glass, wood, and fiber). Craft objects tend to be decorative, while art generally makes a personal statement.

2   Artists and craft workers have tried to break down this barrier at various times. For example, in the 1870s William Morris in England urged artists to turn away from the fine arts and devote their skills to making everyday objects. Most works of art in the West are unique and very expensive things; only the wealthy can afford them while the rest of us visit them in museums or look at copies in books. Morris thought that if artists devoted their skills and taste to the creation of things for common use, then everyone's life would be enriched. Hence the artists in his workshop made dishes, wallpaper, furniture, and fabrics by hand, like craft workers of the Middle Ages. This was Morris's

attempt to bring art and craft together, enriching the lives of ordinary people at the same time. Unfortunately, the shop could never get its prices low enough to please either the founder or the public.

3   A similar idea led to the creation of the Bauhaus in Germany in 1919, though it had a more modern approach. This school was the union of an art academy and a craft workshop. There, too, students and teachers cultivated the fine arts side by side with the applied arts of furniture making, graphic design, typography, and even architecture. The goal was similar to that of the Morris workshop: to bring craft and art together and to let artists use their skills to enrich objects we use every day. But because Adolph Hitler disliked modern art, the school was subject to Nazi harassment in the early 1930s and was forced to close.

4   The most recent push against the separation between art and craft began in the 1970s, when many artists began making unique objects out of craft media for gallery exhibitions. At that time, consumers increasingly appreciated the high level of skill, taste, and labor that go into the best craft work, such as quilts, dishes, and stained glass. Industry and mass production reduced the demand for handmade things for daily use. Craft and art thus began to draw together, and the barrier between them began to break down.

5   This change in attitude brought western thought in line with that of other cultures around the world and throughout history—cultures that have not separated art and craft. Most of the world's cultures have always regarded an excellent piece of pottery as highly as a painting, and a book illustration as equal in merit to a piece of sculpture. Western society is arriving at this view as well. As an example of this change in perspective, in 2002, the American Craft Museum changed its name to the Museum of Contemporary Arts and Design.

Example of an artist/craftsperson

6   In the mid-1950s, Peter Voulkos brought ceramic tradition together with modern art expression, and thus extended the horizons for both art and craft. He and a group of his students broke through preconceptions about the limits of clay as a medium for sculpture. With his rebellious spirit, Voulkos revitalized ceramic art and helped touch off new directions in other craft media. If most movements to unite art and craft involved artists moving toward craft, Voulkos reversed the process. Trained as a potter, he had a studio that sold dishes in upscale stores until the mid-1950s. Then he began to explore abstract art, and he found ways to incorporate some of its techniques into his ceramic work. At first he took a fresh approach to plates: He flexed them out of shape and scratched their surface as if they were paintings, thereby making them useless in the traditional sense. His first exhibition of these works in 1959 caused a great deal of controversy, because most people did not think of stoneware as an art medium, yet none could deny the boldness of his creations. His monumental *Firestone* brings the emotional energy of abstract expressionist painting to three-dimensional form. While ceramic processes have evolved rapidly over the last century, the most significant change has come in the use of clay as a conceptual and sculptural art form.

Peter Voulkos. *Firestone.* 1965.

Source: Frank, P. (2006). *Prebles' artforms: An introduction to the visual arts* (8th ed.). Upper Saddle River, NJ: Pearson Prentice Hall.

Focused Reading

This reading contains many examples of useful phrasal verbs. These combinations of verb + preposition, or occasionally verb + adverb, occur frequently in English, and they are difficult to learn if English is not your first language.

1. *Work with a partner. Use the paragraph references in the left-hand column of the chart to find the verb listed in the middle column that appears in the reading on pages 128–129. Write in the preposition (or adverb) that follows the verb in the text. In the right-hand column, write a short sentence using the phrasal verb. Share your best sentences with the class.*

Paragraph Number	Phrasal Verb (and Meaning)	Your Own Sentence
1	looked __at__ (viewed/saw)	They went to the art gallery and looked at the works of art.
1	thought _____ (considered)	
1	are made _____ (created from)	
2	break _____ (remove or eliminate)	
2	turn away _____ (reject)	
3	bring craft and art _____ (bring craft and art closer)	
4	push _____ (reject)	
4	draw _____ (become closer)	
6	broke _____ (got past or beyond)	
6	touch _____ (to begin something new)	

By now you know the difference between facts and opinions, and you know two patterns of presentation: facts first, opinions second, and opinions first, facts second. These two patterns are usually easy to identify, especially if the speaker or writer uses one of the common opinion indicators (such as *I think that, it seems to me,* or *from my perspective*).

It is more difficult to identify opinions when the speaker or writer does not use one of these common opinion indicators. In fact, sometimes the speaker or writer does not state an opinion directly, but makes statements that help you indirectly determine the opinion.

For example, an author might write, *Is art better than craft? The answer depends on what you want. If you want a skillful use of materials, the craftsperson will achieve that goal every time, because if it isn't skillful, it isn't craft. If you want an emotional response to a work, you might get it from art, but you might not.*

Can you indirectly determine, from these few sentences, what the writer's answer is to her own question: Is art better than craft? In this case, the writer's opinion seems to be that craft is better than art because it more reliably delivers skillful work, while art is not as good because it only inconsistently delivers an emotional response. The adjective *skillful* has a positive meaning and shows the author's opinion.

When you have to identify opinion without a common opinion indicator, you have to look for words that have positive or negative meaning that demonstrate the speaker or writer's opinion.

2. *There are several places in the reading where the author does not directly state an opinion. Read the paragraphs of the text on pages 128–129 again and determine the writer's opinion. Then circle the best answer.*

1. Read Paragraphs 1 and 5. What is the writer's opinion about the change in western thought over the last 400 years?
   a. It is good that western thought about the value of art and craft is in line with that of other cultures.
   b. It is too bad that westerners did not value craft more highly over the last 400 years.
   c. Westerners should continue to value art more highly than craft.

2. Read Paragraph 6. What is the writer's opinion about Peter Voulkos's work?
   a. It is controversial and should not be displayed in art galleries.
   b. It is an unfortunate example of useful craft objects being made non-functional.
   c. It is an important example of how the barrier between art and craft is breaking down.

3. Read Paragraphs 2, 3 and 4. What is the writer's opinion about the attempts to blend art and craft?
   a. They are destined to fail now as they have many times in the past.
   b. They have succeeded because of the many attempts over the years.
   c. They are only a short-term phase in art history, and the distinctions between art and craft will always remain.

Checkpoint 2   PEARSON LONGMAN   myacademicconnectionslab

4
Building Academic Speaking Skills

In this section, you will practice emphasizing important information when speaking. Then you will orally express an opinion about an object and support your opinion with facts that you have learned from the unit. Your short presentation should explain whether you think the object is art, craft, or a blend of the two based on characteristics presented in the unit.

For online assignments, go to

PEARSON LONGMAN
myacademicconnectionslab

Before You Speak

In the unit lecture you learned about the differences between art and craft, as defined by R. G. Collingwood. In the unit reading you learned about the blending of art and craft. In this reading you will learn another reason why craft and art are drawing together.

1. *Read the text and answer the questions.*

JAPANESE SWORDS

Today we are governed by rationalism and efficiency, and we live in the midst of mechanized and mass-produced objects. As a result, traditional crafts are becoming more valuable and important for modern people.

Craftspeople still make traditional craft items one by one with painstaking care. They use elaborate techniques dating back several hundreds or even thousands of years. These crafts are the exact opposite of rationalism and efficiency; they are full of unique beauty that can never be expected of mass production. When we see these traditional craft items, their beauty fascinates us.

In the past, crafts were a combination of function and ornament, while paintings and sculptures were made purely for the expression of beauty and existed only because of their beauty. This was the traditional view held by people who felt that works of craft should be clearly differentiated from the pure works of art like paintings and sculptures. Nevertheless, in modern society, traditional craft items have lost their function. For instance, Japanese swords were originally made to kill the enemy and were never intended to create beauty. Nowadays, however, they have completely lost their function as weapons. Yet because of their very beauty, they are now valued as one of the best of Japan's traditional arts. Excellent craft items with a long tradition necessarily possess superb artistry. We have only to appreciate their artistic value and beauty just as we do with paintings and sculptures.

Source: Japan Times, Ltd. (1972). *Japanese crafts.* Tokyo: The Japan Times.

---

1. Do you believe that modern people are governed by the principles of rationalism and efficiency? Support your opinion with some facts from your own experience. (State your opinion first, and provide facts second.)

2. Why are crafts the opposite of rationalism and efficiency?

3. Over time, what has happened to traditional crafts? Give an example.

2. To help you prepare for your oral presentation, review the unit readings and lecture, and list the characteristics of art, traditional craft, and modern craft in the chart.

	Characteristics of Art	Characteristics of Traditional Craft	Characteristics of Modern Craft
Purpose	*for beauty to express emotion*		
Materials			
Value			
Relationship of creator to object			
Other characteristics			

Focused Speaking

When you give an oral presentation, placing the correct emphasis on key words will help your audience understand what you are saying. To emphasize a word when you are speaking, say the word more slowly and a bit more loudly (but not too loudly). To show emphasis in a written text, we use capitals.

1. 🎧 *Listen to these examples as you read the sentences. Can you hear the emphasis on the key words? If you can't hear the emphasis the first time, listen again.*

   1. According to Collingwood, PORTRAIT paintings that were TRADITIONALLY thought of as ART are really CRAFT.

   2. Everyone thought they were ART simply because they were PAINTINGS.

   3. However, because they were painted for a specific CONSUMER, Collingwood argues they are CRAFT.

   4. Probably, the portrait painter also PLANNED the outcome of the painting carefully to please the BUYER, and PLANNING is also characteristic of CRAFT.

2. 🎧 *Listen to the sentences that are written here without the capitals to show emphasis. Circle the words you hear that have emphasis.*

   1. (Modern) craftspeople are now using traditional craft materials to make art.

   2. Voulkos created pottery plates that were functional, then bent and scratched them so they were non-functional.

   3. Traditional Japanese swords were functional craft. Now they have lost their function and are considered art.

3. *Compare your answers in Exercise 2 with a partner's. Once you have confirmed with your partner which words were emphasized by the speaker, review the circled words. How does the speaker know which words to emphasize? What are the characteristics of the words that are emphasized?*

4. *With your partner, read the sentences and circle the words you think should be emphasized. Then practice reading the sentences out loud to your partner, placing the emphasis on the correct words.*

   1. Takaezu made functional clay tea bowls and then closed the top of the bowl to create an art object.

   2. Initially, this kind of art was very controversial.

   3. People felt that craft materials should not be used to make art.

   4. However, the blending of art and craft is well established now and is no longer controversial.

Integrated Speaking Task

You have read and listened to information about the distinction between and blending of art and craft. You will now use your knowledge of the content, key vocabulary, and skills from this unit to complete an oral report assignment. Here is your assignment: **Give a short oral presentation that explains whether an object is art, craft, or a blend of the two.** Your presentation will include facts about the object, your opinion about the object, and information about art and craft that supports your opinion.

Follow the steps to prepare your presentation.

Step 1: Look at the pictures of three objects. The factual details for each object are provided. Choose one of the objects as the topic of your presentation.

	Details Creator: Hans Holbein the Younger Title: *Henry VIII* Date: 1540 Painted for King Henry VIII Description: Oil on panel Location: Galleria Nazionale d'Arte, Antica, Rome

	Details
	Creator: Meret Oppenheim
	Title: *Object (Le Déjeuner en Fourrure)*
	Date: 1936
	Description: Fur-covered cup, saucer, and
	   spoon
	Location: The Museum of Modern Art,
	   New York City, USA

	Details Creator: Lyubov Sergeevna Popova Title: *Lady with the Guitar* Date: 1914 Description: Oil on canvas Location: Museum of Art, Smolensk, Russia

Step 2: Plan your introduction. This should include the facts and details about the object. As well as the facts, you should describe your object. This is common practice in the field of art history.

Step 3: Consider your opinion about the object and your degree of certainty.

Step 4: Plan the information about art and craft you will use to support your opinion.

Step 5: Plan a conclusion for your presentation. Your conclusion should be a sentence or two that states the name of the object and summarizes your opinion about it.

Step 6: Write out your presentation. Look at the sentences you have written and circle the key words. Circle words that show contrast and words that you would like to emphasize. Practice your presentation. Give emphasis to the words you have circled.

Step 7: Practice your presentation in front of a classmate. Ask your classmate to evaluate your presentation based on the checklist.

Features of an Oral Presentation	Yes	No
In the introduction, does the presenter talk about the details of the object and describe the object?		
Does the presenter clearly express his or her opinion about the object and indicate his or her degree of certainty? What is the presenter's degree of certainty? Write the answer here:_____		
Does the presenter use facts to support his or her opinion? Is this information taken from the unit lecture and reading?		
Does the presenter finish the presentation with a conclusion that states the title of the object and summarizes his or her opinion?		
Does the presenter emphasize content words and contrasting words effectively?		

Step 8: Based on the information in the checklist, revise your presentation and practice it. Then make your presentation to the class.

UNIT 7

Biology
Genetic Testing

Unit Description

Content: This course is designed to familiarize the student with concepts in genetic testing.

Skills: Purpose

- Recognizing a writer's or speaker's primary purpose
- Recognizing a writer's secondary purpose
- Recognizing a speaker's purpose
- Recognizing a speaker's secondary purpose
- Recognizing how thought groups, stress, and intonation help express a speaker's attitude
- Understanding the intended audience

Unit Requirements

Readings: "Principles of Inheritance" (from *Biology of Humans: Concepts, Applications, and Issues,* J. Goodenough, B. McGuire, & R. Wallace, Pearson Prentice Hall)

"Prenatal Genetic Testing" (from *Essential Biology with Physiology*, 2nd Edition, N. Campbell, J. Reece, & E. Simon, Pearson Benjamin Cummings)

Lecture: "Genetic Testing"

Integrated Writing Task: Writing a pamphlet about genetic testing, keeping in mind the purpose and audience

Assignments: www.MyAcademicConnectionsLab.com

1

Preview

For online assignments, go to

PEARSON LONGMAN
myacademicconnectionslab

Key Words

cholesterol *n* a chemical substance found in the blood; too much may cause heart disease

deterioration *n* decreasing function; **deteriorate** *v*

dominant *adj* particular genetic feature of a parent that is visible in a child, even if it has been passed on by only one parent; *opposite of* **recessive**

mucus *n* a thick liquid produced in various parts of the body, such as the nose

recessive *adj* a particular genetic feature that is visible in a child only if both parents pass it on; *opposite of* **dominant**

susceptibility to *n* a tendency to be affected by something; **susceptible** *adj*

Previewing the Academic Content

Improvements in medical technology have made us what is arguably the healthiest generation of humans of all time. We know how to prevent diseases through vaccination, treat cancer with radiation and chemotherapy, and detect internal damage with magnetic resonance imaging (MRI). There have been parallel improvements in the field of genetics. With our greater understanding of genes and chromosomes, we can detect the likelihood that a person will develop a genetic disorder later in life, or determine the chances that a child will be born with a genetic disorder.

With this knowledge comes a series of complicated questions. Should doctors test the genes of unborn children to see if they will be healthy? Should doctors tell people if they will develop a genetic disorder as they get older? Should the results of genetic tests be available to others—for instance, employers and insurance companies? Should governments pass laws about genetic testing, or should people make their own decisions? What would *you* do if you found out *you* had a genetic disorder?

1. *Look at the table. It lists several recessive and dominant genetic disorders, their symptoms, and their incidence rates.*

SOME HUMAN GENETIC DISORDERS		
DISORDER	**MAJOR SYMPTOMS**	**INCIDENCE**
Recessive Disorders		
Albinism	Lack of color in skin, hair, and eyes	1 in 22,000
Cystic fibrosis	Excess mucus in lungs, digestive tract, and liver; increased susceptibility to infections; death in early childhood unless treated	1 in 1,800 European Americans
Tay-Sachs disease	Mental deficiency; blindness, paralysis, death in childhood	1 in 3,500 Jews
Dominant Disorders		
Achondroplasia	Normal growth is slowed down; the individual remains short her/his entire life	1 in 25,000
Alzheimer's disease	Mental deterioration; usually strikes late in life	Not known
Huntington's disease	Mental deterioration and uncontrollable movements; strikes in middle age	1 in 25,000
Hypercholesterolemia	Excess cholesterol in blood; heart disease	1 in 500

Source: Campbell, N., Reece, J., & Simon, E. (2007). *Essential biology with physiology* (2nd ed., p.153). San Francisco: Pearson Benjamin Cummings.

2. *Fill in the blanks with information from the table on the previous page. Then compare your answers with a classmate's.*

1. This table lists _____ three _____ recessive disorders and _____ four _____ dominant disorders.

2. Albinism is a disease characterized by _____.

3. A recessive disorder that causes blindness, paralysis, and death in early childhood is _____. It affects _____ Jews.

4. Cystic fibrosis shows up in _____ European Americans.

5. _____, a dominant genetic disorder, strikes people late in life.

6. Uncontrollable movement is a symptom of _____, which affects one in _____ people.

7. Of all the diseases listed in the table, you are most likely to get _____.

8. With an incidence of one in 25,000, people with achondroplasia remain _____ their entire lives.

3. *Work with a partner. Discuss what you would do if you knew you would develop Huntington's disease in your middle age. Consider the questions.*
- Would you want to know?
- Would you work harder or relax more in your productive lifetime?
- Would you tell your spouse, employer, or friends?
- Would you have children if you knew you might pass on Huntington's disease to them?

In this unit, you will consider a writer's or speaker's purpose. You will also learn about the use of thought groups, stress, and intonation to express intended meaning.

Previewing the Academic Skills Focus

Recognizing a Writer's or Speaker's Primary Purpose

A writer's or speaker's purpose is the *reason why* he or she writes or speaks. Of course, there are many reasons why people write or speak. In an academic setting, usually the *primary* purpose is to inform the audience. For example, an author writes a textbook to inform students, and a professor gives a lecture for the same reason. You may read or hear texts whose *primary* purpose is to persuade the audience as well.

Here are the characteristics of texts that inform or persuade.

(continued on next page)

Writer's Primary Purpose	Characteristics of a Text Written for That Purpose
To inform the reader	Very factual
To persuade the reader	Contains opinions, strong statements (*it is imperative, it is essential*), and modal verbs (*we should/must/ could*)

Good writers and speakers use a variety of strategies to inform their audiences. For example, they may inform audience by entertaining them—for instance, by telling a story that demonstrates a point. Similarly, writers and speakers may persuade audience members by informing them about different options. In these cases, even though the text may sound informative, its primary purpose is to persuade the reader or listener.

Whether their primary purpose is to inform or to persuade, writers and speakers usually begin by *getting the audience's attention*. They may tell a story to personalize the issue, state a startling fact, quote a famous person, or explain why their topic is important. These are ways to attract the audience's attention. You, too, should begin by getting the audience's attention when you write or speak in an academic context.

How writers and speakers choose to achieve their primary purpose will vary, depending on the audience. Later in this unit, you will consider how writers and speakers take their audiences into account to achieve their purposes.

Read the text and answer the questions on the next page.

The Story of Dan and Steve

1   Steve's brother, Dan, is a risk taker. Two years ago, he hiked through the Andes Mountains in Chile with only a backpack and a knife. Four years ago, he learned to scuba dive while on an adventure cruise in Alaska. Recently, he took up skydiving.

2   Dan hasn't always been like this. Six years ago, he was finishing law school and looking forward to a career in politics. Then his father was diagnosed with Huntington's disease, which is caused by the degeneration of brain cells. This devastating disease usually appears in middle age with symptoms of clumsiness and forgetfulness. Now Dan's dad is still able to work, but his handwriting has become uncontrollable, and it is difficult for him to sit for long periods without twitching.

3   The bad news for Dan and Steve is that Huntington's disease is genetic. There is a 50 percent chance that they also carry the gene.[1] Because Huntington's disease is caused by a dominant gene, if Dan and Steve do carry the gene, they will surely develop the disease in middle age. After his father's diagnosis, Dan decided to have his genes analyzed to see if he carried the Huntington's gene. Unfortunately, he did. When Dan finished school, he started to live the life of a risk taker.

---

[1]**carry the gene** *v* to have the gene

"What do I have to lose?" he thought. Steve, on the other hand, was happily married to Jessica. He elected not to have his genes tested but to continue to live the nearly perfect life he and Jessica had always enjoyed. But then Jessica got pregnant. Jessica wanted to have the child, but not if it would be born with the gene for Huntington's disease. She insisted that the baby's genes be tested. Fortunately for Steve, Jessica, and the baby, the test was negative.

4   Most of us do not need to worry about whether we will develop Huntington's disease. However, as you flip though the pages of your family album, you may notice distinctive traits scattered through the generations. Physical characteristics may be the most obvious way in which heredity has shaped you, but they are a very small part of your genetic legacy. The genes you received from your parents influence all the biochemical reactions taking place inside your cells, your susceptibility to disease, certain behavior patterns, and even your life span. Although your environment influences the expression of genes, your genes provide the basic outline for your possibilities and limitations.

Source: Goodenough, J., McGuire, B., & Wallace, R. (2005). *Biology of humans. Concepts, applications, and issues.* Upper Saddle River, NJ: Pearson Prentice Hall.

1. What was the author's primary purpose for writing this text?
   a. to entertain us with the story of Dan and Steve
   b. to persuade us that genetic testing is best
   c. to inform us about how our genes can influence our lives

2. Why did the author start this text with a story?
   a. to tell the reader about her friends Steve and Dan
   b. to get our attention
   c. to make us feel sorry for Dan

3. The writer's move from the narrative about Dan and Steve to a more informative text takes place in which paragraph? How do you know?
   a. 2
   b. 3
   c. 4

4. Why did Dan choose to live the life of a risk taker?
   a. He felt he was going to die soon.
   b. He enjoyed the thrill of danger.
   c. He didn't want to get married.

5. Steve did not get his genes tested for Huntington's disease because he _____.
   a. was already leading a happy life
   b. didn't care
   c. knew he was going to die sometime

6. Steve and Jessica decided to test the genes of their unborn child because they _____.
   a. were looking for a cure for Steve's father
   b. didn't want their child to have Huntington's disease
   c. wanted to have a perfect child

2

Building Academic Reading Skills

In this section, you will learn some common vocabulary related to genetics and how dominant and recessive genes create physical characteristics in individuals. You will also consider the primary and secondary purposes of a textbook excerpt. For online assignments, go to

myacademicconnectionslab

Key Words

allele *n* /əˈliːəl/ one of several possible forms of gene

chromosome *n* /ˈkroʊməsoʊm/ a thread-shaped part of every living cell that contains the genes controlling size, shape, and other physical characteristics

gene *n* /dʒiːn/ a part of a chromosome that controls what an organism looks like, how it grows, and how it develops

Before You Read

*1. Read the key words and their definitions, and look at the illustration. Then read the statements. Decide if they are true or false. Write **T** (true) or **F** (false). Correct the one false statement.*

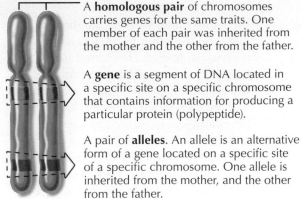

A pair of chromosomes

A **homologous pair** of chromosomes carries genes for the same traits. One member of each pair was inherited from the mother and the other from the father.

A **gene** is a segment of DNA located in a specific site on a specific chromosome that contains information for producing a particular protein (polypeptide).

A pair of **alleles**. An allele is an alternative form of a gene located on a specific site of a specific chromosome. One allele is inherited from the mother, and the other from the father.

_____ 1. Chromosomes come in pairs and contain paired genes. One gene is inherited from the mother, and one comes from the father.

_____

_____ 2. A homologous pair of chromosomes carries genes for the same physical trait.

_____

_____ 3. An allele is a kind of chromosome.

_____

2. Look at the photographs. Then complete the tasks on the next page.

Freckles: *FF* or *Ff*   No freckles: *ff*   Widow's peak: *WW* or *Ww*   Straight hairline: *ww*

Attached earlobes: *EE* or *Ee*   Unattached earlobes: *ee*   *tt*   *Tt*   *TT*
Tongue rolling

Genotypes and phenotypes of selected inherited human traits

Key Words

dominant gene *n*
a gene that causes
a child to have a
particular feature of
a parent even if it has
been passed on by only
one parent; designated
by a capital letter

genotype *n* the exact
genes that are present
in a living thing that
may or may not lead to
a visible characteristic

phenotype *n* a
clearly visible physical
characteristic

recessive gene *n*
a gene that causes
a physical feature,
but only if a child
inherits two of that
gene; designated by a
lowercase letter

1. Read the key words and their definitions

2. Read the statements. Decide if they are true or false. Write **T** (true) or **F** (false). Correct the one false statement.

_____ 1. Scientists indicate dominant genes with capital letters and recessive genes with lowercase letters.

_____

_____ 2. People with *ff* alleles will have freckles.

_____

_____ 3. Phenotype is related to how a person looks and the physical features that you can see.

_____

3. *Confirm your answers from this section with the class. If you don't understand some of the terms, ask about them now.*

Global Reading

1. *Read the text and determine:*
- the author's primary purpose
- how you know the author's primary purpose
- the number of the paragraph in which the author switches from getting the reader's attention to focusing on the main purpose of the text

Principles of Inheritance

1   Why is your brother the only sibling with Mom's widow's peak (a hairline that comes to a point on the forehead) and freckles? How can you have blue eyes when both your parents are brown eyed? Will you be bald at forty, like your dad? A closer look at chromosomes shows how chromosomes and heredity are related.

2   Human cells have twenty-three pairs of chromosomes. One member of each pair is inherited from the female parent, and the other member comes from the male parent. Two chromosomes that carry genes for the same traits are called a **homologous pair of chromosomes**. Chromosomes are made of DNA and protein. Certain segments of the DNA of each chromosome function as genes. A **gene** directs the synthesis of the specific polypeptide (protein) that can play either a structural or a

functional role in the cell. In this way, the gene-determined protein can influence whether a certain **trait**, or physical characteristic, will develop. For instance, the formation of your brother's widow's peak was directed by a protein coded for by a gene that he inherited from your mom.

3   There are different forms of genes, called **alleles**. Alleles produce different versions of the trait they determine. Generally, there are two alleles for each trait in the body's cells—one allele on each homologous

chromosome. One of the several genes that determines eye color, for example, dictates whether the brown pigment melanin will be deposited in the iris, or the colored part of your eye. When this allele is present, eye color will range from green to dark brown, depending on the amount of melanin present. The other allele for eye color does not lead to melanin deposit. If neither homologous chromosome has an allele that directs a melanin deposit, a person's eye color will be blue.

4   When two copies of the same allele of a gene are present in an individual, the alleles are said to be **homozygous** (*homo* = "same"; *zygo* = "joined together") for that trait. When different alleles of the same gene are present, they are said to be **heterozygous** (*hetero* = "different"; *zygo* = "joined together"). When the effects of a certain allele can be seen, regardless of whether an alternative allele is also present, the allele is described as **dominant**. Dimples, freckles, and attached earlobes are human traits dictated by dominant alleles.

5   The allele whose effects are hidden in the heterozygous condition is described as **recessive**. As a result, only the traits associated with homozygous recessive alleles can be seen. Several human disorders result from homozygous recessive alleles. One is cystic fibrosis, in which excessive mucus production impairs lung and pancreatic function. Another disorder is albinism, in which the pigment melanin is missing in a person's hair, skin, and eyes.

6   By convention, the dominant allele is designated with a capital letter, and the recessive allele gets a lowercase letter—*A* and *a*, for example. We observe the dominant form of the trait whether the individual is homozygous dominant (*AA*) or heterozygous (*Aa*) for that trait. Thus, we cannot always tell which alleles are present. We observe the recessive form of the trait only when there are two recessive genes for the same physical characteristic (*aa*).

7   It is often useful to distinguish between an individual's genetic makeup and an individual's appearance. Therefore, the term **genotype** refers to the precise alleles that are present—that is, whether the individual is homozygous or heterozygous for different gene pairs. The term **phenotype**, on the other hand, refers to the observable physical traits of an individual. The table below summarizes terms commonly used in genetics as they apply to the inheritance of freckles, which is a dominant trait.

COMMON TERMS IN GENETICS

GENOTYPE: the alleles that are present	DESCRIPTION	PHENOTYPE: the observable trait
FF	**Homozygous dominant** • two dominant alleles present • dominant phenotype expressed	Freckles
Ff	**Heterozygous** • different alleles present • dominant phenotype expressed	Freckles
ff	**Homozygous recessive** • two recessive alleles present • recessive phenotype expressed	No freckles

Source: Goodenough, J., McGuire, B., & Wallace, R. (2005). *Biology of humans: Concepts, applications, and issues.* Upper Saddle River, NJ: Pearson Prentice Hall.

2. *Read the text again. Answer the questions. Then compare your answers with two other classmates'.*

1. What is a homologous pair of chromosomes?

   _____

2. What do genes do?

   _____

3. What do alleles do?

   _____

4. If you have an allele that deposits melanin in the iris of your eye, what color eyes will you have?

   _____

5. What do the terms *homozygous* and *heterozygous* mean?

   _____

6. What are some human disorders that exist when there are homozygous recessive genes?

   _____

7. When can we see the dominant form of a trait in an individual?

   _____

8. When can we see the recessive form of a trait in an individual?

   _____

9. When you describe what a person looks like, what are you describing?

   _____

10. Write the genotype for the each picture.

Freckles: _____   No freckles: _____   Widow's peak: _____   Straight hairline: _____

Attached earlobe: _____   Free earlobe: _____

Focused Reading

As you have learned, every written text has a *primary* purpose. At a university or college, that primary purpose is most often to inform or to persuade. However, writers may also have *secondary* (or rhetorical) purposes. Generally, to express a *secondary* purpose, writers use the following specific words, phrases, or strategies:

- to introduce a new point: *first, next*
- to explain why something happens: *because, as a result, therefore, in order to, for this reason*
- to provide more information: *in addition, also*
- to provide an alternative explanation: *or, on the other hand;* use of parentheses
- to provide an example: *for example, for instance, such as*
- to quantify a general statement: use of numbers
- to emphasize a point: *it should be noted that, most of all, especially, in particular*
- to contrast ideas: *but, however, although, while, whereas, on the other hand*
- to create a picture for the reader: *imagine, picture this, is like, looks like*

When you think about the writer's secondary purpose, you are thinking about why the writer made a specific point, or why the writer developed the point in a specific way. You need to consider the words, phrases, or sentences in relation to the rest of the text to figure out why the writer presented this information in this particular way.

Determine the writers' secondary purposes from the sections of the texts you have read so far. Circle the correct answers. Then discuss your answers with the class.

From "The Story of Dan and Steve"

> Steve's brother, Dan, is a risk taker. Two years ago, he hiked through the Andes Mountains in Chile with only a backpack and a knife. Four years ago, he learned to scuba dive while on an adventure cruise in Alaska. Recently, he took up skydiving.

1. Why did the writer say that Dan tried hiking, backpacking, scuba diving, and skydiving?
   a. to give examples of Dan's risky behavior
   b. to show that Dan is very athletic
   c. to suggest that Dan likes to travel the world

> This devastating disease usually appears in middle age with symptoms of clumsiness and forgetfulness. Now Dan's dad is still able to work, but his handwriting has become uncontrollable, and it is difficult for him to sit for long periods without twitching.

2. Why does the writer mention that Dan's father's handwriting has become uncontrollable and that it is difficult for him to sit for long periods without twitching?
   a. to show that Dan's father is suffering from Huntington's disease
   b. to suggest that life is not that bad for people with Huntington's disease
   c. to create an image of the disease in the reader's mind

> When Dan finished school, he started to live the life of a risk taker. "What do I have to lose?" he thought. Steve, on the other hand, was happily married to Jessica. He elected not to have his genes tested but to continue to live the nearly perfect life he and Jessica had always enjoyed.

3. Why did the author use the phrase "on the other hand"?
   a. to show that Steve's other hand is fine
   b. to contrast Dan and Steve
   c. to explain why Steve didn't get his genes tested

From "Principles of Inheritance"

> A **gene** directs the synthesis of the specific polypeptide (protein) that can play either a structural or a functional role in the cell. In this way, the gene-determined protein can influence whether a certain **trait**, or physical characteristic, will develop.

4. Why is the word *protein* in parentheses?
   a. to provide more explanation about the polypeptide
   b. to provide an alternative word for *polypeptide*
   c. to provide information that contradicts the polypeptide

> There are different forms of genes, called **alleles**. Generally, there are two alleles for each trait in the body's cells—one allele on each homologous chromosome. One of the several genes that determines eye color, for example, dictates whether the brown pigment melanin will be deposited in the iris, or the colored part of your eye. When this allele is present, eye color will range from green to dark brown, depending on the amount of melanin present. The other allele for eye color does not lead to melanin deposit. If neither homologous chromosome has an allele that directs a melanin deposit, a person's eye color will be blue.

5. Why does the writer use the word *generally* in the text?
   a. to show that there is no need to be specific
   b. to provide more explanation about alleles
   c. to show that this fact is true in the majority of cases

(continued on next page)

6. Why does the writer mention eye color in this section of the text?
   a. to give an example of how alleles work
   b. to show that eye color is an important physical feature
   c. to explain why people have blue eyes

The allele whose effects are hidden in the heterozygous condition is described as **recessive**. As a result, only the traits associated with homozygous recessive alleles can be seen.

7. The writer uses the phrase "As a result" in order to _____.
   a. explain why traits associated with recessive genes are only seen in the homozygous condition
   b. conclude the paragraph with a good point about homozygous genes
   c. provide more information about homozygous genes

By convention, the dominant allele is designated with a capital letter, and the recessive allele gets a lowercase letter—*A* and *a*, for example. We observe the dominant form of the trait whether the individual is homozygous dominant (AA) or heterozygous (Aa) for that trait.

8. Why does the writer use the phrase "By convention" in the first sentence?
   a. to introduce the next point about dominant and recessive alleles
   b. to explain that this method of designating dominant and recessive alleles is traditional
   c. to persuade readers that dominant and recessive alleles should not be designated in this way

It is often useful to distinguish between an individual's genetic makeup and an individual's appearance. Therefore, the term **genotype** refers to the precise alleles that are present—that is, whether the individual is homozygous or heterozygous for different gene pairs. The term **phenotype**, on the other hand, refers to the observable physical traits of an individual.

9. Why does the author start this paragraph with this first sentence?
   a. to emphasize that there must be a distinction between genes and appearance
   b. to provide an alternative explanation for genotypes and phenotypes
   c. to explain why we need the terms *genotype* and *phenotype*

Checkpoint 1   PEARSON LONGMAN myacademicconnectionslab

3

Building Academic Listening Skills

In this section, you will learn how to determine the primary and secondary purposes of the professor's lecture. You will also learn to recognize how English speakers use thought groups, stress, and intonation to express meaning.

For online assignments, go to

myacademicconnectionslab

Before You Listen

You are about to enter the lecture hall where your large biology class will be held in just a few minutes. The students from the previous biology class are leaving the classroom. Those students have just heard the lecture you will hear next. You notice two international students who have stopped briefly to talk about the lecture they have just heard. You decide to listen to their conversation to try to get information about the lecture.

🎧 *Listen to what the students say about the lecture's vocabulary and purpose before they walk away from you. As you listen, you quickly take notes on the information that will help you understand the lecture. Some of the notes are provided in the box. Fill in the blanks in the box to complete the notes. Compare your notes with a classmate's.*

Notes

1. Genetic testing = _____

2. two synonyms for disease: _____

3. *Like a snowball rolling downhill* means _____

4. Lecture purpose: informative or persuasive? _____

Global Listening

Key Words

ethical *adj* morally good or correct

prevalent *adj* common at a particular time or in a particular place; **prevalence** *n*

relieved *adj* feeling happy because you are no longer worried about something; **relieve** *v*

Recognizing a Speaker's Purpose

As you know, a speaker's purpose is the reason why he or she speaks. In a school setting, most often a speaker's primary purpose is to inform, although it may also be to persuade. An informative presentation is characterized by many facts, while a persuasive presentation is often characterized by the use of modal verbs like *must*, *have to,* and *should*.

1. 🎧 *Listen to the lecture once to determine the instructor's primary purpose. Do you think the purpose is informative or persuasive? Discuss with the class.*

Recognizing a Speaker's Secondary Purpose

Just like writers, speakers also have *secondary* (or rhetorical) purposes for their presentations. Generally, to express a *secondary* purpose, speakers use the following specific words, phrases or strategies:

- to introduce a new point: *first, next*
- to explain why something happens: *because, as a result, therefore, in order to, for this reason*

(continued on next page)

- to provide more information: *in addition, also*
- to provide an alternative explanation: *or, on the other hand*
- to provide an example: *for example, for instance, such as*
- to quantify a general statement: use of numbers
- to emphasize a point: *it should be noted that, most of all, especially, in particular*
- to contrast ideas: *but, however, although, while, whereas, on the other hand*
- to create a picture for the listener: *imagine, picture, is like, looks like*

When you think about the speaker's secondary purpose, you are thinking about why the speaker made a specific point, or why the speaker developed the point in a specific way. You need to consider the words, phrases, or sentences in relation to the rest of the text to figure out why the speaker presented this information in this particular way.

2. *Listen to the excerpts from the lecture, and answer the questions about the speaker's secondary purpose. When you have finished, confirm your answers with the class.*

⌒ Excerpt One

The instructor included this analogy to a snowball because he wanted to _____.

a. explain to the students what it is like in a country where there is snow
b. create a picture of how hard it would be to stop genetic testing
c. quantify how hard it would be to stop genetic testing

⌒ Excerpt Two

The word *another* in this spoken text shows that the instructor _____.

a. has already discussed a point and is moving on to the second point
b. is providing an example of an advantage
c. is emphasizing the importance of the advantages of genetic testing

⌒ Excerpt Three

The instructor says "consider, for instance" because he is _____.

a. contrasting information about genetic testing with information about genetic screening
b. introducing a new point about the advantages of genetic testing
c. providing an example of a disease that can be prevented through genetic screening

⌒ Excerpt Four

The instructor uses the phrase "as a result" in order to _____.

a. provide an alternative reason why the disease is not as prevalent today
b. demonstrate a disadvantage of voluntary genetic screening
c. show the outcome of voluntary genetic screening

Excerpt Five

The sentence "However, genetic testing also has a dark side" indicates that the instructor _____.

a. has already presented the advantages of genetic testing
b. is introducing another advantage of genetic testing
c. is providing an example of the advantages of genetic testing

Excerpt Six

Why does the instructor talk about Huntington's disease?

a. He wants to know if you would like to know the cause of your own death.
b. He wants to provide an example of a genetic disease for which there is no prevention or treatment.
c. He wants to emphasize that there are diseases that you certainly do not want to have.

Excerpt Seven

The instructor says, "What would happen if information about your genetic test was available to your employer . . .?" because he is suggesting that _____.

a. this is a real situation
b. this is a possible situation
c. this is an impossible situation

Excerpt Eight

Why does the instructor use so many questions in this part of the lecture?

a. to provide more information about genetic testing
b. to introduce lots of questions for discussion
c. to emphasize that there are many questions about genetic testing

Focused Listening

Recognizing How Thought Groups, Stress, and Intonation Express a Speaker's Attitude

English speakers use thought groups, stress, and intonation to express their attitude. A speaker's attitude is his or her overall opinion about an idea, person, or thing. Understanding a speaker's attitude can help you understand what the speaker is saying. You need to listen carefully to both the words the speaker is using and the speaker's thought groups, stress, and intonation to figure out the speaker's opinion.

Thought groups are groups of words that belong together in a phrase or clause. Often (but not always) a comma, semicolon, colon, or period marks the separation between two thought groups. Good English speakers pause between thought groups; each thought group is a 'chunk' that contains meaning. The pause at the end of each thought group allows listeners time to understand each 'chunk.' The end of a thought group is indicated by a slash (/).

1. 🎧 *Listen to the speaker say this sentence. There are two thought groups. Can you hear the pause between the thought groups?*

Two years ago, / Dan hiked through the Andes.

2. 🎧 *Now the speaker will add information to the sentence. Listen for the pauses in the sentence and mark the separations between thought groups with a slash (/).*

1. Two years ago, Dan hiked through the Andes, which was a dangerous thing to do.

2. Two years ago, Dan hiked through the Andes with only a backpack and a knife.

As you can hear, the speaker is pausing between thought groups that are separated by a move from an introductory phrase to a main clause (*Two years ago,*) or a move to a new
- clause (*which was a dangerous thing to do*)
- prepositional phrase (*with only a backpack*)
- item in a list (*and a knife*)

When you speak, help your listener understand by pausing between thought groups—and *not* at other points in a sentence.

3. *Work with a partner. Read the paragraph and mark a slash (/) between the thought groups. Then practice reading the paragraph to your partner. Can your partner hear the pauses between thought groups?*

Dan hasn't always been like this. Six years ago, he was finishing law school and looking forward to a career in politics. Then his father was diagnosed with Huntington's disease, which is caused by the degeneration of brain cells. This devastating disease usually appears in middle age with symptoms of clumsiness and forgetfulness. Now Dan's dad is still able to work, but his handwriting has become uncontrollable, and it is difficult for him to sit for long periods without twitching.

Good English speakers place **stress** on content words in every sentence. This allows them to emphasize the words that they think are the most important. The stress tells the listener which words are most important.

Generally, content words such as nouns, main verbs, and adjectives are stressed. Words that contrast with preceding words are also stressed. Function words like articles, auxiliary verbs, and prepositions are usually not stressed.

To place stress on words, speakers say the word a bit more loudly (but not too loudly) and a bit more slowly (but not too slowly). Stress in writing is indicated by CAPITAL LETTERS.

4. 🎧 *Listen to the speaker say this sentence. Can you hear the stressed words? With the class, repeat the sentence two or three times using the speaker's stress.*

The BAD news for Dan and Steve is that HUNTINGTON'S disease is GENETIC.

5. 🎧 *Listen to the speaker. Circle the words that are stressed. Then compare your circles with a classmate's. Listen to the paragraph again if you don't agree about which words are stressed.*

Because (Huntington's) disease is caused by a dominant gene, if Dan and Steve do carry the gene, they will surely develop the disease in middle age. After his father's diagnosis, Dan decided to have his genes analyzed to see if he carried the gene that affected their father. Unfortunately, he did. When Dan finished school, he started to live the life of a risk taker. "What do I have to lose?" he thought. Steve, on the other hand, was happily married to Jessica. He elected not to have his genes tested but to continue to live the nearly perfect life he and Jessica had always enjoyed.

6. *When you and your partner agree on which words are stressed, mark the thought groups with a slash (/). Then read the paragraph out loud together to practice thought groups and stress.*

Remember, when you speak with thought groups and stress, you help your listener understand the grammar of what you are saying, as well as the points that you think are important.

Intonation is the rise and fall of the tone of a speaker's voice. Intonation patterns may be difficult to hear, but you will become better at recognizing differences in intonation if you listen for them.

A speaker uses intonation to show his or her attitude about something. If the listener hears the speaker's intonation, the listener can understand the speaker's attitude. Intonation is marked with a line that rises and falls above the words, just as a speaker's voice rises and falls.

Speakers may express enthusiasm by placing greater stress on certain words and raising their intonation on content words more than normal.

Example

Genetic testing is a WONDERFUL technology. / It will allow people to make INFORMED DECISIONS / about whether to have CHILDREN.

Speakers may express worry or concern by speaking more slowly, placing greater stress on words that show uncertainty, and using falling intonation.

(continued on next page)

I LIKE the idea of genetic testing / in PRINCIPLE, / but if LIFE INSURANCE companies found out PERSONAL genetic information, / it might cause PROBLEMS.

Speakers may express strong negative opinions by placing greater stress and rising intonation on words that are negative, and using falling intonation at the end of sentences.

Example

There's NO WAY governments should allow genetic testing. It is MUCH too expensive, and if PERSONAL information ever became PUBLIC, it could RUIN people.

7. *What is your attitude about genetic testing? Put a check (✓) in the chart to show your attitude.*

Your Attitude	Attitude	Intonation Pattern
	Enthusiastic	place greater stress and rising intonation on content words
	Worried and concerned	speak more slowly, place greater stress on words that show uncertainty, and use falling intonation at the end of a sentence
	Strongly negative	place stress and rising intonation on words that are negative, and use falling intonation at the end of a sentence

8. *Write at least two sentences to express your attitude about genetic testing. Ask your teacher or a classmate to proofread your sentences. Revise your sentences if necessary.*

9. *Mark your sentences with a slash (/) between thought groups, CAPITAL LETTERS for stressed words, and a line above the words for the intonation patterns. Practice saying your sentences several times, using pauses, stress, and intonation to make your attitude clear. When you are ready, say your sentences to a classmate or a group of classmates. Can they hear your pauses between thought groups, your stressed words, and your intonation? Can they figure out your attitude about genetic testing?*

Checkpoint 2   PEARSON LONGMAN myacademicconnectionslab

4

Building Academic Writing Skills

In this section, you will learn how to modify your writing based on your purpose and your intended audience.
Then you will write a pamphlet to explain how genes produce traits in individuals and when prenatal and personal genetic tests are justified. You will write your pamphlet for the purpose and audience of your choice.
For online assignments, go to

myacademicconnectionslab

Key Words

fetal *adj* relating to an unborn child

fetus *n* an unborn child

poses some risk *exp* causes some potential problems

prenatal *adj* before birth

run in the family *exp* is common in members of the same family

Before You Write

1. *Read the text about prenatal genetic testing. Then answer the questions on the next page. Compare your answers with a classmate's.*

Prenatal Genetic Testing

1 Few events in life are as exciting as the news that you're having a baby. There are so many decisions to make! How should you prepare your home? What about names? Recent advances in genetics have added yet another question: Should you have the fetus genetically tested? The answer may be *yes* for parents with an increased risk of passing on a genetic disease to their children. For example, women over thirty-five are at an increased risk of having children with Down syndrome.[1] Other couples may be aware that certain genetic diseases run in their families. These prospective parents may wish to know their future children's chances of developing a genetic disorder.

2 Genetic testing before birth usually requires the collection of fetal cells. Doctors can do this by performing amniocentesis between weeks 14 and 20 of pregnancy. During amniocentesis, a physician inserts a needle through the mother's abdomen into her uterus to collect amniotic fluid, or the fluid surrounding the fetus. The doctor then screens the cells for genetic diseases. Certain chemicals in the amniotic fluid can show that a genetic disorder, such as the fatal Tay-Sachs disease, exists. Similarly, physicians may find chromosome abnormalities, such as Down syndrome.

3 Unfortunately, amniocentesis poses some risk of complications, such as maternal bleeding, miscarriage, or premature birth. The complication rate is approximately one percent. Because of the risks, doctors usually reserve amniocentesis for situations in which the possibility of a genetic disease is significantly higher than average. If fetal tests reveal a serious genetic disease, the parents must make a choice—to end the pregnancy or to prepare themselves for a baby with serious problems. Identifying a genetic disease early can give families time to prepare—emotionally, medically, and financially. The decision of whether to have fetal genetic testing is just one example of how genetics affects our lives.

---

[1]**Down syndrome** *n* a disorder resulting from a chromosome abnormality

Source: Campbell, N., Reece, J., & Simon, E. (2007). *Essential biology with physiology* (2nd ed.). San Francisco: Pearson Benjamin Cummings.

1. What is the writer's primary purpose for this text?

2. Why does the writer begin by writing about things people do to prepare for a new baby?

3. What is the purpose of Paragraph 2?

4. What are the choices available to parents who discover that their fetus has a genetic disorder?

2. *Conduct a class survey to determine your classmates' opinions. This survey will provide you with information that you can use in your integrated task.*

Survey question: Would you want to know if your future children might have a genetic disorder? Why?

_____ percent of my classmates would like to know if their future children might have a genetic disorder.

_____ percent of my classmates would not like to know if their future children might have a genetic disorder.

Focused Writing

A pamphlet is a short text that can be found in many places, such as doctor's offices, banks, insurance companies, political offices, and licensing offices. Pamphlets are usually printed on heavy paper and folded two or three times so that they are long and narrow in shape. Their purpose is to inform or to persuade, depending on the intended audience.

Understanding the Intended Audience

When preparing to write or speak, you should think about your audience—the people you are writing or speaking to. Understanding your audience can influence your purpose and affect how you present information. Consider these questions while identifying your audience:

- Who will be your readers/listeners? (children, men, women, students, parents, etc.)
- What do you know about them? (age, interest, gender, feelings toward topics, knowledge about the topic, etc.)

Knowing your audience will help you identify your own purpose and choose the best techniques for sharing information. For example:

- If your audience has opinions that are different from yours, you may try to persuade them.
- If your audience has little knowledge of the subject, you may need to inform them about it or explain it to them. You may also want to use visuals to explain concepts.
- If your audience has little interest in your subject, you may want to entertain them as you give information.

1. Bring two or three pamphlets to class. Your teacher may bring in a selection of pamphlets as well. Work with a partner. Spend a few minutes looking over the pamphlets. For each pamphlet you review, determine:
   - where it was found
   - the topic
   - the intended audience
   - the purpose
   - how the writer gets your attention
   - the characteristics of the writing

Then discuss your ideas with the class.

2. You will be writing a pamphlet about genetic testing. Work with two or three other students. Select an audience from the list.

Possible Audiences

1. prospective parents who have a higher than average chance of passing on a genetic disorder to their future children

2. biology students learning about genetic testing

3. adult children of an older person who has just been diagnosed with a genetic disease

4. government officials who are deciding whether to allow genetic testing

For Each Audience, Decide On:
   - your primary purpose
   - how to get your audience's attention
   - how much space you would devote to explaining basic concepts
   - the use of technical terms
   - the need for visuals

Now compare your points with those of groups that selected different audiences. How are your answers similar or different?

Integrated Writing Task

You have read texts and listened to a lecture about genetic testing. You will now use your knowledge of the content, vocabulary, and audience needs to write a pamphlet that explains how genes produce traits in individuals, and when prenatal and personal genetic testing are justified. You will write your pamphlet for a purpose and audience of your choice.

Follow the steps to create your pamphlet.

Step 1: Select an audience and purpose for your pamphlet from the chart on the next page.

Audience	Purpose
1. prospective parents who have a higher than average chance of passing on a genetic disorder to their future children	to inform the parents of the possible advantages and risks of genetic testing
2. biology students learning about genetic testing	to inform the students of the possible advantages and risks of genetic testing
3. adult children of an older person who has just been diagnosed with a genetic disease	to persuade the person to get genetic testing
4. adult children of an older person who has just been diagnosed with a genetic disease	to persuade the person NOT to get genetic testing
5. government officials who are deciding whether to allow genetic testing	to persuade the government officials to allow genetic testing
6. government officials who are deciding whether to allow genetic testing	to persuade the government officials NOT to allow genetic testing

Step 2: Based on your audience and purpose, decide:
- how to get your audience's attention
- how much space you will devote to explaining basic concepts
- the use of technical terms
- the need for visuals

Step 3: Write the text of your pamphlet. Then work with a partner. Without telling your partner your audience and purpose, ask your partner to read your text and determine the audience and purpose. If your partner is not sure which audience or purpose you selected, rewrite the pamphlet text so that your target audience and purpose are clear.

Step 4: If you can, develop some visuals or graphics to get your audience's attention. Add them to the text of your pamphlet.

Step 5: Proofread your pamphlet. Make revisions if necessary. Then ask your teacher or classmate to review your pamphlet and fill out the checklist on the next page. Based on the feedback from the checklist, revise your pamphlet if necessary.

Features of an Effective Pamphlet	Yes	No
The audience and purpose are clear.		
The writer attracts the audience's attention.		
The text explains how genes produce traits in individuals.		
The text informs or persuades the audience about when genetic testing is justified.		
The visuals are useful.		
The amount of space devoted to explaining basic concepts and the use of technical terms are appropriate for the audience.		
The pamphlet looks professional.		

Step 6: Display your pamphlet in the classroom. Read your classmates' pamphlets. What have you learned about writing with a purpose and writing for various audiences?

UNIT 8

Business
Mediation

Unit Description

Content: This course is designed to familiarize the student with concepts in conflict management.

Skills: Inference
- Collecting information to make inferences
- Inferring a speaker's intentions
- Identifying and using similes and metaphors

Unit Requirements

Readings: "The Best Approach to Mediation" (from *The Conflict Survival Kit: Tools for Resolving Conflict at Work,* C. Goodwin & D.B. Griffith, Pearson Prentice Hall)

"Turning Positions into Interest-Based Statements" (from *Mediation Theory and Practice,* S. McCorkle & M.J. Reece, Pearson Allyn & Bacon)

Lecture: "Mediation Techniques"

Integrated Speaking Task: Mediating (role-playing) a conflict between two disputants (parties)

Assignments: www.MyAcademicConnectionsLab.com

161

1 Preview

For online assignments, go to

PEARSON LONGMAN
myacademicconnectionslab

Previewing the Academic Content

Mediation is what you do when you try to end an argument between two people. Have you ever been caught in the middle of two people having an argument? How did you feel? Were you uncomfortable listening to their dispute? Did you try to help solve their conflict? Were you successful? Almost all people find themselves in this situation at some time in their lives, but not many people know how best to help the arguing parties. How should you help two disputants who are angry with each other? Should you take the side of one friend and oppose the other? Should you remain impartial? What should you say? Are there specific techniques you can use to assist people to resolve their differences?

1. *There are many key words in the introductory paragraph that will help you speak and write fluently about mediation. Work with a partner. Look back at the introductory paragraph to complete these items. They will help you focus on vocabulary that you will find useful for this unit topic.*

1. *Argue* is the verb.

   _____*argument*_____ is the noun.

   The two _____ people will solve their problem eventually. (adjective)

   Two people are _____ an argument. (verb that collocates with *argument*)

2. Find three synonyms for *argument*.

   _____

   _____

   _____

3. Find a synonym for *solve their conflicts*.

   _____

4. Find two nouns that mean *people or groups of people who are involved in a legal dispute*.

   _____

   _____

5. Find an expression that means that you are uncomfortable listening to two people who are arguing.

   _____

6. a. Find an expression that means *to support one person in an argument and oppose the other.*

   _____

   b. Now find the word that means the opposite of the expression in 6a.

   _____

2. *Imagine that you are sharing a small apartment with two other friends while you all attend college. You are all very busy with your studies and don't have a lot of time. One of your friends is very tidy and likes the kitchen to be clean. Your other friend likes to make delicious food but never cleans the kitchen. They are now having an argument about who will clean the dirty kitchen. What do you do? Circle your answer.*

- Do nothing and leave the room.
- Yell at them to stop arguing.
- Clean the kitchen yourself and hope they stop arguing.
- Take the side of your friend who likes a clean kitchen and force the cook to clean up.
- Take the side of your friend who likes to cook and tell your friend who likes a clean kitchen not to worry about the dirty kitchen.
- Remain impartial and help resolve the conflict.

3. *Find two or three other classmates who chose the same response you did. In your group, discuss why this is the best response. Then prepare a statement for the rest of the class that explains why this is the best response.*

4. *Read the text, which provides a definition of conflict. As you read, think about how this definition applies to the description of the three friends in Exercise 2. Be prepared to answer the questions that follow the text on the next page.*

Key Words

compatible *adj* able to exist or be used together without causing problems; *antonym*: **incompatible** *adj*

A Definition of Conflict

Conflict involves *competition* between two or more individuals or groups who have *incompatible interests* and who are *interdependent*. Let us examine this definition further.

Interdependent parties. Each party in a conflict has needs that only the other party can satisfy. For example, an employee and her boss are interdependent. The employee has needs—income, job satisfaction, and other considerations—that can only be met through her relationship with her boss. Her boss needs her to do certain work, which only she is available and capable to do. Conflict arises through their attempts to have their needs met. Without this mutual need, no conflict exists. If the employee finds a job that better meets her needs, or if her boss finds someone who will do the work if she will not, their interdependence ends.

Incompatible interests. Interests are the parties' wants, needs, values, or goals, which represent the source of the disagreement or conflict.

Conflict results from the belief of one or both parties that their interests are not compatible. If there are no incompatible interests, there is no conflict because there is nothing to fight about.

Competition. Conflict occurs when one or more parties perceive that a need is threatened or that resources are insufficient to meet the need. If the parties cannot see a way to resolve their differences immediately, they perceive that any outcome must result in a win-lose situation: One of them must win, and the other must lose. The competition, therefore, results from the rush to be the winner and not the loser. In these cases, often the two parties do not perceive alternative solutions that might lead to a win-win solution.

This definition makes clear that the existence of conflict is often based on perception. It is often the belief that our interests are incompatible, rather than the reality, that sets the stage for conflict. With the right approach, perhaps the parties can find common ground where their interests are not as incompatible as they first thought.

Source: Goodwin, C., & Griffith, D.B. (2007). *The conflict survival kit: Tools for resolving conflict at work.* Upper Saddle River, NJ: Pearson Prentice Hall.

5. *Work with your group to answer the questions based on the situation of the three friends described in Exercise 2 on page 163.*

1. Why are the three friends interdependent?

2. What are the incompatible interests in this situation?

3. What is the competition in this situation?

4. Do you believe that this situation is largely a problem of perception? Why or why not? What possible solution can you see to this conflict?

In this unit, you will practice making inferences based on what people write or say.

Previewing the Academic Skills Focus

Inference

To **infer** is to decide that something is true based on information that you have. This truth may not actually be stated by the writer or speaker; it is something that you figure out based on what you have read or heard.

In the example of the three friends sharing an apartment on page 163, you might have inferred the following possible truths:

- The three friends didn't discuss cleanup rules before they moved in together.
- The friend who likes to cook doesn't like to clean.
- The friend who likes the kitchen clean doesn't like to cook.
- If the two friends cannot resolve their conflict, they will not live together for much longer.

None of these points are actually mentioned, but they are points you can infer, or figure out, based on the information you have.

The verb *infer* is often followed by *that (infer that)*. You can also *make an inference* (noun) *about something*. Making inferences is similar to forming generalizations, drawing conclusions, thinking critically, guessing at meaning, and predicting the outcome.

1. *Read the description of the conflict and complete the activity on the next page.*

Michael and Su-Young are boyfriend and girlfriend, and they love each other very much. They live in South Korea. They met when Michael, who is from Australia, went to South Korea to teach English for a year after he graduated with a degree in engineering. Michael has been happy teaching English in South Korea and going out with Su-Young. They have been together for two years now. Su-Young works with a large international company and makes a lot of money. Michael has recently been offered a job in Australia as a project-management engineer. If he takes the job, he will earn more money than he is earning now, but not as much money as Su-Young makes at her job. He wants Su-Young to leave her job and come with him to Australia, but he understands why Su-Young doesn't want to leave her job.

Check (✓) the statements that you can reasonably infer about Michael and Su-Young's situation. Discuss with the class which statements you can or can't infer and why.

_____ 1. Su-Young doesn't love Michael.

_____ 2. Because Michael has a degree in engineering, he would like to have an engineering job.

_____ 3. Michael believes that his engineering job is more important that Su-Young's current job.

_____ 4. If Michael stays in South Korea with Su-Young, eventually he will be unhappy.

_____ 5. If they break up, Su-Young will meet a South Korean man who makes more money than she does.

_____ 6. If Su-Young moves to Australia with Michael, she will not be able to get a job that pays as well as her current job.

2. *Work with a partner to discuss the questions.*

1. How are Michael and Su-Young interdependent?

2. What are the incompatible interests in this situation?

3. What is the competition in this situation?

4. What are some possible solutions to this conflict? Discuss your best ideas with the class.

Before You Read

1. *In the text you will read in this section (pages 168–169), there are a number of useful collocations—two or more words that occur together frequently. Find these expressions in the text using the clues provided in the chart, and write the expressions in the same row as the clues. Then check your answers with the class.*

Paragraph Number	Structure of the Collocation	Meaning of the Collocation	Collocation
1	verb + adj + noun	to discover two parties have similar opinions or attitudes	*find common ground*
2	verb + determiner + noun	influencing what someone does	

(continued on next page)

In this section, you will learn useful collocations that can be used when you speak or write about mediation. You will also practice forming generalizations, drawing conclusions, and making inferences.
For online assignments, go to

PEARSON LONGMAN
myacademicconnectionslab

2
Building Academic Reading Skills

Paragraph Number	Structure of the Collocation	Meaning of the Collocation	Collocation
4	article + noun + preposition + noun	the result of two opposing sides that refuse to change	
4	article + noun + verb + adjective	to establish a position and be unwilling to change	
4	verb + preposition + possessive pronoun + noun	unable to change opinions	
6	adjective + noun	important but not obvious	
7	verb + preposition + article + noun	to argue about the price of something with someone	
7	verb + adjective + noun	causes unfriendly feelings toward someone	

2. *Use the collocations from the chart to complete the sentences. Then compare your answers with a classmate's.*

1. The car salesperson learned to _____ to get the best price for the car.

2. The positions of the two parties were so far apart that it was difficult for the mediator to _____.

3. As the child began to cry, his parents began to wonder what was

   _____.

4. If a business doesn't satisfy its customers, it _____. The customers will never return to purchase a product from that company again.

5. When _____, it is very difficult for a mediator to get the parties to think of other solutions to their conflict.

6. The child behaved badly in school, but the teacher knew that the

_____ was the child's desire for more attention.

7. In the positional approach, the parties _____, and the mediator

may not be able to resolve their conflict.

8. Her roommate refused to be quiet during the study period, and she refused to

clean the kitchen. It was _____.

Global Reading

Look at the questions and read the text on pages 168–169. Then work with a partner to answer the questions. Compare your answers with another pair's. Resolve any different answers you might have.

1. What is the 'simple yet complex' key to resolving conflicts?

_____

_____

2. Summarize the two examples the authors use to explain the importance of underlying needs in Paragraph 2.

_____

_____

3. What are the two positions on addressing conflict?

_____

_____

4. In which approach do the parties lock into their positions? Once they are locked into their positions, how is it possible to solve any problem?

_____

_____

5. Which approach to mediation should you use when the relationship between the parties is important and must be maintained? How does this approach maintain good relationships?

_____

_____

6. What are the principles that interest-based mediators use to judge any negotiation?

_____

_____

(continued on next page)

7. Read the comments from people who have just resolved conflicts through mediation. Based on their comments, label the form of mediation that you think the parties just completed.

Comments

a. I'm still angry, but that's the way it goes. _____*positional*_____

b. Now I know why he wanted to work over the holidays. _____

c. I won, and he lost. Too bad for him. _____

d. There was no way to satisfy both of us. _____

e. Now I realize she was just trying to be helpful. _____

f. I didn't know that in her culture people yell when they are angry. I thought she was just rude. _____

Key Words

reconcile *v* to have a good relationship with someone again after you have argued with him or her

superficial *adj* on the surface; not deep or substantive

THE BEST APPROACH TO MEDIATION

1   With the right approach, perhaps the disputants can find common ground where their interests are not as incompatible as they first thought. But what is the right approach? If parties have been in conflict for a long time over seemingly unsolvable issues, how will they ever come to realize that they have many interests in common? How will a husband and wife, two neighbors, or an employee and a supervisor ever come to realize that they actually have less to fight about? The answer is both simple and complex: They must communicate.

2   If we look deeper into any conflict, we usually find the real underlying needs the parties want to express. Often, the disputants have common interests that they are not communicating effectively. If we look deeper into why a husband and wife are not communicating and are about to divorce, we uncover their underlying fears, hurts, and unfulfilled needs. If we can help each party to understand the other's concerns, these concerns may disappear. Here is another example. As a manager, you may have to discipline an employee who behaves badly, but it may be beneficial to first talk about what is driving this behavior. Is the employee suffering some personal loss or trouble at home? Does he or she feel threatened by recent organizational changes? As long as the employee's position is not locked in, asking the right questions and providing a sympathetic response may save your relationship with the employee. This could be the first step to restoring him or her as a productive worker.

Two Approaches to Addressing Conflict

3   Individuals generally take one of two distinct approaches to addressing conflict. These are referred to as *positional* and *interest-based*.

Positional

4   In the positional approach, the parties treat the conflict as a contest of wills. They enter a conflict discussion with clear ideas of what they want to achieve and then hold on to these positions. For example, an employee wants a

salary increase of a certain amount and will leave if she does not receive it. The manager will pay only up to a certain amount in salary to keep the employee, and not a penny more. If these amounts are incompatible, the lines are drawn. The positional approach does not take into consideration the underlying concerns, needs, or wants of the parties, which generally prevents any examination of how the parties' positions might be reconciled. Rather, the disputants lock into to their positions. If resolution occurs, it is because the parties realize what they have to lose by not resolving the dispute rather than considering how each might achieve more by working together.

5   The positional approach is the traditional model many people have come to know and accept. This does not mean that it is always the "wrong" approach. Many accomplished lawyers, salespeople, and businesspeople have written volumes on the subject. But the positional approach involves game playing. If you are a customer wanting the best deal on a car or the salesperson wanting the best price, and your relationship with the other party is superficial, you might use this approach. However, if you use this strategy during your next argument with your spouse or coworker, where relationships matter greatly, do not expect positive outcomes.

Interest-Based

6   Mediators who use the interest-based approach consider the underlying needs, wants, values, and goals of the parties. They believe that any useful resolution must preserve, and

perhaps improve, the relationship between the parties. Interest-based mediators establish clear principles that can be used to judge any negotiation. These principles include preserving or improving the relationship between the parties. In addition, any agreement should meet the legitimate interests of the parties, resolve conflicting interests fairly, be long lasting, and take into account the interests of others who may be affected by the agreement. The interest-based approach is more efficient than the traditional positional model because it eliminates game playing, time, and costs.

7   When relationships matter, focusing on interests rather than locking into positions makes sense. We value our relationships and therefore must consider both the short-term and long-term impacts of our agreements. We should not settle for agreements that may benefit our selfish interests in the short run if there are long-term consequences we would not like. Even our salesperson from the previous example may have a few things to learn by using this approach. Does he haggle with the customer for the best price if it creates ill will in the process? Where will the customer purchase his or her next car? Will the customer return for service? While the clever car dealer wants a sale, he places higher value on a long-term relationship and the chance to sell the customer six cars over a lifetime, not just one. Even where positional bargaining appears to make sense, the positional bargainer often has an incentive for engaging in the interest-based approach.

Source: Goodwin, C., & Griffith, D.B. (2007). *The conflict survival kit: Tools for resolving conflict at work*. Upper Saddle River, NJ: Pearson Prentice Hall.

Focused Reading

As you have learned, when you make inferences, you figure out the truth based on information that you have. To help you make inferences, gather as much information as you can from pictures, titles, headings and subheadings, and the full text itself.

1. *Read the questions and circle the correct answers. There may be more than one correct response for some questions. Then confirm your answers with the class.*

1. What do the authors mean when they write (Paragraph 1), "The answer is both simple and complex: They must communicate"?
   a. Communicating is too complicated for most people to achieve.
   b. Communicating is too simple because most people are complex.
   c. Communicating is easy to understand but hard to do.

2. What do the authors mean when they write (Paragraph 5), "However, if you use [the positional strategy] during your next argument with your spouse or coworker, where relationships matter greatly, do not expect positive outcomes"?
   a. The positional approach to mediation is not recommended when relationships are important.
   b. The interest-based approach is better if your relationships are superficial.
   c. The mediator can expect positive outcomes if using the positional approach.

3. What do the authors mean when they write (Paragraph 7), "Even where positional bargaining appears to make sense, the positional bargainer often has an incentive for engaging in the interest-based approach"?
   a. Relationships may matter more than you think they do.
   b. The interest-based approach is better than the positional approach.
   c. There is really never a good time to use the positional approach.

2. *In the Preview section you learned that making inferences is similar to drawing conclusions and making generalizations. Work in a group of three. Read the descriptions of the conflicts and select one conflict you would like to discuss further. Approximately half the class should select Conflict 1, and half should select Conflict 2. When you have made your selections, complete the tasks on the next page.*

Conflict 1: Large Company

You are the president of a large company. You believe that your company is not performing well. You have a meeting with your two vice presidents to discuss this. You would like to take the top management (a group of about 30 people) to a resort town for a week to discuss ways to improve the company's performance. One vice president agrees. She sees the need for improvement and is enthusiastic about setting a program for the weeklong retreat. The other vice president disagrees. He feels he is too busy to take a week away from his regular duties and feels the retreat would be a waste of time. The two vice presidents are locked into their positions.

Conflict 2: Cab Company

You are the manager of a cab company. A family from another country arrives at an airport. The members are looking forward to a week's holiday. The father hires a cab driver from your company to take his family to a hotel. The cab driver charges $100. The father thinks this is expensive but pays the driver. However, the father does not tip the cab driver. When the family returns to the airport to fly home, the father hires another cab driver from your company. This cab driver charges the family $60. The father asks why the cab fare was so expensive the first time, but the second cab driver doesn't know. He says the standard price of a ride from the airport to the hotel is $60. When the father returns home to his own country, he contacts you to begin an investigation into the first cab driver's actions.

1. Use the information in the conflict descriptions to draw a conclusion about which approach to mediation is best. Why do you think this is the best approach? All members of your group should agree.

2. Find a group that discussed the other conflict situation. Share your answers to question 1. Together, form generalizations about when it is best to use each approach. Use the chart to keep track of your discussion. When you have finished, share your answers with the class to complete the chart.

It Is Best to Use the Positional Approach When . . .	It Is Best to Use the Interest-Based Approach When . . .

Checkpoint 1   PEARSON LONGMAN myacademicconnectionslab

Building Academic Listening Skills

In this section, you will continue to practice making inferences—this time based on what you hear.
For online assignments, go to

PEARSON LONGMAN
myacademicconnectionslab

Key Words

mediator *n* a person or organization that tries to end an argument between two people or groups through discussion

Before You Listen

1. *What can you do to help two people resolve a conflict? Work in groups of three to review the possible mediation techniques. Check (✓) the appropriate column to show whether your group thinks the technique would be helpful or unhelpful. Be prepared to explain your answers.*

Helpful	Unhelpful	Possible Mediation Techniques
		1. Repeat something negative that a disputant says to show that you are listening.
		2. Break a large issue into smaller issues.
		3. Make a comment indicating that a disputant is obviously wrong.
		4. Offer a solution to solve the dispute before the parties get a chance to discuss their differences.
		5. Ask a neutral question to encourage discussion.
		6. Paraphrase what a disputant says to try to uncover his or her underlying need.
		7. Find the parties' common interests, opinions, and values.
		8. Encourage one disputant to insult the other to get his or her feelings out in the open.

2. *Take a survey of the class. Do all the groups agree on which techniques might be helpful and which would not? Discuss the reasons for any differences in opinion.*

Global Listening

1. 🎧 *In this lecture, the professor describes five mediation techniques. Listen to the lecture once and write down the five techniques. Then match each technique to its description. Listen to the lecture a second time to check your matches. Then confirm your answers with your class.*

Technique   **Description**

___b___ 1. *fractionation*   a. finding shared opinions, values, and attitudes of the two parties

_____ 2. _____   b. breaking a larger problem into smaller issues

_____ 3. _____   c. asking the parties for a list of all possible proposals that might resolve their problem

_____ 4. _____   d. restating a negative statement in a more positive way

_____ 5. _____   e. asking neutral questions to encourage discussion

2. *How can these images help you remember the key techniques? Label each image with the matching technique. There is one image that will help you remember two techniques.*

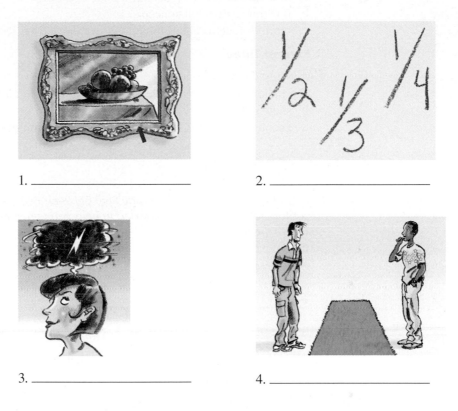

1. _____

2. _____

3. _____

4. _____

Inferring a Speaker's Intentions

In Unit 7, you learned how to recognize a speaker's purpose. You also learned how a speaker or a writer can have more than one purpose. This purpose —or intention— may not be obvious to you, and the professors may not make these intentions explicit. Sometimes, you may need to figure out—or infer—the intention of the lecturer so you can understand the lecture better. You may need to answer the question, "Why did he/she say that?"

To infer a speaker's intentions, ask yourself:

  • What possible purpose(s) did the speaker have?

  • Which one(s) best fit(s) the situation?

3. *Listen to the excerpt from the lecture. Infer the lecturer's intention. Circle the answer that best completes each statement.*

∩ Excerpt One

The lecturer makes this statement because she _____.
  a. is giving a topic from the lecture
  b. wants to discuss a topic from a previous lecture
  c. likes to talk about mediation

Excerpt Two

The lecturer's intention for saying this is to _____.

    a. link current ideas to past knowledge

    b. illustrate a difficult concept

    c. remind students about something from an earlier lecture

Excerpt Three

The lecturer says this to _____.

    a. challenge students to develop their own mediation techniques

    b. show what they need to study for a test

    c. encourage students to apply the mediation techniques in real life

Focused Listening

1. *Listen to the description of an argument between two neighbors. As you listen, take short notes in the space provided to help you remember the description. Then complete the tasks.*

_____

_____

_____

_____

  1. Make inferences about the complaining neighbor's

    • Age: _____

    • Employment: _____

    • Relationship with the basketball-playing neighbor: _____

    _____

  2. Make inferences about the basketball-playing neighbor's

    • Age: _____

    • Employment: _____

    • Relationship with the complaining neighbor: _____

    _____

  3. What would be the best approach to mediating this dispute: positional or interest-based mediation? Why?

    _____

    _____

2. *Work in small groups. Use your knowledge of mediation techniques to answer the questions.*

  1. How could you use fractionation to break this dispute into smaller issues?

  2. What can you say to frame the dispute and encourage the neighbors to begin communicating?

3. What can you say to reframe these comments?
   - The complaining neighbor says, "The bouncing basketball sounds like gunshots going off outside my window. He is so inconsiderate about the noise he is making so early in the morning."
   - The basketball-playing neighbor says, "She thinks she's the queen and everyone has to do what she says."

4. What kind of common ground could you highlight for these neighbors?

5. What kinds of solutions to this problem could the neighbors brainstorm?

Checkpoint 2   PEARSON LONGMAN myacademicconnectionslab

Before You Speak

This text gives you an example of how mediators move complaining parties from positional to interest-based statements. As you read the example, take note of the expression used by the successful mediator. Then answer the questions on the next page.

4

Building Academic Speaking Skills

In this section, you will participate in a role play so that you can practice the mediation techniques you learned in the previous sections. You will learn how to identify and use the rhetorical devices of simile and metaphor and include these rhetorical devices when you speak.
For online assignments, go to

PEARSON LONGMAN
myacademicconnectionslab

Turning Positions into Interest-Based Statements

Disputants all come to the mediation session locked into their positions. Here are some examples of positional statements.

"We won't sign a contract that does not include a dental and vision plan."

"I won't take a dime less than $800 for the damage she did to that carpet."

"He can see the kids every other weekend and two weeks in the summer."

"She needs to move that wreck of a car from in front of my house."

Behind every positional statement is an interest waiting for the mediator to uncover. Interests are what drive positions—the needs that underlie the demands. Skilled mediators listen for positional statements so they can explore the interests that brought the parties to those conclusions. Instead of repeating positional statements, mediators should reframe positions. Here is an example of what mediators should NOT do, followed by an example of a successful reframing.

Restating the Position:
Unhappy Disputant: "I won't pay her a dime for those calls. They're not all mine."

Mediator: "So you don't want to pay her for the calls." [This paraphrase restates the position.]

(continued on next page)

▄▄▟▟▗ Unit 8 ■ Mediation   **175**

By restating the disputant's position, the mediator adds power to that position, making it more difficult for the party to consider other options. Instead, the mediator could reframe the statement into an *interest* and work to clarify more of the story.

Successful Reframing:

Unhappy Disputant: "I won't pay her a dime for those calls. They're not all mine."

Mediator: "You're looking to be treated fairly and have a concern with the request for payment. Tell me, when did you first find out about the phone bill?"

"Fair treatment" is an interest that the mediator can explore and that may lead to a resolution.

Source: McCorkle, S., & Reece, M. J. (2005). *Mediation theory and practice.* Boston: Pearson Allyn & Bacon.

1. What expression did the successful mediator use to introduce the interest-based statement?

   _____

   _____

2. Here are some other expressions that a mediator might use to introduce an interest-based statement. What others can you think of? You can use these expressions in your role play.
   - Do you mean that you would like to be treated fairly . . . ?
   - So you would like to be treated fairly . . .
   - You're hoping to be treated fairly . . .
   - I understand that you would like to be treated fairly . . .

   _____

   _____

Focused Speaking

Identifying and Using Similes and Metaphors

Rhetorical devices are ways of speaking and writing to create a special effect. Two common rhetorical devices are similes and metaphors. Similes and metaphors are methods of comparison that are used to create an image in the receiver's mind. They can make the comparison more interesting for the listener or reader.

- A **simile** is used to compare the action, person, or setting to something else using the word *like* or *as*. Here is an example of a simile:

  "The bouncing basketball sounds *like* gunshots going off outside my window."

- A **metaphor** is used to compare the action, person, or setting to something else by saying that it *is* that thing. A metaphor does not include *like* or *as*. Here is an example of a metaphor:

  "She thinks she's the queen and everyone has to do what she says."

When someone uses a simile or a metaphor, the listener or reader can understand more clearly what the speaker or writer is feeling or experiencing. When you use a simile or metaphor yourself, your own speaking or writing becomes more interesting. Effectively using simile and metaphor is also a sign of a more advanced level of language proficiency.

1. *Read the sentences and decide whether the comparison is a simile or a metaphor. Remember that a simile is a comparison using* like *or* as; *a metaphor makes a straight comparison.*

  1. My ex-husband's sense of humor is as black as night. ___*simile*___

  2. She drove the car like it was a rocket ship. _____

  3. The field was a flat tabletop stretching as far as the horizon. _____

  4. My mother's eyes are X-rays that see straight into my soul. _____

  5. She is as wise as an owl. _____

  6. The tree was my protector, sheltering me through the rainy night. _____

2. *Complete the sentences to create similes (using either* like *or* as) *or metaphors. Then compare your answers with a classmate's. Have your classmate's similes and metaphors created pictures in your mind? Share the best ones with the class.*

  1. My brother/sister is _____.

  2. My grandfather is _____.

  3. My country is _____.

  4. I run like _____.

  5. My cell phone is _____.

Integrated Speaking Task

You have read and listened to information about techniques a mediator can use to assist people in resolving their diferences. You will now work in a group of three students to act out the roles of three people resolving a dispute: the two complaining parties and the mediator. You will use your knowledge of the unit content, vocabulary, and skills as well as similes and/or metaphors to bring your role play to life. Your group may role-play one of the disputes described in this section, or you could create your own dispute. If you create your own dispute, be sure to describe it accurately so that others can understand it.

Descriptions of Disputes

Two roommates have asked a friend to mediate their dispute. Ms. X spends too much money. She likes to buy a lot of clothes. She never has enough for meals or gas, so she is always asking her roommate, Ms. Y, for food or gas money. She wants money to help pay for her books and sometimes doesn't have enough to help pay their housing expenses. Ms. Y is fortunate to have enough money, but thinks it is unfair that her roommate isn't paying her share and asks for money so often. Ms. X often doesn't pay back the money she owes her roommate.

Two roommates have asked a friend to mediate their issue. Mr. X comes home late and rowdy from the local bars on Thursday, Friday, and Saturday nights. When he comes home, he doesn't feel like sleeping right away, so he watches television or listens to music. This wakes up his roommate, Mr. Y, and the neighbors in the apartment next door. Mr. Y needs to go to sleep early these nights because he has Friday classes and has to go to work nearly every weekend. Even worse, the neighbors are angry with both of them and say they will talk to the apartment manager if the late-night noise doesn't stop.

A senior couple has asked their daughter to mediate their conflict. The husband has recently retired and now spends all his time in the house. He doesn't do any household chores and gets in his wife's way. He is lonely, so he wants his wife at home to keep him company. He objects when his wife leaves the house to visit with her friends. He realizes his wife is annoyed, but he doesn't know why.

Your father and his sister (your aunt) have asked you to mediate their dispute. Your father thinks that his sister took an expensive piece of furniture from their father's house after he passed away without discussing it with him. Your aunt took care of their father in his final days and had a key to his house. Your aunt was also in control of their father's finances, and your father thinks she took all his money during his father's final days. Now your father is angry at his sister.

Source: Cahn, D., & Abigail, R.A. (2007). *Managing conflict through communication* (3rd ed.). Boston: Pearson Allyn & Bacon.

Follow the steps to complete your role play.

Step 1: Work in groups of three. Select the description of the dispute that you would like to role-play, or develop your own description of a dispute.

Step 2: Decide who will play which role. Two students will be unhappy parties, and one will be the mediator.

Step 3: Make inferences about the parties' age, employment, relationships, etc., so you can imagine their characters.

Step 4: Plan what each of you will say. You do not need to write out what you will say, but you should take notes to remind you.

- The mediator should review the techniques of fractionation, framing, reframing, highlighting common ground, and brainstorming, as well as the useful reframing expressions on page 176.
- The parties should plan their versions of the dispute and their positional statements. They should each use at least one simile or metaphor to create a picture for the listeners.

Step 5: Practice your role play. You should follow this process during your role play.

1. The mediator brings the two parties together and makes an opening statement. The opening statement indicates the rules for the mediation session: no interrupting, no insulting the other party, and no more mediation if the conflict escalates.

2. The mediator asks each party to describe the dispute from his or her point of view. The other party must listen and not speak.

3. The mediator uses fractionation, framing, reframing, highlighting common ground, and brainstorming to find a solution.

4. The mediator clearly states the final agreement.

5. The mediator concludes the mediating session.

Step 6: Ask your teacher or a classmate to evaluate your role play based on the features in the checklist.

Role Play Evaluation Checklist	Yes	No
Does the mediator make an opening statement indicating the rules for the mediation session?		
Do the two parties make their positional statements and describe their versions of the dispute?		
Do the two parties use similes and/or metaphors to make their statements more interesting?		
Does the mediator use one or more of the following mediation techniques: fractionation, framing, reframing, highlighting common ground, and brainstorming?		
Does the mediator resolve the conflict?		
Does the mediator clearly state the final solution and conclude the mediating session?		

Step 7: Based on the information in the checklist, revise and practice your role play. Then perform it for the class.

AUDIOSCRIPT

UNIT 1

Biology: Brains and Gender

Before You Listen

Exercise 1, Page 13

Professor: So there we have it. We've seen some of the ways that modern brain imaging techniques are helping us improve our understanding of the brain, but we've also seen that we still have a very long way to go. It's a new and exciting area of research, and I'm sure discoveries will come thick and fast over the next few years.

In the next lecture, we'll look at some recent results of ongoing work. Specifically, we'll look at pain and mental health—two areas where there seem to be some very surprising differences between males and females.

Global Listening

Exercise 1, Page 15

Professor: Hello, everyone. Welcome to the next neuroscience lecture. As we mentioned last time, male–female brain differences are a really exciting field of research. We're finding out things that completely contradict some points that scientists used to feel sure about. In today's lecture, we'll look at two areas where male–female brain differences may have some quite radical implications for medicine: perception of pain and mental health.

Lecture: Different genders, different medicines?[1]

Professor: Hello, everyone. Welcome to the next neuroscience lecture. As we mentioned last time, male–female brain differences are a really exciting field of research. We're finding out things that completely contradict some points that scientists used to feel sure about. In today's lecture, we'll look at two areas where male–female brain differences may have some quite radical implications for medicine: perception of pain and mental health.

First, pain. This is a really fascinating area of brain research. Research suggests that the brain circuits that suppress pain may be different in males and females. In fact, a lot of research—but not all—suggests that females experience more pain than males.

Two researchers, separately from each other, have looked for the reasons behind this. They are Anne Murphy at the

University of Georgia in the U.S. and Jeff Mogil at McGill University in Canada. An important finding was that males and females appear to use different circuits in the brain to block pain.

This finding may explain something else that has caused confusion in the medical world. As we mentioned before, painkilling drugs are generally tested on men. However, some time ago, doctors noticed that some painkillers have different effects on men and women. For example, nalbuphine works better for women than for men—in fact, it sometimes actually *increases* pain in men! Others appear to work better on men.

So, with increasing understanding of how painkillers work, in the future we may be able to create painkillers that are more effective for women. Developing drugs is very expensive though, so we will probably have to wait for more research to show whether this will be financially worthwhile.

Another area where there are gender differences is mental health. Let's take depression, for example. Women appear to suffer from depression twice as often as men, and their brains typically produce about half as much serotonin—a brain chemical linked to depression. Recently, Anna–Lena Nordström from the Karolinska Institute in Stockholm, Sweden, found that there seem to be significant differences in how male and female brains process serotonin. There are no firm conclusions yet, but this is of special interest for two reasons. First, common antidepressants like Prozac work on serotonin. Second, there is evidence that women respond better to these common antidepressants than those that work on neurotransmitters other than serotonin.

Males may be less likely to suffer from depression, but this is balanced by other issues. Boys are more likely than girls to be diagnosed with a wide range of problems affecting brain systems, such as: autism, Tourette's syndrome, dyslexia, stuttering, attention–deficit disorder, and early–onset schizophrenia. So, a new approach to designing medicines, with one gender in mind may also benefit males in the future. Again, we have to wait for further research.

OK. To sum up, there's still a lot to learn. We're just beginning to find out how pain control and mental health are different in men and women. One thing that is still astonishing is that so many researchers failed to include females in their studies. This is especially strange when it comes to pain research. Women are the most common sufferers of pain and yet most basic pain research is carried out only on males. In many areas, there seem to be more and more reports that the results of earlier research are actually only true for males, thus making the earlier researchers look rather foolish. Anyway,

---

[1] Hoag, H. (2008). Sex on the brain. *New Scientist, Australasian Edition, 2665,* 28–31.

what's important is that researchers are now beginning to take women into account. We may well see medicines better suited to female physiology in the future. In a few decades' time, women and men with the same illnesses could be treated in different ways. And this may apply to more than just the brain. So, it's an exciting field to explore—and one that could make a real difference to people's lives. OK, for next time please . . .

UNIT 2

Business: Pricing

Lecture: Pricing[2]

Professor: OK. Pricing is today's topic. In fact, as you'll see, it's one of the most important topics we'll cover—and when you finish this course and start your career in business, price setting could well be one of the biggest decisions you'll make. The main thing we'll do today will be to examine two types of pricing—cost–based pricing and value–based pricing—and to discuss the issues around them. We will see that, in most cases, value based pricing is the most useful. But before that, we'll take a look at why pricing is so important.

So, first of all, let's look at the importance of careful price–setting. Choice of prices can make or break a company. Set the price too high, and people might buy a competitor's products instead of yours, right? But, set it too low, and you won't make a profit—or your profit will be too small. Price can make a very big difference to profit. One expert, a guy named Paul Hunt, claims that, for most organizations, a one percent price change generates a 12.5 percent profit improvement. You can believe that.

Perhaps for this reason, some managers see pricing as a big headache. However, clever managers use pricing as a key tool. Price plays an important role in how much value customers see in a product—higher prices often send the message that quality is higher, even if it isn't. It also plays a role in building customer relationships, which is great: customers often like to associate themselves with products that project a high–quality image, and price can have a role in this. Can you think of any products like that in your life?

Let's move on now to look at strategies for pricing. The first we'll consider is rather old fashioned. It's called *cost–based pricing*. In cost–based pricing, first a company designs a product. Then it works out how much each item costs to make, plus all the other costs such as delivery, packaging, and design. Finally, a margin is added, to produce the profit. That seems pretty easy, right?

However, there are many disadvantages to cost–based pricing. A very big one is that it doesn't consider the customers—that is, the market, the people out there. Customers might not want

to pay the price. Or competitors' products may have better features for the same price. Alternatively, your product may have extra features, but not ones that people are happy to pay extra money for. Or, you may find that people buy your competitors' products just because their brand is stronger. All of these factors could have a big effect on sales. Pricing based just on cost ignores all of these important factors.

But there is an alternative approach. It's called *value–based pricing* and is, in fact, what most leading companies use today. To understand it, we first need to understand what value really means. It's important to remember that "good value" is not the same as "low price." Here's an example: some car buyers consider a Bentley, a luxury car now, to be a very good value, even at an eye–popping price of $150,000. You heard me right. For a hand–built vehicle, the quality is as good as cars that sell for twice the price.

Value–based pricing reverses the process of cost–based pricing. Instead of starting with a price, the marketers first consider what the customers want, and how much people are happy to pay for it. This may come from market research. From this, all aspects of the product are chosen, including its features and a target price. The product is then designed with this target price in mind. Thus, the customer comes first, and the product is designed to fit what the customer wants, at the price the customer is happy to pay. And we can make sure there is plenty of room for a profit.

The advantages of this are so clear. With a value–based strategy, you can be more certain that people will be happy to pay for your product. Furthermore, you have a good idea in advance whether a product is going to turn a profit. Value–based pricing may be a bit more difficult than cost–based pricing, but it's worth going to the extra trouble, as it is more likely to lead to a successful product.

So, in conclusion, careful consideration of pricing is important. And we've seen that out of the two main ways to go about choosing prices, value–based pricing is the most likely to result in success. In your reading for next week, you'll look more deeply at value–based pricing, and you'll see that there are quite a number of different ways to do this. Enjoy your reading everybody!

Before You Speak
Exercise 1, Page 43

Student: Good morning, everyone. In this talk, I'm going to briefly describe to you a purchase decision I made recently. After that, I'll explain how and why the shop encouraged me to make that decision.

OK. So, I'll give the situation first. I wanted to buy a new digital camera, and saw an advertisement for one at a very low price. So, off I went to the store, thinking I would quickly pop in, and be out again within a few minutes. But it didn't quite happen like that. The sales person, first of all, told me that the camera wasn't very good! This was a surprise, but then

---

[2] Armstrong, G., & Kotler, P. (2007). *Marketing: An introduction* (8th ed.). Upper Saddle River, NJ: Pearson Prentice Hall.

he started talking about a different camera, which he said was only $50 more, but much, much better. Well, I was in a hurry, and of course I want to take good photos, so I bought the one he recommended, and became $50 poorer than I expected!

Exercise 2, Page 43

Student: So, why did they do this? Well, this is almost a kind of bait–and–switch advertising. The low price was just to tempt people into the store; they actually wanted to avoid selling this product as they might even have made a loss on it. Really, the idea was to talk people into buying a much more profitable model.

Focused Speaking

Exercise 2, Page 45

Reporter: Ever wondered why so many price stickers end in .99 or .95? Surely retailers don't really believe we'll think that something priced at $19.95 is much different from $20? We're not dumb! We can see through that trick straight away . . . right?

Well, it seems that the psychology of pricing is very subtle. Even when the logical part of our minds tells us one thing, the emotional part may do something else—at least for some of us. Price stickers ending in .99 or .95 do actually work. People do buy more when the price ends like that. Otherwise, we wouldn't still see *so* many stickers with these prices!

This is just one example of psychological pricing. Another is common with supermarkets. You know that loaf of bread that only costs a couple of dollars? Well, the supermarket might actually be losing money on it. But it'll make people think the supermarket has some good prices, and more people will visit. That's when they make their money! These loss–making goods are called loss leaders.

Many clothing retailers have a different psychological trick. You know how department stores often have several different departments for women's clothes? And how each projects a very different image—some more upmarket than others? Well, who's to say the clothes actually cost any more to make? People will assume that the clothes in the more expensive department are better quality than elsewhere, and will often pay more for them.

Tricky people, these marketers, eh?

UNIT 3

Social Psychology: Conformity

Global Listening

Exercise 3, Page 63

Professor: Good morning, everyone. Now, what was today's topic? . . . Oh yes, conformity. Well, conformity has both positive and negative sides. Society runs more smoothly

when people know the usual rules of behavior, and also when they share the same attitudes. If you conform in clothing, preferences, and ideas, you're more likely to feel in tune with friends and colleagues. But conformity can also have some negative effects. It can suppress critical thinking and creativity. In a group, it can lead to bad decision making. As we'll see throughout the rest of this lecture, groupthink is one concept that can help us understand these negative effects. We'll look first at what groupthink is, then the circumstances in which it happens; we'll look at some examples of groupthink, and how to recognize it, and finally, how to avoid it.

Lecture: Groupthink[3]

Professor: Good morning, everyone. Now, what was today's topic? . . . Oh yes, conformity. Well, conformity has both positive and negative sides. Society runs more smoothly when people know the usual rules of behavior, and also when they share the same attitudes. If you conform in clothing, preferences, and ideas, you're more likely to feel in tune with friends and colleagues. But conformity can also have some negative effects. It can suppress critical thinking and creativity. In a group, it can lead to bad decision making. As we'll see throughout the rest of this lecture, groupthink is one concept that can help us understand these negative effects. We'll look first at what groupthink is, then the circumstances in which it happens; we'll look at some examples of groupthink, and how to recognize it, and finally, how to avoid it.

So, what is groupthink? Well, the concept was first developed to help understand some controversial decisions made by the U.S. Government. Groupthink tends to occur when members of a group have strong rapport with each other—in other words, it occurs in highly cohesive groups where the members see relationships as very important. This often means that ideas are not examined carefully, and that other possible courses of action are sometimes not even considered. In short, groupthink occurs when members of a group change their opinions to match the consensus of the group. And they do this even when it goes completely against their original opinion.

Well, you might ask, why would someone change their opinion like this? Some do so because they identify with group members and want to be like them. Some want to be liked. Some believe the group has knowledge that is better than their own. And some conform to keep their jobs, get promoted, or win votes. Also, social pressure is often very strong, and being a nonconformist can be uncomfortable.

Let's look now at when groupthink happens. The psychologist most associated with groupthink is Irving Janis. He identified several conditions likely to promote groupthink. The most important is high group cohesiveness. Related to this is similarity of members' social backgrounds and values. Then

[3] Wade, C., & Tavris, C. (2008). *Psychology* (9th ed.). Upper Saddle River, NJ: Pearson Prentice Hall.
Zimbardo, P. et al. (2007). *Psychology: AP Edition.* Boston: Pearson Allyn & Bacon.

there's group isolation. Groups having little contact with outside people are more likely to be affected by groupthink. Leaders who order their team around also encourage groupthink. And so does the presence of external factors causing a high level of stress, as well as anything else that makes it difficult to reach a decision.

There are many examples of important events in which some people say groupthink played a role in decision–making. These include the space shuttle disasters and the collapse of Enron Corporation. In situations such as these, group members were often uncomfortable with dissenters. In the end, groups might punish, isolate, or even throw out the nonconformist.

Now, you're probably asking yourself, "How can I know when groupthink is happening?" Well, Irving Janis also did some work in this area. He identified a number of symptoms of groupthink. I'll list a few to watch out for. First, there's a feeling of invulnerability across the group. When a group feels that it can do nothing wrong, there's likely to be a problem. Second, there's self–censorship. Dissenters choose to keep quiet rather than speak their mind, so that they don't cause trouble or risk negative opinions from other group members. Another danger sign is when there's pressure on dissenters to conform. Maybe the leader makes fun of doubters, or makes them feel uncomfortable in some way. This often takes the form of accusations of "disloyalty" or not being a "team player."

This all sounds rather scary, doesn't it? But all is not lost. There are a few things you can do to avoid groupthink—well, if you're a leader, anyway. One is to encourage and even reward expressions of doubt and dissent. Another is to try to bring out as many different ideas as possible. Well . . . maybe you could ask people to come up with counter–arguments. Or you could bring in people from outside who may have fresh ideas. Being clear about the role of group members can help, too. If people think of themselves as open–minded problem solvers, they are more likely to deal with different ideas than if they think their purpose in the group is just to justify their own opinion.

So, in summary, now you know the dangers of groupthink, how to recognize it, and how to avoid it. Good luck with your future group decision–making!

Focused Listening

Exercise 1, Page 64

EXCERPT ONE
So, what is groupthink? Well, the concept was first developed to help understand some controversial decisions made by the U.S. Government. Groupthink tends to occur when members of a group have strong rapport with each other—in other words, it occurs in highly cohesive groups where the members see relationships as very important.

EXCERPT TWO
In short, groupthink occurs when members of a group change their opinions to match the consensus of the group. And they

do this even when it goes completely against their original opinion.

EXCERPT THREE
Well, you might ask, why would someone change their opinion like this? Some do so because they identify with group members and want to be like them . . . .

EXCERPT FOUR
There are many examples of important events in which some people say groupthink played a role in decision–making. These include the space shuttle disasters and the collapse of Enron Corporation.

UNIT 4

Architecture: Aesthetics

Global Listening

Exercise 2, Page 81

Professor: Good buildings should inspire strong emotional responses. Think about the Taj Mahal, serene and relaxed. Who could fail to feel peace and calm when looking at it? In comparison, the Sydney Opera House with its elegant sail–shaped roofs projects a livelier, energetic feeling. So, what aspects of a building inspire these feelings? Three factors which appear to strongly affect this are form, texture, and scale. Today I'm going to talk a little about each.

Lecture: Architecture for the People: Emotional Responses

Professor: Good buildings should inspire strong emotional responses. Think about the Taj Mahal, serene and relaxed. Who could fail to feel peace and calm when looking at it? In comparison, the Sydney Opera House with its elegant sail-shaped roofs projects a livelier, energetic feeling. So, what aspects of a building inspire these feelings? Three factors which appear to strongly affect this are form, texture, and scale. Today I'm going to talk a little about each.

So, let's begin with form. Let's look at two examples. First, a building from the so–called "modern" era, a typical skyscraper—the MLC Centre in Sydney. It's pretty rectangular, isn't it? And what emotions does it inspire? Interest? Boredom? Anger—at how something so ugly could be allowed? Perhaps it's so plain you just feel nothing? Let's compare it with the Sydney Opera House. These buildings were both designed at around the same time, but they could hardly be more different from one another. The curved roofs of the Opera House form a far more interesting shape. And the shape actually means something—the curved roofs remind us of the sails of the yachts on Sydney Harbor. I think that explains why people feel so much more affectionate toward the Opera House! A lovely building, isn't it? Now, which building would you be most proud to work in?

OK. Now, here's another building—the Chrysler Building, in New York City, which, incidentally, is still the world's tallest brick building. Just like the MLC Centre, it's an office building. Now, the MLC Centre is just a plain block, a box. But look at the variety on the Chrysler Building—far more curves, complex shapes at the top . . . in short, more interest! There's far more to look at in the older building, isn't there?

That leads us to our next theme, texture. See how the windows and decoration of the Chrysler Building create repeated patterns? And look again at the MLC Centre. Notice there's also a lot of repetition there—in fact, the same pattern for the whole height of the building. Now, I would call that effect a texture. I don't mean the close–up texture that comes from the materials; I mean patterns that can be seen from a distance, from where people usually view buildings. Yes, there's also repetition, a texture, on the Chrysler Building, but not the exact same effect repeated over the whole building. I think you'll agree that there's something much more interesting about the surfaces of the Chrysler Building compared with the MLC tower. I think texture goes a long way toward explaining why more people like the Chrysler Building than most "modern" architecture—and why the Chrysler Building generates a more positive emotional response. I can see why this building was recently ranked the ninth most popular building in the U.S.

It's worth looking further at texture. It's often said that older buildings look much better than modern ones. So let's examine that opinion in terms of texture. First, here's Durham Cathedral in England, which is a great example of a European cathedral. Durham's a wonderful place to visit by the way. It's a great little town, very friendly. I spent some time there a few years ago. Really enjoyed it! And here's Todai–ji in Japan, one of the most famous temples in that country. Now, the texture of these buildings is far richer and more detailed than on most modern buildings, isn't it? There's still some repetition, but there's also a lot more variety. And there are no large areas with the same monotonous texture. Having the same texture all over just inspires boredom. I believe this is a key point that many modern architects have forgotten.

OK. The third factor, as I mentioned, is scale. Think about a small house and a large one on the same street. Which one would you prefer to live in? Which one projects the best image? And would the Taj Mahal create such strong emotions if it were only 12 feet high? That's not to say that big is necessarily beautiful, just that the emotional response is different. Architects of older religious buildings knew the effect of scale on emotional response very well. A sense of power and importance is one reason that towers are so popular in these buildings, and why temples, mosques, and churches often dominate their towns.

So, to conclude, we have looked at three of the things that allow an architect to affect people's emotional responses to buildings. I say again—people's emotional response is often the most important thing to think about when considering a building's appearance. Get that right, and you'll have a building that people remember and like.

Alright, our time is up. For next time, please read chapter. . .

Focused Listening

Exercise 1, Page 83

EXCERPT ONE

The curved roofs of the Opera House form a far more interesting shape. And the shape actually means something—the curved roofs remind us of the sails of the yachts on Sydney Harbor. I think that explains why people feel so much more affectionate toward the Opera House! A lovely building, isn't it? Now, which building would you be most proud to work in?

EXCERPT TWO

Now, here's another building, the Chrysler Building, in New York City, which, incidentally, is still the world's tallest brick building. Just like the MLC Centre, it's an office building. Now, the MLC Centre is just a plain block, a box. But look at the variety on the Chrysler Building.

EXCERPT THREE

I think texture goes a long way toward explaining why more people like the Chrysler Building than most "modern" architecture—and why the Chrysler Building generates a more positive emotional response. I can see why this building was recently ranked the ninth most popular building in the U.S.

EXCERPT FOUR

First, here's Durham Cathedral in England, which is a great example of a European cathedral. Durham's a wonderful place to visit by the way. It's a great little town, very friendly. I spent some time there a few years ago. Really enjoyed it!

UNIT 5

Transportation Engineering: Managing Traffic Flow

Global Listening

Exercise 1, Page 104

Professor: Good morning. Let's get started. As you know, efficient, cost–effective, environmentally responsible, and safe transportation systems contribute to a nation's economy and quality of life. However, designing these kinds of networks is not easy. In this lecture, we will look at the challenges that transportation engineers face when they design transportation systems, or networks.

Lecture: Transportation Challenges

Professor: Good morning. Let's get started. As you know, efficient, cost–effective, environmentally responsible, and safe transportation systems contribute to a nation's economy and quality of life. However, designing these kinds of networks is not easy. In this lecture, we will look at the challenges that transportation engineers face when they design transportation systems, or networks.

First, let's consider efficiency, which is related to location utility and time utility. Essentially, vehicle use of roads is inefficient due to the normal highs and lows of travel demand. We all know that for about two hours each morning and afternoon, on weekdays only, we need wide roads, large numbers of buses, more drivers, and so on—but during the other 20 hours a day, and on weekends and holidays, we only need a fraction of this capacity. So how big do we have to build? This problem becomes even more complicated when a city is growing. Large, growing cities such as Beijing, Berlin, Dubai, Los Angeles, Mexico City, Toronto, and so on, must consider how big their transportation systems need to be to meet their needs today, and tomorrow. Of course, the size of a transportation system is directly related to its cost.

Now, we can talk about the cost utility of transportation projects; it's *very* expensive to build roads, subways, airports, and train tracks. And we don't often have all the money to build all the projects we need. So right away we must consider which projects will bring the most benefit, and we start looking at trade-offs. For example, a city may need a bigger airport, but if the local highway isn't wide enough to carry the rush hour flow of vehicles, then it might be better to spend money on widening the highway. So engineers must make trade-offs.

Our third challenge is that transportation projects usually involve some damage to the environment. Land that could be used for agriculture, retail, residential, or recreational purposes is used for roads, tunnels, and tracks. Also, there are pollution concerns. All vehicles require some kind of energy mostly the burning of fossil fuels—which creates air pollution. Similarly, transportation creates noise, and many people will fight to prevent noise pollution near their homes. For instance, in Thailand, transportation engineers had to complete an environmental impact plan before building Suvarnabhumi Airport to service Bangkok City. The environmental plan considered noise pollution, air quality, traffic congestion, wastewater production, and even bird migration impacts. It's not easy to balance environmental concerns with efficient and affordable transportation.

And finally, transportation projects must be as safe as possible. To make transportation systems safe, you may need to build them bigger. Wider roads, longer airport runways, and bigger bridges may be safest for people traveling and people living nearby; and of course, all of these require more money and more space. Again, there are trade-offs that must be made between safety and cost or safety and the environment. You can see how safe projects may not be the cheapest or most environmentally friendly. However, it is still possible to build safe transportation projects that are also cost-effective. In many cities, there are transportation safety committees that consider how to build local roads, freeways, and airports both safely and cost effectively. This is one of the major goals of transportation engineers.

Now, as you know, conventional approaches to traffic problems have included building new roads, or new lanes onto existing roads, increasing public transit, encouraging carpooling and high-occupancy vehicle lanes, and providing radio and TV traffic reports. However, these solutions have only been able to help so much; there are still significant increases in traffic. So now, transportation engineers are looking for new solutions to old problems. Recently, a wide range of advanced electronic technologies have been combined into what we now call Intelligent Transportation Systems (ITS). This will be the subject of your next reading. See you next class.

Focused Listening, Page 105

Student 1: It makes sense that one of the challenges is environmental responsibility. Everyone is worried about the environment these days.

Student 2: I was so tired in that lecture, I nearly fell asleep. I really need to get more rest.

Student 3: I think the four challenges were well explained. These four things must be challenges for every transportation project.

Student 4: The four challenges are really difficult to overcome. I think that applying electronic and communications technology to transportation problems will give us new ways to build roads and travel efficiently.

Student 5: There must be more than four transportation challenges. Only four sounds too simple.

UNIT 6

Art History: Art versus Craft

Previewing the Academic Skills Focus
Exercise 1, Page 120

Audio Tour Guide: The *Ardabil Carpet* was produced in Islamic Persia during the Safavid Dynasty in the 16th century. It was made with about three hundred knots per square inch of carpet, or approximately 25 million knots in total. It is one of the greatest of all Persian carpets.

The quilt *Tar Beach*, made by Faith Ringgold in 1988, shows a poor family and their friends on a hot night. They are on the roof of their apartment building—their "beach"—because there is no air conditioning in their apartments. There are two children on a blanket; their parents are playing cards and eating. Ringgold explained that the girl child dreams she can give her father the job he didn't get because of his race, and let her mother sleep late and eat ice cream every day. Art critics believe that the combination of fantasy and hard reality makes this quilt special. Ringgold is telling us that imagination is the key to overcoming obstacles.

Gustave Courbet painted *The Stone Breakers* in 1849. Courbet was a realist painter. Realists disliked "romantic" art which showed extraordinary, historical, religious, or heroic events. Realists focused on ordinary things and common life. *The Stone Breakers* shows the real life scene of men building a road. Many people felt that realists caused artistic and moral decline by painting unpleasant and unimportant subjects. Some believed realists were enemies of true art.

Lecture: Collingwood's Theory of Art and Craft[4]

Professor: Good day! In this lecture I will talk about the characteristics of art and craft as defined by R. G. Collingwood in the 1930s. Before the 1930s, ordinary people believed that art was art because it was made of specific materials—so painting and sculpture were arts, but sewing, furniture making, or metalworking were crafts. However, Collingwood developed a theory of art and craft that was independent of the materials used. This meant that his theory could be applied to many forms of artistic creation.

Let us begin with defining craft more exactly. Craft means the skillful application of a technique to some kind of material. But the application must be done by hand—in person. Craft is *not* something that can be produced en masse with the use of technology. For example, the mass production of coffee mugs is not craft, but the creation of a single coffee mug—skillfully done—is craft. So when I talk about craft, I mean an object that is skillfully made by the human hand, not through the use of technology.

Also, craft has historically meant the production of practical objects that have some functional value. Art has historically meant the creation of objects that have no specific function. The craftsperson's teapot should hold tea, or the vase should hold flowers. A craft may be pretty or even beautiful, but its beauty is separate from its function. *Art* is typically *not* practical or functional.

These two characteristics of crafts—that they are made with the skillful application of the human hand and that they have practical use—are generally accepted as fact. However, these facts don't help us separate craft from art. Why? Because many works of art also require skill and still have enormous practical value—for example, works of architecture. You must agree that buildings are tremendously practical.

In the 1930s, the British philosopher R. G. Collingwood made a distinction between art and craft. The main distinction was related to *planning*. Craftspeople, he stated, know what they want to make before they make it. This means they also know when they are finished making it. And they make it for a consumer—they have a particular consumer in mind.

To demonstrate this point, let's compare the carpenter with a painter. When the carpenter sets out to make a table, he has a plan. He knows exactly how long the legs should be and the exact dimensions of the tabletop. When the plan is achieved, the table is finished. The craftsperson plans the table, builds the table according to the plan, and stops building when the table is finished. The outcome of a craft is dependable, reliable, predictable. Also, carpenters make tables for customers. There is a market for tables of this particular size and shape. These are characteristics of crafts.

On the other hand, the painter may begin her painting with an idea, but probably not a plan. As she paints, she explores the possibilities of her subject, her materials, and the light. She is not certain what the painting will look like when she is finished. In fact, she may not know when the painting is finished. She could always keep painting, keep adding details, color, subjects. In this way, the painter is part of her own audience. Just as a viewer cannot know the outcome of her painting, she does not know the outcome of her painting. This is very important in defining art. And finally, she may paint the painting without knowing who will buy it. She has no specific consumer in mind. Painting is an exploration, *not* a product for market. These are characteristics of art.

Of course, another key idea that Collingwood proposes is that art creates emotion in the viewer, while craft does not. A painting may make a viewer feel a certain emotion, and this is a characteristic of art. It may make different viewers feel different emotions—emotions the painter could not have predicted. This is art. However, if a painting was planned and painted in a specific way to create a specific emotion in specific viewers, then according to Collingwood, it is a craft.

So let's just recap these key points. Craft and art can both be skillful and useful. However, craft is planned, with an obvious end point to the creative process, and made for a consumer. Art is an unplanned exploration of the creative process; it may make viewers feel a variety of emotions unanticipated by the artist. Its creation has no clear end point, and no obvious consumer. And as a result, the artist is part of her own audience.

Now, one of the interesting things about Collingwood's theory is that much of what has been considered art in the past is really not art. For example, many religious paintings and portraits were commissioned by specific churches or wealthy people—kings, for example. These paintings have always been considered art, but not according to Collingwood. If these paintings were planned, painted to create a specific predictable outcome—with an obvious end point—and painted with a purchaser in mind—then they are *not* art—they are *craft*.

To conclude, one reason Collingwood's theory of art and craft has been so influential is that it explains that the difference between art and craft is *not* related to the materials used, the style of the object, the gender, or social status of the creator. Instead, the distinction is based on the *kind* of creating. And

---

[4] Adapted from Dutton, D. (1990, July 4). The difference between art and craft. Retrieved October 15, 2008, from http://www.denisdutton.com/rnz_craft.htm.

you should notice that this distinction is not always clear. You can often argue about whether an object is art or craft.

Focused Listening

Exercise 2, Page 126

Viewer 1: This is a decorative panel from the Alhambra Palace in Granada, Spain. It was created in the 14th century by an unknown craftsperson. The detail is fantastic. I am certain that this panel will fascinate mathematicians for centuries to come.

Viewer 2: This work of art titled *Tar Beach* was made by Faith Ringgold. It's beautifully made with cloth, acrylic paint, and pieces of fabric stitched together to make a quilt. This quilt should inspire many fabric artists.

Viewer 3: This is a ceramic bowl with a closed top made by artist Toshiko Takaezu. It's a functional item made into an art object. In the beginning, objects like this were considered controversial because they used craft materials to make works of art. This object will never be considered a functional object.

Viewer 4: The audio tour says that Utamaro Kitagawa painted *Reflected Beauty* in 1790. The painting is memorable because of the composition—the main focus is not in the middle of the painting. The curved line of the mirror is strong, and the figure leaning in from the right is cut off by the frame. I think that in the future, it's unlikely that this kind of composition will seem so unusual.

Viewer 5: Barbara Kruger created this work of art in 1987. It's called *Untitled (I shop therefore I am)*. This work makes a serious statement about our consumer society. This kind of anti-consumer statement may be better understood by people who reject capitalism.

UNIT 7

Biology: Genetic Testing

Before You Listen, Page 149

Student 1: So genetic testing means the same thing as genetic screening?

Student 2: Yes, the instructor said that right at the beginning. Did you hear it?

Student 1: I must have missed that part, but I'm glad I knew all the synonyms for the word *disease*. Did you hear those words? There were two.

Student 2: Ummm . . . *disease* and *disorder*, right? What was the second synonym for *disease*?

Student 1: *Condition* . . . You can have a condition like Huntington's disease.

Student 2: Right. I laughed about the image the instructor used for genetic testing. What was it again? . . . oh yeah, he said genetic testing was a technology whose time has come, that it was gaining momentum like a snowball rolling down a hill. I guess he meant that genetic testing can't be easily stopped, like a snowball rolling down a hill is hard to stop.

Student 1: You have to come from a country where there's snow to understand that expression. But what was the instructor's primary purpose for that lecture—was it informative or persuasive?

Student 2: Well, I'm not sure. I thought it was informative, but at the end, maybe it was persuasive. What did you think?

Student 1: I'm not sure either.

Lecture: Genetic Testing[5]

Professor: Hello, everyone. Today I want to talk about genetic testing or genetic screening. Genetic screening is the testing of people who have no symptoms to determine if they carry genes that will increase their chances of developing certain genetic diseases. It's a technology whose time has come. Like a snowball rolling downhill, the practice is gaining momentum. However, genetic screening raises many ethical issues, and we have to think about these now so we can make informed decisions about genetic testing.

Certainly, there are advantages to genetic testing. One is that if you know you have a treatable or preventable condition, you can take steps to reduce the risk of developing the disorder. Another advantage is that you are informed about the likelihood of passing on a genetic disorder. You could choose to prevent suffering in future generations if the disorder is caused by a recessive allele that can remain hidden for generations or by a dominant allele that is not expressed until late in life. Consider, for instance, Tay–Sachs disease. Now, this disorder causes the death of children, usually by the age of five. The infant appears healthy at birth, but at about six months old it gradually stops smiling, crawling, or turning over. Eventually, the child becomes blind, paralyzed, and unaware of its surroundings. This terrible condition is especially prevalent in descendants from Jewish communities from Eastern Europe. Many people in these communities have volunteered to be genetically tested, and as a result, the number of children born with Tay–Sachs disease has decreased by tenfold in many communities.

However, genetic testing also has a dark side. The psychological consequences of test results can be devastating. Many genetic disorders cannot be prevented or treated. So do you really want to know now what will cause your death? For example, Huntington's disease is caused by a dominant allele that provides no hint of its existence until relatively late in

---

[5] Adapted from Goodenough, J., McGuire, B., & Wallace, R. (2005). *Biology of humans: Concepts, applications, and issues.* Upper Saddle River, NJ: Pearson Prentice Hall.

life. About 60 percent of the people with Huntington's disease are diagnosed between the ages of 35 and 50. The gene causes degeneration of the brain, leading to muscle spasms, personality disorders, and death, usually within 10 to 15 years. Because Huntington's disease is caused by a dominant allele, a bearer has a 50 percent chance of passing it to children. Thus, a person whose parent dies of Huntington's disease could be relieved if a gene test did not detect the allele. But it's equally likely that the allele will show up. Many people at risk for Huntington's disease prefer to live without the knowledge of their possible future. Also, a genetic test that confirms the risk of a serious disease can cause anxiety and depression in carriers and feelings of guilt in siblings who do not carry the allele.

OK. There is also the possibility that the results of gene tests will not remain private. What would happen if information about your genetic test was available to your employer or health insurer? As an employer, if you had information about the genetic test of someone you might hire, would you choose to invest time and money in training a person who carried an allele that increased the risk of cancer, heart disease, Alzheimer's disease, or alcoholism? As an insurer, would you knowingly insure a carrier of these genes?

There are also a large number of unanswered questions about genetic testing. Who should decide whether screening should be done, for which gene, on whom, and in which communities? Could we make laws to clarify the answers to these questions? Should we leave ethical issues to judges and legislators? Should moral matters be decided by society or clergy—or should they be personal decisions?

So, if genetic testing is done, who should be told the results? If the affected person is an infant, should the parents always be told the results, even if the condition is poorly understood? Would that be helping or hurting the child?

Also, unfortunately, we live in a world of limited resources. So, as soon as we decide who should be tested, we must decide who should pay the bill. Both testing and treatment are expensive. Should testing be done only when treatment or preventative measures are available? And if there is bad news, who pays for the medical treatment?

As you can see, there are no easy answers. We must all think about the issues raised by these and similar questions.

OK now. . . our time is up. For next class, please read unit eight and . . .

Global Listening

Exercise 2, Page 150

EXCERPT ONE
It is a technology whose time has come. Like a snowball rolling downhill, the practice is gaining momentum.

EXCERPT TWO
Certainly, there are advantages to genetic testing. One is that if you know you have a treatable or preventable condition, you can take steps to reduce the risk of developing the disorder. Another advantage is that you are informed about the likelihood of passing on a genetic disorder.

EXCERPT THREE
Consider, for instance, Tay–Sachs disease. Now, this disorder causes the death of children, usually by the age of five.

EXCERPT FOUR
Many people in these communities have volunteered to be genetically tested, and as a result, the number of children born with Tay–Sachs disease has decreased by tenfold in many communities.

EXCERPT FIVE
However, genetic testing also has a dark side. The psychological consequences of test results can be devastating.

EXCERPT SIX
Many genetic disorders cannot be prevented or treated. So do you really want to know now what will cause your death? For example, Huntington's disease is caused by a dominant allele that provides no hint of its existence until relatively late in life.

EXCERPT SEVEN
There is also the possibility that the results of gene tests will not remain private. What would happen if information about your genetic test was available to your employer or health insurer?

EXCERPT EIGHT
Who should decide whether screening should be done, for which gene, on whom, and in which communities? Could we make laws to clarify the answers to these questions? Should we leave ethical issues to judges and legislators? Should moral matters be decided by society or clergy—or should they be personal decisions?

So, if genetic testing is done, who should be told the results? If the affected person is an infant, should the parents always be told the results, even if the condition is poorly understood? Would that be helping or hurting the child?

UNIT 8

Business: Mediation

Lecture: Mediation Techniques[6]

Professor: Good day, everyone. As you may guess, being a mediator is not easy. Today I want to talk to you about what a mediator actually does to help people resolve their disputes. Mediation sessions usually begin with a broad and confused

---

[6] Cahn, D., & Abigail, R.A. (2007). *Managing conflict through communication* (3rd ed.). Boston: Pearson Allyn & Bacon.

discussion of issues seen from competing perspectives. What the mediator wants to do is to move the general discussion to a more detailed and specific discussion. Based on these specifics, cooperation and shared values can emerge. To move the discussion from general to specific, mediators use techniques such as fractionation, framing, reframing, highlighting common ground, and brainstorming.

To start, mediators use fractionation. This technique involves breaking down complex issues into smaller, more manageable ones. After separating issues into their smallest components, the mediators can ask the disputants to deal with each issue one at a time. Hopefully, the parties can resolve some of these smaller conflicts, which will build a feeling of success, and give the parties some confidence in the process by the time they get to resolving the larger issues. For example, two roommates might decide that they are not getting along. But after the discussion moves from the general to the specific, the mediator discovers that they have a number of specific differences. They disagree about the music they play on their stereo, what they like to eat, when they have visitors, when they wake up, and when they study. Some of these issues should be easier to resolve than others, so the mediator will start with those issues. This is fractionation.

Another mediation technique is known as framing, where mediators ask neutral or friendly questions that avoid blame or passing judgment. These questions should help the parties open discussion or summarize their issues. Returning to our example of the two roommates, the mediator might frame the problem like this: "You clearly have some problems living together, but you are both here trying to resolve these problems, and that's a step in the right direction."

One more technique is reframing, where mediators restate negative, biased, or insulting statements made by one of the parties. The mediator reframes the statement using neutral vocabulary, or restates positions in a way that makes the parties look at the issues differently. For example, if one of the roommates says, "He always comes in late and makes noise just when I need to study the most," the mediator could reframe this statement by saying, "Getting good grades is important to you, and you need some quiet time to study—is that right?"

Finally, mediators highlight common ground, by finding shared attitudes, values, behaviors, expectations, and goals. This can help lay the ground for a possible agreement. Getting back to our roommate example, the mediator might discover that although the roommates prefer to study at different times of the day, receiving good grades is important to both of them. The mediator will highlight this common ground between the two roommates by saying something like, "Both of you want to get good grades and need some quiet time to study—you're similar in this way."

As the discussion progresses, the mediators brainstorm proposals or solutions to the problem that would satisfy the interests and needs of both parties. The mediators also help the parties brainstorm alternative proposals. The idea is not to criticize or limit the proposals in any way, but simply to create as long a list as possible. Sometimes one suggestion, even if ridiculous, triggers the parties to think of something better. Brainstorming plays an important role in expanding the range of options for reaching an agreement.

Throughout the discussion, mediators use fractionation, framing and reframing, and highlighting common ground to encourage discussion. They use brainstorming to identify possible solutions. And of course, they encourage positive contributions, and show attentiveness by responding verbally or nonverbally to comments by both parties. This positive feedback encourages the parties to continue the mediation and work toward agreement. These are some techniques that serve mediators well when they help to resolve disputes. Your challenge now is to practice some of these techniques yourselves.

Global Listening
Exercise 3, Page 173

EXCERPT ONE
Today I want to talk to you about what a mediator actually does to help people resolve their disputes.

EXCERPT TWO
For example, two roommates might decide that they are not getting along. But after the discussion moves from the general to the specific, the mediator discovers that they have a number of specific differences. They disagree about the music they play on their stereo, what they like to eat, when they have visitors, when they wake up, and when they study. Some of these issues should be easier to resolve than others, so the mediator will start with those issues. This is fractionation.

EXCERPT THREE
Your challenge now is to practice some of these techniques yourselves.

Focused Listening
Exercise 1, Page 174

You are a neighbor to two people who have asked you to mediate their dispute. The complaining neighbor wants the other neighbor to stop playing basketball from 6:30 to 8:30 every morning and not to move her garbage cans away from the road on garbage collection days. She says she needs to sleep in the mornings; furthermore, the garbage doesn't get collected if the garbage can is not next to the road, and her garbage is piling up. The basketball–playing neighbor insists he needs to practice basketball every day. On garbage collection days, her garbage can is at the edge of the basketball court, so he moves her garbage can out of his way before he plays basketball.[7]

---

[7] Based on a dispute described in Cahn, D., & Abigail, R.A. (2007). *Managing conflict through communication* (3rd ed.). Boston: Pearson Allyn & Bacon.

REVIEWERS

For the comments and insights they graciously offered to help shape the direction of *Academic Connections*, the publisher would like to thank the following reviewers and institutions.

Donette Artenie, Georgetown University; **Jennifer Castello**, Cañada College; **Carol A. Chapelle**, Iowa State University; **JoAnn (Jodi) Crandall**, University of Maryland; **Wendy Crockett**, J. W. North High School; **Lois Darlington**, Columbia University; **Christopher Davis**, John Jay College; **Robert Dickey**, Gyeongju University, Gyeongju, Korea; **Deborah B. Gordon**, Santa Barbara City College; **Mike Hammond**, University of California, San Diego; **Ian Hosack**, Ritsumeikan University, Kyoto; **Sylvie Huneault-Schultze**, Fresno City College; **Barbara Inerfeld**, Rutgers University; **Joan Jamieson**, Northern Arizona University; **Scott Jenison**, Antelope Valley College; **Mandy Kama**, Georgetown University; **Dr. Jose Lai**, The Chinese University of Hong Kong; **Rama Mathew**, Delhi University, Delhi, India; **Mitchell Mirkin**, Baltimore City Community College; **Carla Billings Nyssen**, California State University, Long Beach; **Yannick O'Neill**, Gyeongnam Education Board, Changwon, South Korea; **Gretchen Owens**, San Francisco State University; **Angela Parrino**, Hunter College; **Sarah C. Saxer**, Howard Community College; **Diane Schmitt**, Nottingham Trent University, Nottingham U.K.; **Gail Schmitt**, Montgomery College; **Fred Servito**, University of Washington; **Janet Shanks Van Suntum**, Fordham University, Pace University; **Karen Shimoda**, Freelance ESL Development Editor; **Dean E. Stafford**, Sanho Elementary School, Mason, South Korea; **Fredricka L. Stoller**, Northern Arizona University; **Richmond Stroupe**, Soka University, Tokyo; **Jessica Williams**, University of Illinois; **Kirsten Windahl**, Cuyahoga Community College

CREDITS

Text Credits: pp. 6–8 "He thinks, she thinks," in *Discover Magazine*, by L. Marsa, 2007. Retrieved August 14, 2008 from HYPERLINK "http://discovermagazine.com" http://discovermagazine.com; **pp. 6–8, 13, 15–17** "Sex on the brain" in *New Scientist, Australasian Edition*, by H. Hoag, 2008, No 2665, 28–31; **pp. 34, 37–38, 43, 45** *Marketing: An Introduction*, 8th Edition, by G. Armstrong and P. Kotler, 2007. Pearson Prentice Hall: Upper Saddle River, NJ; **p. 51** *Psychology*, by J. Ciccarelli and G. Meyer, 2006. Pearson Prentice Hall: Upper Saddle River, NJ; **pp. 61–65** "The Enron cult: 'Groupthink' caused everyone associated with Enron to contribute to its downfall," by Roger Brunswick, MD and Gary E. Hayes, PhD, 2009. Retrieved from HYPERLINK "http://www.hayesbrunswick.com/articles.html#enron" http://www.hayesbrunswick.com/articles.html#enron; "Google: 10 golden rules: Getting the most out of knowledge workers," by Eric Schmidt and Hal Varian, 2009. Retrieved from http://1000advices.com/guru/organization_cs_google_10rules.html; **p. 70** *Mastering the world of psychology*, 2nd Edition, by S.E. Wood, G. Wood, and D. Boyd, 2006. Allyn & Bacon: Boston, MA; **pp. 100–102, 109–112** *Fundamentals of transportation engineering: a multimodal systems approach*, by J.D. Fricker and R.K. Whitford, 2004, 10–13, 252–253, 739–750, 758. Pearson Prentice Hall: Upper Saddle River, NJ; **pp. 120, 126, 128–129** *Prebles' artforms: An introduction to the visual arts*, 8th edition, by P. Frank, 2006, 14, 191–192, 195–196, 200, 202–205, 357. Pearson Prentice Hall: Upper Saddle River, NJ; **p. 122** "The difference between art and craft," by D. Dutton, 1990. Retrieved October 15, 2008 from http://www.denisdutton.com/rnz_craft.htm; **p. 127** "Handcrafts," in *Today's Education*, by J. Coyne, November–December 1976. From *Prebles' artforms: An introduction to the visual arts*, 8th edition, by P. Frank, 2006, 196. Pearson Prentice Hall: Upper Saddle River, NJ; **p. 132** From *Japanese Crafts*, 5–6, in Japan Times, Ltd., 1972. The Japan Times: Tokyo; **pp. 138, 155** *Essential biology with physiology*, 2nd Edition, by N. Campbell, J. Reece, and E. Simon, 2007, 144, 153. Pearson Benjamin Cummings: San Francisco, CA; **pp. 140–141, 143–144, 149–151** *Biology of humans: Concepts, applications, and issues*, by J. Goodenough, B. McGuire, and R. Wallace, 2005, 460–462, 472. Pearson Prentice Hall: Upper Saddle River, NJ; **pp. 163, 168–169** *The conflict survival kit: Tools for resolving conflict at work*, by C. Goodwin and D.B. Griffith, 2007, 6–8. Pearson Prentice Hall: Upper Saddle River, NJ; **pp. 172–174, 178** *Managing conflict through communication*, 3rd Edition, by D. Cahn and R.A. Abigail, 2007, 260–261, 266. Allyn & Bacon: Boston, MA; **pp. 175–176** *Mediation theory and practice*, by S. McCorkle and M.J. Reece, 2005, 113–115. Allyn & Bacon: Boston, MA

Photo Credits: Cover: Art on File/Corbis; **p. 1** (TR) Shutterstock, (T) Shutterstock, (B) Peter Arnold Inc./Alamy; **p. 2** Shutterstock; **p. 3** Shutterstock; **p. 4** (T) www.CartoonStock.com, (B) www.CartoonStock.com; **p. 7** Shutterstock; **p. 14** Shutterstock; **p. 19** (T) Marcus E. Raichle, M.D.; (M) Peter Arnold Inc./Alamy, (B) Shutterstock; **p. 23** (TR) Shutterstock, (M) Shutterstock, (BR) iStockphoto.com; **p. 24** (L) Courtesy of Bentley Motors, (R) Dorling Kindersley; **p. 30** Ilian Car/Alamy; **p. 37** Shutterstock; **p. 40** iStockphoto.com; **p. 47** Shutterstock; **p. 49** (TR) Shutterstock, (T) Fancy/Alamy, (M) Photodisc/Alamy, (B) Bob Daemmrich Photography Inc.; **p. 50** Fancy/Alamy; **p. 54** (T) Photodisc/Alamy, (B) ©2000 Ted Goff, **p. 55** Bob Daemmrich Photography Inc.; **p. 73** (TR) Shutterstock, (B) ©David Hill; **p. 74** (L) Shutterstock, (M) Shutterstock, (R) Dreamstime.com; **p. 76** Dreamstime.com; **p. 77** (T) ©David Hill, (B) ©David Hill; **p. 78** (T) Shutterstock, (MT) Shutterstock, (MB) Dreamstime.com, (B) Shutterstock; **p. 86** (L) Art on File/Corbis, (M) BigStockPhoto.com, (R) ©David Hill; **p. 87** Shutterstock; **p. 88** BigStockPhoto.com; **p. 89** Shutterstock; **p. 99** (TR) Shutterstock, (L) Shutterstock, (T) Shutterstock, (M) Shutterstock, (B) Dreamstime.com; **p. 103** Dreamstime.com; **p. 104** Shutterstock; **p. 109** Shutterstock; **p. 117** (TR) Shutterstock, (M) Faith Ringgold/The Solomon R. Guggenheim Museum, New York; **p. 118** (L) Hirshhorn Museum and Sculpture Garden/Smithsonian Institution, (R) Shutterstock; **p. 120** (L) V&A Images, (M) Faith Ringgold/The Solomon R. Guggenheim Museum, New York, (R) The Bridgeman Art Library; **p. 121** (L) Shutterstock, (M) Hirshhorn Museum and Sculpture Garden/Smithsonian Institution, (R) National Museum of Women In the Arts; **p. 126** (T) Dreamstime.com, (MT) Faith Ringgold/The Solomon R. Guggenheim Museum, New York, (M) Charles Cowles Gallery, (MB) Honolulu Academy of Arts, (B) Mary Boone Gallery; **p. 127** Charles Cowles Gallery; **p. 129** Art on File/Corbis; **p. 132** Shutterstock; **p. 135** (T) Art Resource, N.Y., (M) The Museum of Modern Art/Art Resource, N.Y., (B) SuperStock/SuperStock; **p. 137** (TR) Shutterstock, (T) Dreamstime.com, (M) Shutterstock, (B) Shutterstock; **p. 142** (T) Shutterstock, Shutterstock, Shutterstock, Shutterstock, (B) Shutterstock, Shutterstock, Bert Krages/Visuals Unlimited; **p. 143** (T) Shutterstock, (B) Shutterstock; **p. 145** (T) Shutterstock, Shutterstock, Shutterstock, Shutterstock, (B) Shutterstock, Shutterstock; **p. 161** (TR) Shutterstock, (T) Jon Feingersh/agefotostock, (B) Shutterstock; **p. 162** Pixtal/agefotostock; **p. 168** Shutterstock.

AUDIO CD TRACKING GUIDE